Body and Gender

Body and Gender

Sociological Perspectives

Roberta Sassatelli
Rossella Ghigi

polity

The right of Roberta Sassatelli & Rossella Ghigi to be identified as Authors of this Work has been asserted in accordance with the UK Copyright, Designs and Patents Act 1988.

First published in 2024 by Polity Press

Polity Press
65 Bridge Street
Cambridge CB2 1UR, UK

Polity Press
111 River Street
Hoboken, NJ 07030, USA

ISBN-13: 978-1-5095-5007-4
ISBN-13: 978-1-5095-5008-1(pb)

A catalogue record for this book is available from the British Library.

Library of Congress Control Number: 2023936948

Typeset in 10.5 on 12pt Sabon
by Fakenham Prepress Solutions, Fakenham, Norfolk NR21 8NL
Printed and bound in the UK by CPI Group (UK) Ltd, Croydon

The publisher has used its best endeavours to ensure that the URLs for external websites referred to in this book are correct and active at the time of going to press. However, the publisher has no responsibility for the websites and can make no guarantee that a site will remain live or that the content is or will remain appropriate.

Every effort has been made to trace all copyright holders, but if any have been overlooked the publisher will be pleased to include any necessary credits in any subsequent reprint or edition.

For further information on Polity, visit our website:
politybooks.com

Contents

Acknowledgements

Writing this book has been a laborious pleasure, fuelled by many years of research and teaching as well as continuous fertile exchange between ourselves. We would like to thank all those who have provided help and inspiration for the writing of this book. Several friends and colleagues have read and commented on earlier drafts of the manuscript and offered advice and suggestions. In particular, we would like to thank Elia Arfini and Monica Greco for detailed observations on some chapters and sections of the book. We also would like to express our gratitude to Jonathan Skerrett at Polity for his valuable editing and sustained encouragement and to Karina Jákupsdóttir who provided helpful assistance during the publishing process. The limits of the book are ours alone, but the support and suggestions we have received remain priceless.

Introduction:
Embodying Gender

Bodies are constructed. They take on form as our lives and relations develop, we model them actively in our everyday choices, while institutions mould them by their demands, whether tacit or overbearing. Yet our bodies also strike us as an essential given, something unchosen preceding us, something 'natural', prior to human will or decision. On closer inspection, however, that natural body turns out to be made up of many conflicting truths, played out in our bodily practices and social relations. Thus when, in some trepidation, we scan our medical tests, the values may read like so many obscure signals needing a professional to interpret them, whereas how we feel tells us how we are, and how we look will convey to other people the image of what we are. Medical know-how, embodied feelings, our management of impressions are, alike, truths about our body linking to various dimensions of social existence: interaction, culture, institutions. Navigating through constructionist approaches from classic to contemporary sociology, this book will investigate how the body is moulded by all these dimensions and how in turn it contributes to modify them.

This is not to claim there is no materiality situated in time and space. Yet we only have access to materiality insofar as we are social beings, and society inevitably unfolds through the work we do on our bodies. Interaction, culture and institutions demand that different individuals show emotions in different ways according to the situation, or expect differing degrees of body control, or again use differentiated and highly normative codes to represent body images. In so doing, society makes some processes meaningful and others trite, some experiences imbued with authenticity and difference and others banal or indistinguishable. To our human species materiality is never immediate nor inert. Phenomenologically, it exists and becomes active insofar as we understand and feel it, but our understanding and feeling are mired in social practices. The human being is a social and political animal right to the inner depths of its bodily experience. Even when on our own, face to face with our own material being, we observe it with eyes that culture has fashioned for us, we move in ways we have absorbed in the ordinary rounds of our existence, and we feel by emotional codes that we have been learning since the first day of our lives. By its gestures, movements and make-up, our body acts upon and reflects the pattern our life has taken, stamped in its turn by the web of relations in which we are immersed.

The body thus stands as not just a legitimate, but a necessary object of sociological analysis. As the French philosopher Maurice Merleau-Ponty (1962 [1945]) points out, the body's anatomical organization leaves a great deal of scope open; the way it is used is not something laid down once and for all; its meanings and reactions always need interpreting. For humans one cannot imagine a bedrock of natural behaviour onto which a social or cultural superstructure then gets grafted. Nature and culture are inextricably bound up in our species. One might say that the body's various ways of deployment are *both* natural – in being made possible by physiological mechanisms – *and* social – in that they are arbitrary and conventional.

The kind of approach we shall be adopting – sociological yet also materialistic, phenomenological and critical – investigates the social construction of the body or *embodiment* in its concrete, historically situated, culturally defined processes. Considering the body as a social construct does not mean that the individual or subject can act upon it at will. Nor that it can be reduced to a text. What it does mean is that embodied subjects living in space and time come about in a diverse, unequal, social manner. They play their part in the social world by consolidating or altering the practical regulations and classification schemas that initially defined their embodied subjectivity. When we come to look at certain features of embodiment as a social process, we shall see that it is scalar, circular, active, incessant and contested.

- *Scalar*, in that our bodies are forged by social relations at different scales pertaining to appearance and posture, ability and limitations, emotions and physique itself.
- *Circular*, since in being human we tend to incorporate the differences fostered by interaction, culture and institutions and then act upon those differences beginning with our embodied feelings and experiences.
- *Active*, because we are fully the subjects of that embodiment – hence not just bound by the power of social organization and classification, but capable of a subjective role upon our own skins when it comes to reproducing, altering or defying the social norms.
- *Incessant*, since we are not only constantly constructing our body for ourselves and others, but also because it is itself incapable of playing dumb: it will speak for us even when we don't seem to be saying anything.
- *Contested*, given that our own ways of experiencing our body are fundamental, if tacit, modes of expressing our identities which in turn are set within hierarchical systems allowing for power and conflict.

A crucial dimension of embodiment is *gender*. In this book we shall be using gender to reveal the features of embodiment as a social process. The richness of a focus on the embodiment of gender is twofold: it both illuminates the process of embodiment, and it also helps in understanding the deep workings of gender differences, shedding light on invisible hierarchies and power effects in social interaction, culture and institutions that unmask the neutrality of subjectivity. In so doing, we will rely extensively on feminist studies of the past fifty years.

We thus will focus on the phenomenon of naturalization that makes gender both taken-for-granted and powerful. One small experiment suffices: close your eyes and imagine a human body. You may have succeeded in imagining one without a specific race or age, but is it possible to imagine one that is not identifiable with a sexual category? In everyday life, whenever we fill in a form, need a lavatory or even are working out on a treadmill, our eye will be caught, implicitly or explicitly, by an image referring to gender. The boxes on a standard form, the symbols on the toilet doors, the stylized body on a fitness machine depict a human shape that is posited as fundamentally and naturally gendered. Such signs may typically be identifiably male or female, or apparently neuter (tending to take the male to represent the species); or again other categories may be admitted, and left to us to specify, in recognition of the idea that gender identity may nowadays be multiple. But bodies only exist when they measure up to the cultural categorizations of 'female' or 'male', or such other sexual categories as a society may define. A gender approach to the social construction of the body thus leaves room for the gamut of forms in which gender is expressed, and at the same time highlights its filigree character, now visible, now hidden, in relationships and social structures. As we shall see, then, being a man or a woman is not to do with a natural quality but a constantly enacted taking place or positioning: via the slightest gesture of interaction, by long-established meanings in culture, and according to role and function at an institutional level. Feminist thought and gender studies first challenged the idea that the different social conditions of men and women were based on their biology. They thereby foregrounded the issue of the social construction of the body, although with a variety of different emphases, each pondering on a fundamental question: where does nature end and where does culture begin? In other words, to what extent are the differences (and, as we shall see, the inequalities) between men and women down to biological bodies, and how much does society not only elaborate the biological body but contribute to creating it?

As we shall see in the first chapter, considering the body as socially constructed and embodiment as a social process opens the way to a reappraisal of many aspects of social life. Western modernity itself is not just about large institutions and broad social dynamics, but also about how our gendered bodies have been forged and transformed by the process of rationalization. Historically, body rationalization has been most evident in the sphere of production which has been dominated by men, while women have often been confined to the domain of consumption and reproduction. Raewyn Connell (2021), one of the authors who inform this book, indeed defines gender as a practice of constant positioning within the 'reproductive arena' – that is, the field in which embodied individuals take their stand according to their relation to human reproduction. So, in this perspective gender is a 'doing' (West & Zimmerman 1987) and intersects other social forms of being in the body, such as race, class and age, to realize a complex process of embodiment which produces a multi-faceted landscape of embodied difference and inequality (West & Ferstermaker 1995). As Judith Lorber (2021) underlines in her *The New Gender Paradox*, we are now witnessing both the fragmentation of the gender binary and its persistence. Gender is not as such a binary status. However, despite the multiplicity of intersections and the fragmentation of gender at individual level, at the social level, in legal arrangements and social practices, representations and institutions, the contemporary Western world is still in many ways a bi-gendered world.

Gender has to do with the body and is the source of what Colette Guillaumin (1993, 41; see also 2016 [1992]) called the 'fabrication of the sexed body'. This highlights the *work of making the body sexed* and thus the fact that the ongoing process of subjects becoming embodied sorts them into sexual categories that are accorded to unequal, typically (and normatively) binary and hierarchically arranged gender roles. This is reflected and reflects dominant embodied subjectivities that appear as dependent on such categorization, which is thereby naturalized: thus, in Western culture, on the one hand we find female bodies that take care, look on fondly, caress and make room for other bodies, while, on the other hand, we have male bodies expecting room and attention, and exhibiting strength, command and action.

Gendered bodies are constructed first of all in interaction: in the countless rituals of everyday life, it is chiefly through our bodies, their demeanour, appearance and capacity to fit in or stand out, that we build our sense of self, our *subjectivity*. As we shall see in the second chapter, there arises the basic question of the individuals' room for manoeuvre, their capacity and desire to work on their bodies. Anthony Giddens (1991) showed how, in Western societies, gradually over the late modern age the body became a project on which individuals act, reflexively, constructing an identity for themselves and for other people. Yet the details of everyday ceremonies as coded by gender (Goffman 1963; 1982 [1967]; 2010 [1971]) and the habitual manners of our gendered bodies (Bourdieu 1990 [1980]; 2001 [1998]) represent elements which both allow and limit the expression of self in everyday life. Thus, reflexive self-constitution is gendered and works on whatever has already been set up for us in daily interaction and on the conventions we have unreflexively embodied. The result is that we are given differentiated access to body projects, especially those rated highest by our social world.

Such reflexivity is therefore bounded, above all by the gender order, which transpires in even greater clarity if we focus on the emotions, associated as they so typically are with corporeality. A framework in which to consider emotions as accessible to socio-logical study has been provided by Arlie Russell Hochschild (2003). Hochschild focused on the constant daily work that goes into making us sentient selves. We will see that what appears as deeply engrained in embodied subjectivity is in fact socially mediated and that different feeling rules apply to men and to women. We will also see how both men and women work on their feelings, bolstering or at times altering the forms in which one may appropriately experience and express feeling, and in so doing abide by, reproduce and modify gender relations.

Gender relations are in turn enmeshed with power. Power works not just on the embodied subject, sorting it into categories, but also through it, via its feeling, desires and acts in the social world. Our bodies are never inert or neutral, they are constantly caught in power relations. As we shall see in the third chapter, *bodies are political*. Body and power are intimately connected, and inequality in daily life is played out on bodies. They bear the marks of hierarchical classification that is taken for granted: they are moulded, as Michel Foucault (1977 [1975]; 1978 [1976]) argues, by many disciplinary devices making them flesh to redeem, a workforce to employ, or organisms to heal. Foucault played a key role in highlighting some of the power mechanisms in the modern world and the development of a form of power that he called 'biopolitics'. Ranging from the rules for artificial insemination and assisted death, to policies favouring families with children or closing frontiers to migrants, biopolitics has a direct impact on life, delimits its range of action, moulds skills, forges desires, including the most intimate such as sexuality.

Yet Foucault left gender in the half-light, skating over the specific place of women in sexual classification and biopolitical dynamics. His toolbox would thus subsequently be used by feminist studies which have revealed that what on the face of it seems an innocuous, obvious, even liberating difference actually gets translated into a far more problematic form of inequality. Feminist authors as diverse as Judith Butler (1993; 2006 [1990]), Elizabeth Grosz (1994) and Catharine MacKinnon (1987; 1989; 1993) have pointed to the disproportionate weight of society on women's bodies. A certain kind of masculinity, that Connell (1987; 2005a) aptly called 'hegemonic', hogs the central role and tends to downgrade both femininity in its various forms and the many other ways of being a man. The process of *gendered embodiment* is hence not just *relational* – femininity and masculinity being continually correlating – but also *hierarchized*. Feminist thought has endeavoured to uncover such hierarchies and has explored the possibilities of resistance which female bodies and bodily practices may harbour for female subjectivity.

As we have seen, in everyday life gender is often understood as predicated upon *sex categorization*, and yet the gender order is at the basis of such categorization. Sex and gender are further articulated on sexuality. The fourth chapter will investigate how gender differences relate both to sexual categorization and its naturalization, and to a particular organization of sexuality and erotic attraction. We start with Harold Garfinkel's (1999 [1967]) study of Agnes, the first transgender person to be studied sociologically, and we consider its importance in establishing a constructivist reading of sex and gender. This in turn opens the space for a sociological analysis of *sexuality*. The work on transgender and intersex subjectivities has been important to stress that, in considering gender, sex and sexuality, we have to move from a psychologizing attitude, concerned with what is inside people, to relations and the way they unfold in interaction, culture and institutions. Such an approach is also fundamental to consider heterosexuality as a normative frame which is increasingly put into question by the diffusion of alternative ways of experiencing and embodying sexuality. Heterosexuality has long been taken for granted and underexplored in sociology, while we now understand how important it is to shed light on sexual experiences and embodiment and their varieties.

Sex, gender and sexuality intersect other important aspects of corporeality. Corporeality can be defined along *vertical* and *horizontal* axes, as it were. Bodies are typically sorted vertically, distinguishing generations and various stages of life, from childhood to old age and at the same time they are sorted horizontally by gender, sex, sexuality, race, ethnicity, class and disability. Such categories are by no means independent from one another, nor are they neutral with respect to power: embodied *differences* are caught in intersecting systems of privilege and domination which transform them into *inequalities*.

The coming together of many dimensions of inequality can be properly understood through the concept of 'intersectionality'. In its original version proposed by Kimberlé Crenshaw (1989), this notion was developed to consider how interwoven systems of power are reflected in different elements of subjectivity – especially gender and race – and affect those who are most marginalized in society, combining to perpetuate various forms of discrimination and privilege. All these differences among and in bodies indeed become inequalities. That is, they are assigned a basic value and weight in terms of power, importance and esteem. In the fifth chapter, many examples applying the intersectional approach to the study of embodiment will help to demonstrate how the political side of gender works out in all its concrete details, conditioned by factors of age, race, social class and sexual orientation, and also determined by generation, age and lifetime experience. Sexuality will be a clear example of a domain where such dynamics are deployed.

Corporeality is constructed in *depth*, by our work on the emotions and desires, and on the *surface*, by work on appearance. While, as we have suggested, spotlighting the emotions leads us to explore how what is seemingly most deep-seated in the body gets socially moulded, the sixth chapter will explore the surface of the body and how individuals, women above all, are induced to work upon it. The social pressures to shape one's own appearance and the issue about where power really lies, whether in the looked-at subject or in the famous 'eye of the beholder', have been studied by sociologists since the beginning of the discipline. In the case of female beauty, those dynamics are further interwoven with the codes of recognition of female identity itself. We will then revert more directly to the body politics issue from a feminist angle, exploring the politics of appearances. The well-known observations by a variety of authors such as Susan Bordo (2003 [1993]), Catherine Hakim (2010) and Naomi Wolf (2002 [1990]) will help us through an analysis of contemporary ways of embodying, presenting and managing beauty and ugliness which stress powerful asymmetries between masculinity and femininity. Our body projects – ranging from the practices of daily consumerism such as make-up and fitness, to more invasive and extraordinary acts of alteration such as cosmetic surgery or body art – are based on ideals of beauty, degrees of reflexivity and levels of cogency that are heavily marked by gender. The issue, we shall see, is closely bound up with the whole construction of female identity in that, as many authors have pointed out, a woman's body if unkempt is the less feminine, while nothing similar applies to a man.

A perspective on bodily appearances leads us to consider body representation. How far culture weighs on the body is perhaps most sharply recognized if we look closely at how the body is *represented*. In studying the various ways bodies are depicted we gain a clearer idea of how cultural products – from the noble peaks of art down to the prosaic business of marketing goods – play their part in putting forward ideals of masculinity and femininity that speak to our gendered ways of inhabiting the body and show us how to move, what expressions to assume, how to accost other people. In the final chapter we will go into the way the gendered body is staged in cultural products, especially those of a visual nature. From the classic depiction of the female nude in Western figurative art, and likewise from women in classic Hollywood cinema, there turns out to be a masculine gaze which, as Laura Mulvey (1989 [1975]) pointed out, casts women in the passive, decorative camp, whilst eroticizing them voyeuristically. The media often reproduce the visual codes in extreme form, as Erving Goffman (1979) wrote regarding commercial messages where gender features are *hyper-ritualized*. While we still find commodities being advertised by pictures of docile, decorative and playful female bodies or active, dominant, serious-looking male bodies, there is a growing trend for images subverting conventional gender images, picking up feminist ideas and tailoring them commercially to consumer demand.

Indeed, under the pressure of feminist consciousness and a shifting gender order, Kirsten Kohrs and Rosalind Gill (2021) have documented the development of a 'confident appearing' which is particularly appealing to a white middle-class audience of self-conscious women. The way bodies are gendered and represented in the media is a decisive battlefield to reflect, reinforce and continuously reorganize our perceptions of embodiment. Developing on the backdrop of the neoliberal embracing of the reflexive investment of the body as a project, current trends in visual representation intensify the monitoring and disciplining of bodies, especially the female ones, despite todays' growing rhetoric on body positivity and free expression of our 'true self' through the body.

All in all, the literature on bodies and gender in sociology is now vast and it embraces many aspects of our social experience. We wanted to offer a taste of some fundamental theoretical contributions by digging into some of the texts that influenced a constructivist thinking on the body, but we also wanted to show the richness of the empirical research on the body and gender that is unfolding before our eyes. We are dealing with concepts and realities in transition, both because bodies are increasingly scrutinized and because gender is continuously being remade and questioned. In this book we have endeavoured to offer a primer to such a complex problematic.

Of course, like all books, this one too has limitations. First of all, our choice to give ample space to the classical authors of our discipline, sociology, has inevitably led to treating many white, Western, heterosexual male authors. Our aim was precisely to allow studies on the body and gender dialogue with classical sociological literature on the body, since in our opinion this dialogue is extremely fertile for both fields of knowledge. As we teach and research bodies and gender, we are convinced that the gender (and intersectional) perspective cannot be neglected by those in the field of general sociology, and vice versa that the awareness of the androcentrism and ethnocentrism of the discipline should not lead those in gender and feminist studies to throw the baby out with the bathwater: their perspective can be deepened by learning what the classics of our discipline have to teach us about social processes.

The second limit derives from the first. We are very aware that the reference literature is unbalanced to Western production (classics and feminist sociologies inspired by classics) and to the contexts of the Global North. We will try to underline, again from an intersectional perspective, the factors of inequality that cross Western societies but in the awareness that the greatest inequality is between the Global North and the Global South. Despite the forceful critique of sociology that postcolonial theory contains, we agree with those authors who suggest that the two can productively interact (Go 2013). And we believe that this interaction does not entail only studying non-Western societies and colonialism, but rather adopting a theoretical approach and 'ontology that emphasizes the interactional constitution of social units, processes, and practices across space' (ibid., 28). Of course, we had to make reductions in complexity and choose a single focus, which is gender and embodiment, from classic authors in sociology to contemporary intersectional research in Western societies. Nevertheless, we try to adopt what we think is particularly precious in the postcolonial posture, the capacity to question received frames and classification at the roots of the often taken-for-granted power imbalances which are either blind to difference as specificity or naturalize it as inequality. We look at Western modernity and its impact on embodiment trying to provincialize our glance: all in all, many of the critiques that postcolonial thought levels at classical sociologists (first of all, their Eurocentric universalism and their portraying non-Western societies as a 'generalized "other"') has much in common with both the post-structuralist critique of subjectivity and with the feminist critique of androcentric universalism as well as standpoint epistemology, which inspires this book.

Third, we have made choices between authors and themes, inevitably neglecting many: the aim is not to reduce the text to a pure list of names and topics, but to make it understood, by deepening some examples from empirical research, especially ethnographic, of how the body and gender are mutually constructed, marking the first with the asymmetries of the second, and the second with the materiality of the first.

Looking at bodies and embodiment we have chosen to concentrate on gender since it is a fundamental experience which remains crucial for the constitution of embodied subjectivity, intersects with other fundamental dimensions of social differentiation such as race, class and age, and traverses both everyday experience and social institutions. Gender differences have themselves become the object of much reflection in the social sciences and actions in politics and public life.

This has greatly contributed to a continuous evolution of the way we live the gendered body. A call to go beyond gender is becoming significant in our societies as the gender binary is simultaneously under dispute and persistent. We reckon that in contemporary Western society, we still cannot easily think of a body without assigning it a gender. In most social and cultural settings gender, and its dichotomous organization, is the prime way of differentiating bodies. As mentioned, we will argue that such differentiation brings with itself the badges of hierarchy. Gender brands bodies as difference; social dynamics turn difference into inequality. Our view of the sociology of the body inclines us to explore such dynamics. We believe that a gender approach to embodiment, tracing the fast evolution, mutual construction and incessant interweaving of masculinity and femininity as they take bodily form, will enable us to capture the whole social fabric in its deeper as well as its apparently shallower facets, bringing to light conflicts, ambivalences and opportunities.

1

The Social Body

Hailed as 'the Sistine Chapel of the ancients', in 2019 a formidable collection of prehistoric rock art was discovered in Colombia in the midst of the Amazonian rainforest. One of the most captivating traces of the earliest humans to have come down to us is indeed prehistoric graffiti. These first visual representations of the body give a lively and expressive glimpse of our ancestors' everyday experience. The simple outlines reveal a human body that appears as fully socialized, acting in scenes that depict the organization of everyday life. The emphasis is on certain physical properties, linked to the body's biological endowment, of course, but properties socially acquired: thus, what we sometimes call primitive art is all arms and legs since those are the body parts chiefly being used in a task of vital importance for those societies. Among those first populations we know of, posing triumphant beside a large mammal that one was hoping to bring home for oneself and one's clan served as an auspicious ritual that naturalized the body depicted. We gaze at these images, and the human body takes on a neutral, universal appearance, though in point of fact it is a hunter or warrior: a man rather than a woman, adult but not elderly, forged by a specific culture and its practices and wearing headgear and decorations to denote his rank in it.

As the centuries passed, society's impact on bodies grew above all because societies became more complex: a whole range of material developments called for manual skills, enhancing some of our physical powers and atrophying others. As the ability of people to communicate grew and diversified, we became more subtle in how we presented our body and read other people through their physical attributes. Techniques of representation, manipulation and control multiplied, making bodies a mobile frontier of knowledge, experience and power. The just over eight billion human beings now inhabiting our planet lead widely diverse lives and have diverse access to technology increasingly enabling people to see, check and tweak their bodies the way they wish, or as their social life requires. Tomorrow's archaeologist will be faced with a gamut of often competing representations designed to fix today's truth about the body.

In today's societies of the so-called Global North – basically the post-industrial West steeped in capitalist consumerism – more and more objects are being bought and used to decorate and care for the body, which is at the same time expected to respond submissively to the demands of work and serve as an authentic reservoir of experience and emotion. Ever since the Second World War, and especially for the last three decades, this increasingly central role of the body and the care we lavish on it has coincided with sociology's flourishing attention to bodies and embodiment as *socially-mediated processes* (Adelman & Ruggi 2016; Blackman 2021; Boero & Manson 2020; Burkitt 1999; Cregan 2006; Featherstone, Hepworth & Turner 1991; Fraser & Greco 2004; Howson 2013; Moore & Kosut 2010; Moore & Lorber 2011; Shilling 2012; 2016; Thomas 2013; Turner 2008). Sociology, in short, has taken stock of the infinite scope that body culture and body modification provide as an expression of our acts and desires. In societies that are incessantly, blatantly, self-reflexively attentive to the body, sociology above all – the branch of knowledge that reflects on how we live together – could not fail to notice that human bodies are moulded by social organization, the practices that it structures and the meanings it sustains. Conversely, embodied subjects with their lived experience of their own embodied subjectivity contribute to define the limits and possibilities of social organization.

This first chapter focuses on the co-constitution of bodies and society, something that often goes under the rubric of the social construction of the body. We will complicate the nature/culture divide, showing that the body – which may seem like a biological given – is in fact always socialized, experienced and understood in a social context. We will see this in relation to the evolving under-standing of the body in the West, which has been shaped by the development of modernity and capitalism. We will see how the body has assumed a central importance in social organization and how the world of consumerism and mass consumption has increased the opportunities and pressures to present our bodies to the world. The production/consumption divide has historically been articulated by and mapped onto gender. Gender has been a fundamental category for figuring out bodies and society: drawing on the work of, among others, Raewyn Connell and Colette Guillaumin, we will explore how its understanding helps us to define the contours of embodiment. The gender approach to embodiment which we introduce in this chapter will allow us, throughout the book, to consider issues of power and the way embodied subjects collaborate in the reproduction (or otherwise) of the social structure through their very bodily experi-ences and practices.

1. Embodiment, nature and culture

When we claim that the human body is socially constructed, we suggest that it is primarily experienced and managed in ways that differ from culture to culture and epoch to epoch. To consider the human body as mediated by society implies a recognition that, flesh and blood though it manifestly is, it cannot be reduced to a brute fact unconditioned by the social environment in which it grows, acts and interacts. What we experience as its characteristics varies according to the changing forms of social organization and classification.

As anthropology has shown, different cultures inculcate differing notions of person, the relation between person and body, between human body and nature, between the body and its parts, and so on – differing notions that descend from different forms of social organization and correspond to equally distinct forms of individual experience (Mascia-Lees 2011). Traditionally, Western thought separated the body's material side from intangible thought and culture. It decreed a fundamental rift between what pertains to 'nature' and to 'culture', casting the body in the former domain. From ancient times, the body was separated from the soul (Ferguson 2000; Judovitz 2001; Ruberg 2020). Gradually, the body ceased to be explained in terms of myth or a circular animistic view of nature in favour of maps of the body based on the anatomy and physiology of its parts. From the primitive symbolic ambivalence of the body, whereby it was seen as belonging to a cosmic order preventing it from being recognized as an isolated singularity, we arrived at a society of individuals where the individual body, not the social group, is the insurmountable boundary for each and every one of us. The human mind – socialized, rational, detached, the organ of knowledge and truth – came more and more to be placed at one pole of a pair of opposites, the other being the body, the natural seat of desire, pleasure, suffering and indiscipline.

The seventeenth-century philosopher René Descartes picked up on the Platonic-Christian dualism of body and soul, stripping away the mythical and religious overtones and casting the body once more as *res extensa*, an expression of animal rather than human nature. In the philosophy of the Enlightenment, the body is objectified on a par with the outside world, and hence must be governed by the same laws of physics. But it was modern Western science, modern medicine in particular, that played the greatest part in cementing the objective status of the body, which it reduced to a mere biological effigy (Turner 2008). The scientific view of the body, which only admits physical and chemical relations that can be exactly calculated, has become our reality, such that we routinely measure our subjective experience by counting calories and measuring temperatures: these are now largely considered as the objective indexes the condition and internal processes of our body.

Thus, the typical modern Western view of the body rested on a specific conception of the human being: separate from the cosmos, from other people, and from its own body (Bordo 2003 [1993]). Science, religion and even our domestic habits, the rules of etiquette or the educational values instilled in school, became so many ways of culturally socializing people into this understanding of the body and prescribed ways of experiencing our bodies, even at the most personal and intimate level, such as pain and pleasure.

Social science serves to uncover the cultural frames by which these attitudes are *socially mediated*. In an influential sociological study conducted at an American hospital, Mark Zborowski (1969) showed how different ethnic groups had a different reaction to pain. Italians, Jews and third-generation Americans had a quite dissimilar way of experiencing pain: the specific cultural frameworks by which they faced illness and physical suffering made their experience of pain and how to cope with it well-nigh impossible to compare. Elaine Denny (2018) explores the structural and interpretive perspectives on pain to challenge the objectivity of the biomedical approach, testifying to variations across gender, ethnicity, culture, age and disability. Yet in medical contexts attempts at measuring pain by the use of pain scales is widespread, resulting in an experience of marginalization which increases the pain of those whose pain does not fit a clear medical diagnosis.[1]

Pleasure, too, is an experience mediated by the social context which surrounds it and the significance we attach to it. Here the classic study is Howard Becker's (1953) on marijuana smokers. Becker explained that to derive pleasure from the substance it is not enough to smoke it; you need to master a ritual approach to smoking, relishing it, describing and understanding its effects, handling it in a group situation, and so forth. Far from being instantly able to enjoy the experience, the youngsters that Becker studied were learning to appreciate it by trial and error via a proper social apprenticeship which gave them the tools, the taste buds and the language. Recent works support the case. Angela Jones' (2020) *Camming: Money, Power, and Pleasure in the Sex Work Industry* looks at the erotic webcam industry and at the way workers, called cam models, engage with the job. Pleasure is a fundamental element of camming, and it is constructed through the very experience of the interactive computer-mediated sex, which asks and allows freedoms that would not be possible in face-to-face interaction. The online context makes it easier for cam models to deliver embodied authenticity to clients, fostering a space in which workers have a greater potential to experience various pleasures. Jones demonstrates that pleasure itself reflects a complex interplay of social and cultural arrangements: '(f)or cam models, there is pleasure in simultaneously being good capitalist entrepreneurs and sex workers who also have orgasms for a living' (ibid., 40).

Even death is by no means independent of social circumstance and takes specific forms in different ways in contemporary societies despite being linked to the materiality of the body (Walter 2020). Judith Lasker, Brenda Egolf and Stewart Wolf (1994) showed, for instance, that the rate of deaths by heart attack will tend to vary according to the degree of social cohesion. At Loseto, a small town in Pennsylvania inhabited by a compact community of Italian Americans, the heart attack index long remained about half that of the rest of the country. What protected that community from heart attack was not diet or physical exercise, but the town's close social cohesion: attendance at the local church was keenly kept up, as were family links and an extremely active community life. Leen Van Brussel and Nico Carpentier (2014) show how various aspects of dying, from the experience of life ending to management of the corpse, are experienced through negotiation of typically medicalized frames of understanding that nonetheless converge into a precise image of a good death, connected to values such as independence, control and awareness (see chapter 5).

Placed as it is on the uncertain boundary between the social and biological sciences, the body or, better, embodiment is first of all a set of processes, whose boundaries are never set once and for all but are continually constructed in ongoing practices, through institutions and objects, images and discourses, interaction and social relations. This is increasingly being recognized by fields as diverse as epigenetics, neuroscience, microbiology and immunology, where novel research is 'making starkly visible how the assumption that a self is located in a bounded, unitary body is in fact ... a naturalised legal and political fiction' (Frost 2020, 4; see also Blackman 2016 and Rose 2013). Let us therefore look more closely at that constructivist position which views bodies as socially constructed.

The social construction of the body

In broad terms, the constructivist position has developed in two theoretical directions: one *symbolic* and *communicative*, the other *practical* and *mimetic*. In the first theoretical direction the body looks like a system of signs and symbols, a written text or surface to write upon. Anthropologist Mary Douglas (2003 [1973]) is a key figure in this tradition. Douglas showed that in many cultures the body acts as *a system of natural symbols* used to mean or communicate something else: the sick body stands for social malaise, the healthy body indicates moral uprightness, the confines of the body are social confines, its detritus is what our societies discard. No natural way of considering the body exists without also implying a social dimension: the individual body and the social body dialogue with one another in a constant interplay of symbolic reference. Hence, argues Douglas, investigating the individual's experience of the body's structure, margins and boundaries means we must look at the symbol constructed by the society to which that individual belongs: '(w)hat is being carved in human flesh is an image of society' (Douglas 1984 [1966], 117; for a discussion, see Duschinsky, Schnall & Weiss 2016). The more intimately that experience is felt and the more expressive its message, the more eloquently it will reveal the structures of society itself, like in the case of individual disease which becomes a symbol of social disorder. As a set of symbols, the body is also a highly standardized means of individual expression, reflecting the cultural and social pressures bearing upon it.

In the second theoretical direction, the body is seen as the subject's main vehicle for cultural development. Subjects are fleshed out by a process of *embodiment*: individuals' materiality and disposition are moulded by social interaction and institutions and, circularly, via their embodied subjectivities, individuals take their place within society. In other words, the embodied subject finds its social being via physical techniques that reproduce differences and hierarchies (of gender, age, ethnic background, class and so on). This approach is a radical development of sociologist and anthropologist Marcel Mauss's suggestions in his classic essay on 'techniques of the body'. Techniques of the body, writes Mauss (1973 [1934], 70), are 'ways in which from society to society men [sic] know how to use their bodies'. The way we walk, sleep, feed, swim or laugh, wash ourselves or make love may seem spontaneous and somehow pre-social; but they change from culture to culture and between different groups within the same community. The norms that regulate the use of the body are deeply ingrained in individual subjectivities, but they are communal and are transmitted by learning and imitation. They are central to how we differently occupy the social space, something which will be picked up by Pierre Bourdieu (1977; 1992 [1980]) in his reflections on embodiment and society (see chapter 2).

In all cultures different body features and practices are regulated more or less bindingly; they are thus classified, sorted and organized, often in such a way that what is dubbed as 'natural' acts as a prop or pedestal to an overall view of the world. We may be persuaded by the thought that certain tribal societies' ideas of sickness – for example, that it is punishment for some sacrilege – are symbolic constructions framing reality via cognitive tools devised by a particular organization of knowledge and social behaviour, yet we are much less prepared to accept that our own way of perceiving the body and looking after it is likewise a social construction. For instance, Western science and modern medicine are dominantly presented as universal forms of knowledge, objective in being tested by the rigorous procedures of an experimental method. Yet, sociologists have highlighted the potential perils of universalizing particular bodies and embodiments. For example, by understanding male physiology as universal, advancements in medicine and health care fail to consider how differences between male and female pathophysiology may mean that men's and women's bodies display symptoms of illness differently or respond differentially – qualitatively and quantitatively – to medications (Annandale 2021; Bird & Rieker 2012). It also appears counterintuitive to hold that pain and pleasure are not essential, pre-social data bearing upon us according to a biological substratum that determines and defines their basic characteristics, but as we have seen above, this has been challenged by social scientists.

In contemporary Western culture, where the body is regarded as 'natural', it is important to remember that the natural is perceived both as an objective datum – something that does not depend on us – and as a *moral* datum – something right or wrong, to the point where, in order to denigrate some action, we claim it is 'against nature'. Thus 'naturalness' acts as the last frontier of people's room for manoeuvre. We invoke nature when we want to terminate discussion by a self-evident, unfathomable value, when we want to come up with a definitive judgement or justification. The construction of a nature/culture divide is thereby an inherently political issue. Many studies have laid bare the politics of the natural, in science and culture (Franklin, Lury & Stacey 2000; Latour 1999). As Nigel Thrift (2000) has suggested, modern Western society is relying on 'nature' even more than previous societies. To ponder the boundary between nature and culture and see how they construct one another is particularly urgent in an age when technology is altering what is held to be natural about the body, the environmental crisis is making us reappraise the changing limits of human existence, and the experience of the pandemic has pointed to the interlocking of the limits of human embodiment and social organization.

2. The body in the rise of Western modernity

Despite being considered a natural, pre-social datum, the modern body in the capitalist West is primarily the fruit of a long historical development in which its appearance, postures and gestures gradually changed. In his seminal work on the process of civilization, Norbert Elias (2021 [1939]; see also Shilling 2012) demonstrated how, in the course of time, there arose a special 'civilized' body behaviour connected with certain forms of control or management of the body, apparently distancing humans from animals. The development of the modern State and of its monopoly on physical violence resulted in the spread of 'pacified' social spaces whereby the individual's prime object of fear was no longer physical violence, but that of not giving the right impression. The ensuing conflict and cooperation dynamics between social classes led to the genesis of modern Western society, the catalyst of the 'civilizing process' being when the dominant nobility turned from being a class of knights into one of courtiers whose bodies were increasingly *rationalized*. Court life called for and produced different qualities from those needed in armed combat. One needed constant 'reflection and forethought', and 'stricter regulation of one's emotions', because every greeting and every conversation has an importance far exceeding the single occurrence as they reveal one's own status and contribute to social standing in the court. Courtiers learnt to foresee others' acts from tiny signals in their interaction: in 'psychologizing' the other and guessing their motives by an increasingly subtle ability to read body language, they held their emotions in check as strategic counters to be played in the social dance; they pursued carefully contrived personal objectives by their ability to keep self-expression under tight control.

In the early modern age, the transformation of nobles into courtiers went with a steady rise in the middle classes, making it necessary for the former to distinguish themselves from the latter. Unconsciously felt 'rejection of vulgarity' permeated the conduct of the superior courtier class for whom, like 'good taste', it held 'prestige value'. Later, in the nineteenth century, the commercial and industrial bourgeoisie gained the upper hand. Instead of the courtier's skills, the bourgeoisie's 'code of conduct' privileged professional competence, possession of money and, in general, customs prizing self-control above refinement, again communicated through rationalization of the body.

Given the colonial setting it operated in, the rationalized body was also uncompromisingly white. More and more, the Black body came to figure as a savage 'other', excessive in its prosperous form and at the same time sexualized as a deviant object (Gilroy 1993; hooks 1992; McClintock 1995; Stoler 1995; Strings 2019).[2] As African people had been turned into commodities in the Atlantic slave trade, Western countries identified some specific bodily differences to justify their subjugation: dark skin was at the negative pole in the dichotomy of white and good versus black and evil, broad facial features stood for undue sexual appetites, unruliness or stupidity, muscularity cried for hard labour. Such rationalization of the body, which was first and foremost male, white and bourgeois, translated into a means of domination on a global scale. As Edward Said (2003 [1975], 207) showed in his influential work *Orientalism*, non-Western people featured *en masse* as the 'Orient', being variously 'designated as backward, degenerated, uncivilized and retarded, the Orientals were viewed in a framework constructed out of biological determinism and moral-political admonishment'. The body in Western modernity has indeed been the central site for the process of racialization whereby bodily differences are naturalized and inscribed with social meaning and value. Even today, blackness is often constructed as being trapped within the web of nature while the white body has freedom to disembody itself, locating whiteness (and masculinity) firmly within modernity and rationalization. Black embodiment still arguably battles against what Frantz Fanon (2021 [1952]) suggested characterizes Black consciousness: that the Black body is *objectified* in representation, rather than perceived as the *subject* of experience (see chapters 5 and 7).

In its white, Western form, the ideal of the embodied subject of modernity corresponds to an increased rationalization that embraces all aspects of life and is imposed on all social classes. As argued by Chris Shilling (2012), classical sociology could not ignore completely the issue of the body. Sociology was born in the age of industrialization and thus it studied labouring bodies, how they were strictly moulded by the capitalist manufacturing system and the rise of Western rationalism. Typically, interest focused on the male body complying with the demands of capitalist production. Thus, Karl Marx thought work enabled human beings to fulfil themselves in harmony with nature, or else be alienated from themselves and their body, as in the capitalist manufacturing system. With the development of manufacturing, the labourer 'performs one and the same operation' all his life and converts 'his whole body into the automatic, specialized implement of that operation' (Marx 1977 [1887], 321). Factory discipline 'exhausts the nervous system to the uttermost, it does away with the many-sided play of the muscles, and confiscates every atom of freedom, both in bodily and intellectual activity' (ibid., 398). Capitalism thus steals corporeality of its meaning: the worker 'only feels himself freely active in his animal function – eating, drinking, procreating, or at most in his dwelling and dressing-up, etc.; in his human functions he no longer feels himself to be anything but an animal' (ibid., 66). Marx proposes the idea that the boundaries between animality and humanity are socially constructed. This construction is, however, the result of domination and exploitation, something to be criticized on the basis of a truly human and natural way of being in one's own body and deploying one's own labour.

Max Weber (1992 [1922]) in turn considered the modern factory an example of rational conditioning of labour activities. As a result, he reckoned that the human body had become totally geared to the demands of work, a 'function', a 'tool': workers are stripped of their natural rhythm and completely recast to suit the work conditions, adjusting their bodies to the task for the creation of a better 'economy of strength'. This rational conditioning of the body in factories forms part of the Western development of 'discipline' which has its roots in the early modern age. Seen as 'uniform', 'exact', 'consistently rationalized', 'methodically trained' conduct, discipline is found in any society whenever the masses need continuous management, but it especially developed via the bureaucratic and productive systems of modernity.

However, modern bureaucratic discipline is not just rationalized; it is also based on individual aspirations working via individuals instead of simply upon them; it is not only repressive but also expansive, boosting the body's performance while subjecting it to strict routines responding to the requirements of institutions which are chiefly economic and political. Indeed, in Weber's view, Protestant bourgeois men in the Western modern age welcomed discipline and turned it into a project. It thus came to be an important stepping-stone to mobility in the capitalist social order. Discipline was not just a means of bureaucratic domination, therefore, but also a factor that brought growing influence and legitimation to a particular social class, the bourgeoisie; it spurred them to reform, justifying social change in the name of ever-increasing rationalization. In Weber's view, it was the 'sober and rational Puritan discipline' of Oliver Cromwell's army in the English Civil War that meant they proved technically superior to their Royalist opponents, undisciplined 'men of honour' (Weber 2002 [1904]). Just as the mediaeval 'holy anorexics' (Bell 1987) had managed to get over the disadvantage of being women by deliberately allowing themselves to starve to death as a proof of spiritual superiority, so the nascent bourgeoisie of early modern times seem to have exploited their ascetic regime as a way of legitimizing social mobility. Deliberate denaturalizing of the body through extraordinary behaviour and discipline has served in all cultures to divide the elect from the rest of the population. As society increasingly secularized and was imbued with capitalism, certain ways of managing the body to make it docile, responsive to professional needs in the economy and to participation in politics were employed as techniques for governing the population, as well as individual and collective strategies towards emancipation and power (see chapter 3).

In the nineteenth century the opposite extreme to the rational bourgeois man was in many ways the prostitute, the fallen woman, prey to and eliciting irrational desires (see also chapter 3). It was a figure that increasingly fascinated art and artistic representation in that it both repelled and fascinated, the symbol of urban development and its slum areas, a warning to proper-living bourgeois ladies who were still largely debarred from the public domain and relegated to the domestic area which the patriarchal order (a social system in which positions of privilege and dominance are primarily held by men) and the new capitalist economy ordained for them (Clayson 2003). Indeed, both Marx and Weber's classic analyses of body rationalization do not consider closely the way capitalist accumulation and rationalization might have impacted on women and their bodies.[3] According to Anne Witz (2000), classical sociology constructed for the most part a 'masculinist ontology' where the body was at the same time present and absent: female corporeality was a naturalized given that served as a backdrop to male sociality, which in turn limited the possibility of considering male embodiment in all its facets. In *Caliban and the Witch*, feminist activist and scholar Silvia Federici (2014 [2004], 16) looks at the transition from the Middle Ages to capitalism and provocatively writes that 'the body has been for women in capitalist society what the factory has been for male waged workers: the primary ground of their exploitation and resistance, as the female body has been appropriated by the state and men and forced to function as a means for the reproduction and accumulation of labour'. Sketching analogies between features bestowed to witches in Europe and the portrayals of African and Indigenous American peoples as 'cannibals' and 'devil worshippers', she juxtaposes the suffering of witch-burning to the experience of enslavement. She contends that witch-hunting was deployed to break community resistance to the transition to a capitalist economy that sharply divided private from public life and relegated women's knowledge and role to 'otherness'.

Bodies, minds and emotions were all shaped by the process of modernization. From the end of the nineteenth century onwards, the expansion of the great Western metropolises led to uprooting from one's background, urban anonymity, specialization and differentiation of functions. The burgeoning spectacle of the goods for sale allowed for the development of what Georg Simmel (1950 [1903]) defined as a *blasé* attitude fostering increased intellectualization and rationalization. The metropolis thus had a profound effect on embodied subjectivity. The senses changed, sight coming to dominate experience; people became less sensory and more sensitive. The same author describes a prevailing 'aspiration to hygiene' (Simmel 2009 [1908]). Far from a mere reflection of scientific progress, this served a distinct social and political purpose, as social classes were distinguished and recognized by a different capacity to manage one's own body. With the rise of consumer culture, the body became the stake in a match where the market beckoned to the individual in a thousand leisure areas organized around goods and services. Thus – to go back to Elias – we see how, as the civilizing process advanced in contemporary society, the body became the point of application for forms of self-control that may always have existed, but now turned more 'all-inclusive' – applying to relations with everybody – and 'complex' in being 'more dispassionate', that is, more detached yet also 'highly differentiated'. Growing importance attached to areas designed for the 'controlled de-control of emotions', like sport or the 'exciting' pastimes that made up for what was 'missing' in everyday life (Elias & Dunning 1986). People had to learn how to curb their body yet simultaneously let it live in forms permitted by the worlds of entertainment, leisure time and consumerism which opened the way to new forms of both freedom and domination (see also chapter 2).[4]

Gender and the rise of consumer culture

All in all, the very structure of modern capitalism is based on a division between public and private, production and consumption, which is deeply intertwined with the gender order. For gender not only makes for differences in the consumer cultures of different times and places but played its part in how consumer capitalism came into being from the early modern age down to our present day. It not only stemmed from the industrial revolution peaking in the late nineteenth century, or the calculating ascetic mentality of the eighteenth-century petty bourgeoisie, or even from international commerce and early colonial pursuits in the seventeenth century, but also from changes in consumer practice and culture setting in at the very end of the late Middle Ages – and all the time coinciding with a gradual shift of the woman's role (Sassatelli 2007a).

In a classic essay on luxury and the genesis of capitalism, Werner Sombart (1967 [1922]) analysed art and literature in mediaeval Europe and the Italian Renaissance, suggesting that, as early as the end of the fourteenth century, a connection appears between the 'secularization of love' – meaning its slow but steady emancipation from religious goals, rules or institutions – and the luxury-related use of goods and wealth. Love gradually becomes more justifiable in its own right and, as a result, in that society still overtly biased in favour of male power and strictly heterosexual, a new aestheticism and hedonism come to be attached to women and love, paving the way for greater refinement of the pleasures of life. So, the consumer society seems to have been spurred not just by men risking greater and greater capital in fitting out ocean-going vessels to trade with the colonies, but also, writes Sombart, by a specific category of women: 'courtesans'. They spread and embodied a new femininity based more and more on the calculated use of sophisticated pleasures; in the end the whole of society was infected with a desire for elegant entertainment and sumptuous living.

Though bourgeois women felt the heaviest yoke of patriarchal ideology relegating them to domestic affairs, it was they who fired city life as they scoured the new-born shops and stores for the wares required by the new fashion for elegant domesticity and aesthetic femininity (Glennie & Thrift 1996). For many middle-class house-wives in Victorian England, for example, shopping was their first taste of real freedom, and the starting point for their push into public life (Rappaport 1999). The truly modern consumer culture thrived and spread upon a wave of hedonism and sophistication, fed by certain forms of cultural consumption that were heavily gender-related.[5] It is important to remember, however, how closely women's consumer capacity was linked to power dynamics within the family where it had to be somehow functional and subsidiary to the production of income, man's domain. The proper middle-class wife, as Thorstein Veblen (1994 [1899]) describes, was expected to consume, to cultivate her body and above all to lend lustre to her husband becoming actively complicit in the marriage between consumer capitalism and patriarchy (see chapter 5).[6]

More and more, with the twentieth century and down to our day, the body has become a territory to be explored, a place for regaining self-esteem and developing one's own self (Ruberg 2020). The surface and the interior of the body are open more than ever to recon-struction or re-incorporation through products and services available in the market in new, ever more rationalized fashion (Featherstone 1982; Sassatelli 2012). Body management is geared to *increase* bodies' capacity to feel, to act and to realize self-identity. The dualist paradigm – or divide between body and mind/self – has not been transcended but the ratio between its two poles has changed. Subjects have been encouraged to seek not containment within their body, but expansion via its potential. Traditionally in Western thought the mind and spirit were the seat of intelligence and potential salvation, while the body, especially when deviating from the social rules in its acts and features, tended to be a sign and even a cause of depravity (Bordo 2003 [1993]; Feher, Nadaff & Tazi 1989; Synnott 2002 [1993]). Now, however, it has also become an area of potential self-fulfilment. Self-fulfilment and self-identity are now derived not so much from work and production, as from consumption: we do not simply consume according to what we are, but we become what we consume. This is intrinsically related to the current structuring of the economy, based on information technologies, global production and the imperatives of adaptability. According to Emily Martin (1994), the mantra of flexibility now includes everyone's personality, body and organization, not only the job market. To some extent, the body thus becomes plastic, a sort of lifestyle accessory, a matter to be shaped and 'stylized' (Ghigi & Sassatelli 2018; see also chapters 2 and 6).

We shall see, though, that even the body as a place of personal fulfilment was intensely rationalized and tied to a vision of masculine and racial power. Such a body is still white, male, slim, athletic, hetero-sexual and disciplined in its quest for fulfilment. It stands opposed to deviant bodily forms often associated with ethnic minorities, LGBTQ subjects and women (see chapters 4 and 5).

3. Gender and social relations

Despite the normative force of a rationalized, white, male body, the body that the modern age has built for us is neither neutral nor undifferentiated. In everyday life, the family, school, the workplace, sports field, etc.: everywhere is still organized by fundamental boundaries separating men from women, boys from girls. It is true that, especially in countries shaped by liberal democracy, women currently enjoy a series of important rights on a par with men, and that various spheres of social action are formally regulated by equal opportunity legislation trying to promote real as well as formal equality among people. Yet it is no exaggeration to say, and easily observed, that gender differences remain, loud and clear, when it comes to reproducing the social structure as well as managing personal identity. A focus on gender helps us to under-stand how interaction, institutions and culture mould our bodies, and conversely how interaction, institutions and culture work via gendered bodies.

Gender can be understood in many ways, as a *relational structure*, a dimension of *identity* and a *practice* or process. Far from being a body property, gender is a relational structure.[7] Raewyn Connell (2021, 11) suggests that to understand gender '(t)he key is to move from a focus on difference to a focus on *relations*'. These include relations among individuals endowed with bodies who occupy different positions in social organization due to their reproductive capacity, as well as relations of those individuals with their own body. This set of relations establishes a 'gender order', which fixes a network of possibilities and courses of action that impinge on inter-action, culture and institutions and crystallize power differences.

The notion of gender arose from the need for a term to do justice to differences between men and women. However, the gender order goes beyond relations between men and women: gender relations do include difference and dichotomy, but also many other configurations. In the contemporary world, for example, gender entails hierarchies among men and among women, often coded by class, race, ethnicity, age, sexuality and so on, which can in no way be reduced to a difference between the male and the female (Connell 2021). The notion of gender has in time enabled us to go beyond the male/female dichotomy and envisage a plurality of ways of experiencing the body, sexual identity, erotic desire, femininity and masculinity, as occurred with gay and lesbian studies and more recently queer studies (Beemyn & Eliason 1996; Green 2007; Sullivan 2003) (see chapter 4). Introducing gender as a tool of social analysis has meant that, alongside studies on women with their focus on the barriers to full citizenship, we now have a burgeoning field of men's studies and masculinities (Connell 2005a; 2005b; Connell & Messerschmidt 2005; Gough 2018; Messerschmidt 2018, see chapter 5).

Gender is likewise a basic dimension of identity that is constantly being forged, and played upon, in different ways and contexts according to social organization. While gender underpins all social arrangements, its workings are in many ways dependent on the specificity of the situation at hand. Thus, Connell (2021, 11–12) notices:

> Sometimes cultural patterns do express bodily differences, for example when they celebrate first menstruation as a distinction between girl and woman. But often they do more than that, or less than that. Social practices sometimes exaggerate a distinction of female from male (e.g. maternity clothes), sometimes deny the distinction (many employment practices), sometimes mythologize it (computer games), and sometimes complicate it ('third-gender' customs). So, we cannot say that social arrangements routinely 'express' biological difference.

Furthermore, how gender differences are viewed and experienced and gender equality between the genders promoted varies in different social groups: African Americans, for example, express greater criticism of gender inequality than whites (Kane 2000), while among elite social groups women often occupy traditional roles within the family as compared to the middle class (Keister, Thébaud & Yavorsky 2022). As suggested by Judith Lorber (2021), the gender binary is currently challenged by a proliferation of gender identities which favour fluidity. And yet the paradox cries out: while increasingly destabilized, the gender binary remains fundamental in institutions, everyday life and the legal apparatus, even in the presence of a pluralization and fragmentation of gender identities.

As we shall see in more detail in the third chapter, the origin of the notion of gender dates back to the consolidating of feminist thinking during the 1970s and the widespread realization by social science – sociology, history, anthropology – that differences between men and women are bolstered by many social institutions and essentially go back to an imbalance of power. Rather than seeing gender as the cultural representation of a biological dichotomy between male and female, contemporary feminism prefers the view of a social process producing sexual identities, including our perception that there are two distinct, different and complementary sexes. Gender is thus seen as intertwined with two other defining aspects: sex (and classifications assigning bodies to a sexual category) and sexuality (and classifications sorting bodies according to the organization of erotic desire). The relationship between gender, sex and sexuality is a crucial one; it is hard to talk of one without referring to the others (see chapter 4).

Beginning with Margaret Mead (2003 [1935]) and her famous study on certain tribes in Papua New Guinea, anthropology studies have confirmed not just that male and female behaviour and attitudes vary culturally, but that there exist other sexual classificatory systems that are less rigidly dichotomous than the one which has long been dominant in the West. One need only think how many times a 'third sex' has been posited through history and cultures, with periods of homosexuality long having been seen as normal in several cultures and social circumstances (D'Anglure 2018 [2006]; Herdt 1993; Moodie 1994; Totman 2011; Weston 1993). By contrast, in modern Western culture an alignment between gender, sex and sexuality, if disputed, is still largely dominant, and that alignment posits women and men as essentially distinct entities with complementary functions, behavioural characteristics and diverging physical attributes, each pole being attracted by the other. This alignment is strongly normative: it is often presented as 'normal', and also 'morally right'. Today, in everyday life if a person succeeds in behaving convincingly as a woman, she is gendered as a woman. Attribution to one gender or the other usually works in such a way that what decides whether a person belongs to one category or the other is neither their assignment to a sexual category at birth, nor (since the genitals are customarily hidden) any real conformity with the criterion of assignment. Nonetheless, a woman's actions may cause her femininity to be doubted if she indulges in compromising behaviour, such as homoerotic relations or displaying overt aggressiveness (see chapter 4).

It is thus very apt to say, following the seminal article by Candace West and Don Zimmerman (1987), that gender is a practice and a process: it is a 'doing' stemming from a routine performed in daily interaction (ibid., 126):

> the 'doing' of gender is undertaken by women and men whose competence as members of society is hostage to its production. Doing gender involves a complex of socially guided perceptual, interactional, and micropolitical activities that cast particular pursuits as expressions of masculine and feminine 'natures' ... it is a situated doing, carried out in the virtual or real presence of others who are presumed to be oriented to its production. Rather than as a property of individuals, we conceive of gender as an emergent feature of social situations: both as an outcome of and a rationale for various social arrangements and as a means of legitimating one of the most fundamental divisions of society.

West and Zimmerman's elaboration has been very influential in establishing that gender is an ensemble of ritualized expressions that need to be actualized by interaction (see chapters 2 and 3). So, it is the fruit of conditions situated and determined by interaction and its organization. For this reason, the performers assume it is shared. Doing gender 'furnishes the interactional scaffolding of social structure': 'in appreciating the institutional forces that maintain distinctions between women and men, we must not lose sight of the interactional validation of those distinctions that confers upon them their sense of "naturalness" and "rightness"' (ibid., 147). Contemporary sociology has more and more espoused the view that how our social life and experience are organized makes us not so much express natural differences, as steadily, practically *produce* those differences.

Though all societies share some form of body-related distinction between male and female (and third or multiple categories, in some cases), they may have different perceptions of the difference – the body, its form and potential – and forge embodiment in a variety of ways. In short, the biological endowment is itself moulded socially, and not just by medical or other forms of knowledge, but through practice and institutions.

Gendering the body

Sociology recognizes today that there are a variety of more or less sophisticated institutional frames through which our being a man or a woman is accomplished as a normal, natural fact. Take, for example, the persisting sexual segregation in public toilets, which is still dominant despite the development of gender-neutral bathrooms. This sexual segregation is clearly to do with the functioning of different private parts and dictated by a particular need for modesty related to sexual difference, rather than emphasizing the similarity of what and how we excrete. This plays its part in stressing and naturalizing the differences between men and women, ruling out points of identity that are found between the two categories. So much so that the development of gender-neutral bathrooms has become a battlefield, first supported by feminists, and then demanded by gender-variant people whose use of conventional toilets typically receives a shocking response (Cavanagh 2010).

Even where biological differences are glimpsed between the two sexes (as in physical strength and size), it can be shown that the actuality of gender differences – their working as inequalities, we might add – is upheld by social organization and institutions. For example, it is true that males are on average taller and sturdier than women, but that relative difference between men and women is above all reproduced and underpinned by the social norm of 'selective mating' (Goffman 1977a), whereby most people tend to find it 'odd' when the woman of the couple is visibly taller and bulkier than the man. The fact is, as we have seen, that unlike the laws of physics, sexual difference is bolstered by practical structures of social organization that construct and naturalize gender distinctions and render them consequential. We might even say that the greater the social pressure, the greater the difference between bodies (Guillaumin 1993; 2016 [1992]).[8]

Gender is not an individual or body property, but it is *realized through the body*. As such, gender is a basic social construct and hence, as Judith Butler (1993) and Pierre Bourdieu (2001 [1998]) have written, it cannot be reduced to a whim: embodying gender is a process or practice accomplished in the various social settings in which individuals find themselves; such identity gets consolidated by material traits – deportment, body size, way of talking, etc. – and symbolic aspects – discourse, classification and categories – which people cannot easily slough off without relinquishing a fundamental part of themselves (see also chapter 3).

Thus, for example, as Iris Marion Young's seminal essay *Throwing like a Girl* (2005 [1980]) showed, considering female embodiment, women learn to experience space and movement in particular ways. From our earliest infant play, they learn to bunch their fist or 'throw like a girl', so that it comes to seem quite natural that a girl should throw 'underarm' rather than overarm, while in sporting lore throwing a ball, such as in baseball, is from the outset a different style of throwing according to the male or female versions of the game. More generally, through the organization of spatiality, women have typically come to restrict their movements as they perceive themselves as the object rather than the subject of action, viewing their bodies as something that needs protecting and being taught to live in their enclosed inner space. 'The modalities of feminine bodily existence', suggests Young (ibid., 153),

> are not merely privative, however, and thus their source is not merely in lack of practice, though this is certainly an important element. There is a specific positive style of feminine body comportment and movement, which is learned as the girl comes to understand that she is a girl. The young girl acquires many subtle habits of feminine body demeanour – walking like a girl, tilting her head like a girl, standing and sitting like a girl, gesturing like a girl, and so on.

Feminist scholar Colette Guillaumin (2016 [1992]; see also Guillaumin 1993) explored the way the embodiment of gender is both social and material. Gender is implanted in the body by a social process of embodiment that, as suggested, Guillaumin called the 'fabrication of the sexed body'. Such fabrication, or the 'work of making the body sexed', is a social process of physical differentiation that situates people via their bodies, dividing them into gender categories, typically stressing a dichotomy between masculinity and femininity. Guillaumin's constructivism is firmly anchored in the 'material' nature of our experience: our gendered bodies take shape via a complex system of differentiation which involves the management of time, space and relations. The gender order dictates the fabrication of the sexed body, which is, in short, the inevitable 'practices of formation of a woman's or a man's body correctly inserted into its society' (Guillaumin 1993, 42). Conversely, Guillaumin sees gender as essentially a matter of constructing the body and naturalizing the differences (ibid., 40):

> around the external reproductive apparatus (female or male), a material and symbolic construction is elaborated, destined first to express, then to emphasize and finally to separate the sexes. This construction duplicates a material social relationship that is not at all symbolic: the socio-sexual division of labour and the social distribution of power. Such construction makes men and women appear to be heterogeneous, that is, essentially different. This material and symbolic structure implies a constant intervention by social institutions throughout the life of the individual, beginning

at birth and even before birth, ever since it has been possible to know the sex of an infant in the womb. The intervening social construction is inscribed in the body itself. The body is constructed as a sexed body.

Thus, the binary fabrication of a body that fits the gender order is a long-term operation beginning very early on, with something new added at each stage. It is a steady process, constantly deciding what is appropriate for a woman's body and what for a man's; and it assigns women a subordinate position. Such fabrication results in a 'sexualization' which is for Guillaumin (1995; see also Juteau-Lee 1995) analogous to racialization: just like race is inscribed in the body through racism and its order, sex is inscribed in the body through the practical and cultural ways in which gender and gender relations are organized.

Guillaumin argues that the fabrication of the body as a sexed body is forged in three ambits. First, 'direct interventions' upon the body, including techniques to modify it, fashion, distribution of food and checking up on respective sizes, all differing according to gender. Second, what is called 'indirect interventions', training the body to handle its own physical space, posture, mobility, use of utensils and objects, tone of voice, etc. For example, children's games are a basic means of setting a gender-specific posture: physical games prescribe that 'a girl does not kick or punch as boys do. Since it is equally forbidden to both sexes to bite or pull hair, girls find themselves without a coherent defence in children's fights, in which they are not supposed to participate anyway' (Guillaumin 1993, 46). Play is itself typically dichotomously gendered: boys have more time and room for playing than girls, which will reflect on subjective features like posture, boldness, range of spontaneous movements, so that male embodiment gets defined differently from femininity. It will later be reflected in different embodied attitudes once the children grow up: 'women ceaselessly restrict their use of space, men maximize it. Look at the arms and legs of the latter, which extend widely on seats, chair backs and their open – even brusque – gestures while moving about. By contrast, look at the joined legs, the parallel feet, the elbows held close to the body, the measured movements of women even when they are in a hurry' (ibid., 50).

Lastly, the fabrication of the sexed body proceeds along the axis of 'the body for others'. This includes handling the proximity between men and women, ways of being reciprocally interrelated and acting as a couple. Here Guillaumin stresses how boys and girls go through a different bodily apprenticeship during socialization. The former learn to cooperate on an equal basis via informal games that keep them physically close in a rough-and-tumble, not fearing contact but seeing it as natural and spontaneous, while their games lead them to occupy public places for sports that require cooperation; the latter learn to avoid wrestling or confrontation, they are groomed for a body they will keep as adults, 'close to babies, the sick, invalids, old people, the sexuality of men', which asymmetrically isolates them in the roles of caregiving, attentiveness and devotion. This is how the process of fabrication of the sexed body tacitly reproduces subordination and inequality of power.

In this chapter we have considered the way the body is socially constructed. In Western modernity, the body has been rationalized and has appeared more and more as a 'natural' object to be disciplined to the needs of a variety of institutions. Discipline and rationalization have worked not only as ways of controlling the population but also as techniques of legitimation, in particular for the white male bourgeois which came to dominate economy and society. While the Black body was typically excluded from this process, women were assigned to the consuming pole of the equation and relegated to the private sphere. The gender order, which organizes the relations between genders, works as to make different bodily capacities grow for the different genders. Women's bodies bear the burden of inequality, being constructed in ways which stress subordination in countless ordinary practices. Ordinary practices and interaction are fundamental for the constitution of embodied subjectivities and gender. This we shall discuss in the next chapter.

2

Gendered Bodies and Subjectivity

In *Sorry We Missed You*, a 2019 film directed by British director and playwright Ken Loach, we are faced with society's power to stretch the limits of the body. The protagonist, Ricky, runs a franchise as a self-employed delivery driver but gets robbed and violently assaulted while making deliveries: he should see a doctor, rest and recover but he is compelled by his supervisor to go back to work no matter what. As the male breadwinner who is in charge of saving his family from debt, he feels obliged to continue working despite the injuries and manages his own feelings to go back to work. In the interactions we witness between Ricky and his wife, colleagues and supervisor, we understand that the limits of his body, his medical condition, are not acceptable to him. A doctor's note on the contrary would have established how long he could not, and must not, be held responsible for his absence or, in other words, for his body's incapacity. Once allowed, the medical perspective would have liberated the worker from the responsibility of their body and its tasks: certified as unfit, the body goes beyond human will. The worker would have had to wait, recover, follow medical prescriptions and endeavour to get back to a state of health where the body is under control, a docile instrument of work and other daily occupations.

There are two different relations to the body contained in this scenario. In contemporary Western societies we tend to see the world either as the upshot of 'natural' events, or else as a 'social' phenomenon bound up with people's will, acts and interactions. Two broad, primary frameworks or perspectives are thus enshrined in our minds and our symbols, as well as in the material resources and organizational rules of institutions (Goffman 1986 [1974]). By these two basic frameworks we understand and manage ourselves, our acts and our feelings in everyday life. 'Natural frameworks' attribute events and characteristics entirely to natural factors – hence 'purely physical', not intentional or animate – whereas 'social frameworks' explain phenomena according to human will and design, performing 'guided actions' which in turn subject those performing them to social norms like efficiency, honesty, good taste, tactfulness and so on. The two kinds of perspective frame embodied subjects differently: in the natural kind, people are not responsible for their body since it eludes their will; in social frames, people are custodians of it, manipulating it to their own ends or to appear in the best light. In our everyday dealings with others, we use both kinds of frameworks, more or less credibly according to practical circumstances consolidated into social conventions. This interplay of perspectives is part and parcel of how we manage our bodies in everyday life.

This example points to the relation between bodies, gender and *subjectivity*. We live our bodies and account for them in a variety of ways which are coded by gender and realize ourselves as subjects. Subjectivity is constituted through the way we live, experience and play out our bodies, and this takes place first and foremost at the level of *interaction*. The body is marshalled in countless ways of interaction, which help us construct self-identity and an image of ourselves for ourselves and the others. In everyday life, on the one hand, the body is transformed into an *instrument* for work and labour, a utility, a function. On the other hand, the body continues to operate as the paramount *symbol* for subjects to demonstrate their being self-possessed, civilized or otherwise valuable. We continuously denaturalize the body to take up our social roles in everyday life, and yet we often refer to 'nature' to define aspects of embodiment which are indeed constructed by the rules of interaction, the way we are asked to manage emotions, and the way our body has been shaped throughout our biographies depending on social position as defined notably by gender.

In this chapter, we begin by looking at the body in social inter-action and at people's efforts to manage the conflict between different perspectives on the body. In order to stand as a respectable subject, it is the subject's fundamental responsibility to have a body that is responsive to the needs of interaction, culture and institutions. Subjects need a capable, polished, presentable body within the dictates of their social world. Such norms that dictate what is socially acceptable differ in content and in cogency, depending on gender. We shall thus consider Erving Goffman's work on the constitution of the embodied self in interaction through gender lenses. Gendered embodiment is typically related to emotions. The management of emotions is a fundamental aspect of body management as related to subjectivity, both as it defines the subject's personal experience and its self-presentation in everyday life. We shall then address emotions and the different expectations on our capacity to feel and manage emotions, and how they are related to masculinity and femininity.

There are numerous pressures on how subjects should seek to consciously shape and present their bodies to realize a valuable self in society, including the power of the market and consumer society, to which we will then turn. In late modernity, subjects have become increasingly reflexive in their capacity to work on the body to respond to social requirements to the point that the body has become a reflexive project to be managed and perfected. And yet, in daily life, the embodied construction of subjectivity is, to a large degree, an unreflexive game. We shall thus conclude the chapter by considering Pierre Bourdieu's observations on embodiment and gender. Inscribed in the body is a balance of power that establishes inequality between genders and classes and is only partly accessible to conscious designs. For the body is only partly governable by the subject even in a society like ours that incessantly works at the plasticity of the flesh giving value to and commercializing countless ways of caring for and modifying the body.

1. Interaction and the construction of gender

When we act in and move through public areas in modern cities of the Global North, we are assured of anonymity and polite distancing. Even on private occasions we hold a number of expectations about our bodily manners. Interaction is based largely on our capacity to manage our bodies according to the expectations which are built into social situations. In the first chapter, we referred to Norbert Elias's thesis of the 'civilizing process'. As societies became less violent, an individual's vulnerability in face-to-face relations became ceremonial instead of purely physical, with body language becoming more and more elaborate (Elias 2021 [1939]). We are less afraid than our mediaeval ancestors of being physically attacked; however, we are all of us afraid of behaving out of kilter with our role in any situation and incurring social ostracism. As Erving Goffman pointed out (1982 [1967]; see Crossley 2022), more and more sophisticated body signals – our way of looking and speaking, our gait and posture and so on – indicate both 'diffuse social status', like gender, age or class, and 'individual character', i.e. our self-opinion, our fitting in or standing out.

The contradictions of living with the natural yet social body

These embodied forms are far from superficial: they provide a foundation, as emotionally charged as they are taken for granted, conveying our all-important 'humanity' which we associate with human rights, freedom and tolerance (Schneider 1996). Taken for granted as the material basis of subjectivity, the body and its language cannot, however, be completely controlled by the subject. Our body can be handled, but it is never silent. Although 'an individual can stop talking, he cannot stop communicating through body idiom; he must say either the right thing or the wrong thing. He cannot say nothing' (Goffman 1963, 35). The body, then, is always a tool and measure of the subject. We use it to meet other people, we work on it to give ourselves a certain identity, and all along it is telling other people about us. In other words, the body classifies us as we seek our place in the social rankings, acting on and with that body of ours.

From the moment of our birth, we learn to move and conduct ourselves differently, negotiating our own style within the rules of the category – gender, race, class, sexuality, etc. – to which we have been assigned. Defined at birth on a naturalistic medical frame (weight, length, sex judged by genitals, etc.), the body somehow becomes social as an aspect of other framings ('daughter' or 'son', 'brother' or 'sister' in a family, for example). The medical, naturalistic perspective never ceases to accompany us, though. That is one of the typical features of modernity, in which medical experts have acquired the right to approach the naked human body armed with a naturalistic rather than social gaze (Turner 2008). As a natural frame, the medical gaze works as a resolutely practical fact rather than simply a cognitive or symbolic label. It acts via tools for inspecting the body (blood tests, X-rays, scans, MRIs and so on) which arrive at a concrete definition of that body via markers interpretable by expert knowledge enshrined in the doctor.

In the modern West within the context of the development of modern medical discourse and technologies, there has been, for example, an increasing visualization of the pregnant interior of the woman as a natural given (Shaw 2012). Doctors in turn pose as the expert possessors of objective truth about the body endowed with their own clear bodily signals (white coat, stethoscope, etc.) and special arrangements for the medical interaction (time spent in a waiting room, lack of power symmetry in the way the patient is interviewed and spoken to, etc.).

But some medical situations do strike an ambiguous note, where the natural framework is less stable – situations where we are less likely to let ourselves be treated as mere bodies submitting to detached scientific know-how. This chiefly occurs when patient and doctor are of different genders, and it is harder to filter out the sexual overtones of their respective bodies. A prime example is the gynaecological appointment, where it is often a male doctor handling a female patient and parts of her body that never entirely lose their erotic connotation. For the interaction between male gynaecologist and female patient to go smoothly, the latter's body must be set in a natural framework, desexualized in practice (Henslin & Biggs 1971). So, before the examination the patient may undress with the help of a female nurse or behind a screen which filters out all portions of her person that are irrelevant to the scene; then the woman will adopt a suitable position on the bed with a sheet to cover her body down to the genitals; and during the examination the doctor will tend to avoid eye contact and ignore the patient apart from a few questions tending to keep the situation objective. For her part, the patient will go along with her temporary role, reduced to a non-social-person-with-a-natural-body, abstaining from moving or starting up a conversation. To cope with the ambiguity of the situation, both doctor and patient will thus tend to stick rigidly to their role, using all possible practical resources to frame the body in question as a natural item undergoing medical examination.

A medical examination is but one – albeit glaring – example of the kind of delicate social situation that a human body encounters in normal life. At times, for the interaction to run smoothly, the body has to be put in the background, desexualized, rendered somehow inert. For instance, in a gym changing room (Sassatelli 2010a) or swimming pool (Scott 2010), it will be necessary to pay no attention to bodies, filter out the gender attributes and put their erotic potential in the background. At other times our body will become a major emitter of signals about ourselves, our qualities and skills, including, of course, signalling distinctions of gender or our ability to attract potential partners. Evenings at dancing classes are social occasions in point, where each one is on show and male or female bodies take part in a game of reciprocity, moving and feeling and appearing (Hanna 1988), which is heightened in some genres such as tango (Savigliano 1995). Again, beach establishments, where women can cast off a bikini top while indulging in a ballet of glances and ceremonies controlling nudity and the effect of a gesture which cannot be just an act of liberation (Kaufmann 2001 [1995]). Thus, in ordinary life the body is constantly involved in our self-representation as subjects: it may be assimilated to the self as its symbol or objectified as a natural datum.

A feminist reading of Goffman and the body in interaction

The human body is fundamental in supplying impressions of who we are in everyday life (including identities of gender, race, class, sexuality, etc.), and not only in direct and deliberate social interactions (what Goffman calls 'focused interactions'). The same is true in 'unfocused' interaction, an example of which would include 'civil inattention': strangers who are in close proximity demonstrating that they are aware of one another, without engaging or imposing on each other, as when someone abstains from staring at the person sat opposite them on the bus. In such settings, all contrive to be close and yet distant, anonymous (Goffman 1963; 2010 [1971]).[1] Management of one's body, gaze and posture in crowded public places is essential if one would give the impression of being 'normal'. And 'normal appearances' (Goffman 2010 [1971]) begin from the body above all. On the 'stage', the public area in which we encounter other people, the body supplies a series of tools by which to express the self, an embodied vocabulary acting as a non-verbal language, essential in defining the situation as well as the actor's character. Bodily signals lend substance to respect, or materially construct that 'bubble' around us, especially in public places; they help us project a 'deep' self to be respected as something 'sacred' (Goffman 1963; 1982 [1967]).

The body is a kind of 'expressive equipment' (Goffman 1959) with which the subject presents itself on the social stage. In his famous essay *The Presentation of Self in Everyday Life*, Goffman (ibid., 245) argues that the self is the *product* of a scene which is performed and not a *cause* of it: 'it is not something organic that has a specific location, whose fundamental fate is to be born, to mature, and to die; it is a dramatic effect arising diffusely from a scene that is presented, and the characteristic issue, the crucial concern, is whether it will be credited or discredited'. With our gaze, our face (what individuals are fielding when communicating and relating with other people, namely their self-image – and note the expression 'to lose face') and posture, we show our demeanour (i.e., a demonstration of self-regard) and at the same time assure the bystanders of our deference (i.e., a demonstration of respect for the other), which we expect in return (Goffman 1982 [1967]). The body, then, is fundamental in keeping up orderly interaction and reproducing social roles and identities. Yet, as mentioned, it can only partly be handled instrumentally: the body's lapses are as ordinary as is our ability to control it.[2]

Men and women, however, follow somewhat different rituals in keeping the codes laid down for either sex; meanwhile, precisely in following certain rituals the male/female difference is reaffirmed and socially recreated. In *The Presentation of Self in Everyday Life* (1959), Goffman uses gender codes precisely as an example to show how ambiguous the distinction is between reality and fiction in personal identity construction. He suggests that what we deem authentic is actually a construction, or rather a performance, the fruit of elaborate ceremony, where the body is put to work in specific but normally non-instrumental ways. As he puts it (ibid., 81),

> when we observe a young middle-class American girl playing dumb for the benefit of her boyfriend, we are ready to point to items of guile and contrivance in her behavior. But like herself and her boyfriend, we accept as an unperformed fact that this performer is a young American middle-class girl. But surely here we neglect the greater part of the performance.

The part missed includes the performances of gender identity and sexual categorization themselves. Gender codes underpin the belonging to one particular sexual category, while they map out the scope for the kind of dating and courting strategy in Goffman's example. Being a woman may appear like an essential obvious fact, situated before or at the root of what, consequently, seem like superficial ploys connected with seduction. 'It is commonplace', Goffman goes on (ibid., 81–2), 'to say that different social groupings express in different ways such attributes as age, sex, territory, and class status', but each of these attributes 'is not a material thing, to be possessed and then displayed; it is a pattern of appropriate conduct, coherent, embellished, and well-articulated. Performed with ease or clumsiness, awareness or not, guile or good faith, it is nonetheless something that must be realized'. Even though it may remain in the background, the staging of 'essential' attributes like sex, race or age, all anchored in the body, is a crucial form of personal identity constitution which continuously contributes to placing the subject in different positions in different social situations.

We may, indeed, read Goffman in a feminist perspective as suggested by Candace West (1996) and appreciate the relevance of Goffman's work for an analysis of gender (Brickell 2022).[3] In addition to the major social institutions and structures – such as the labour market, the divide in educational choices, the division of tasks within the family, etc. – Goffman in fact tells us that gender differences are constructed on a daily basis through 'institutional reflexivity', which actualizes body differences in a constant, pervasive, ceremonial ritualization acting through our bodies, and which also renders the differences obvious and immediately recognizable (Goffman 1977a; 1979). By 'institutional reflexivity', Goffman (1977a, 302) means all the facets of social organization that go to confirm our gender stereotypes and bolster the prevailing trend in relations between the sexes: 'it is not then, the social consequences of innate sex differences that must be explained, but the way in which these differences were (and are) put forward as a warrant for our social arrangements, and, most important of all, the way in which the institutional workings of society ensured that this accounting would seem sound'. In Goffman's view, gender difference proves a decisive dimension for subjectivity constitution, as it goes to the heart of distinction and recognition mechanisms during primary socialization: in the hetero-sexual family

each sex becomes a training device for the other, a device that is brought right into the house; and what will serve to structure wider social life is thus given its shape and its impetus in a very small and very cosy circle. And it also follows that the deepest sense of what one is – one's gender identity – is something that is given its initial character from ingredients that do not bear on ethnicity or socio-economic stratification, in consequence of which we all acquire a deep capacity to shield ourselves from what we gain and lose by virtue of our placement in the overall social hierarchy. Brothers will have a way of defining themselves in terms of their differences from persons like their sisters, and sisters will have a way of defining themselves in terms of their differences from persons like their brothers, in both cases turning perception away from how it is the sibs in one family are socially situated in a fundamentally different way from the sibs of another family. Gender, not religion, is the opiate of the masses. (ibid., 314–15)

The ways of addressing the other as a subject codified by gender, or of handling one's body as a gendered body, the interplay of looks and moves in the various scenes of everyday life, and the game itself of heteronormative seduction, are all ritualized reinforcers of gender differences, culturally fixing them as natural. As we shall see better later (see chapter 7), Goffman is intrigued by the ways these ceremonial differences get staged, and actually distilled, in the media.

Gender codes are not just enacted by subjects, but also something imposed and leaving room for numerous contradictions, because in daily reality they are mixed with other identity attributes and a host of roles. In his famous essay on the rituals surrounding the self in contemporary society, Goffman (1982 [1967]) took the example of gender to show the sometimes contradictory interweaving of rules of demeanour and deference. Thus, he noticed that when a man made to get up and leave his seat to a lady, showing his 'respect' for the 'fair sex', she could halt him, showing she did not want to take advantage of her woman's 'privileges' and was ready to define the situation on equal grounds of parity. While by now such gesture may be largely out of fashion, Goffman's example ironically points out how ambivalent the polite gestures are towards women, and hence the ambivalence they need to handle if they are both to show femininity and take an active part in social life. He suggested that 'every indulgence society shows to women can be seen as a mixed blessing' (Goffman 1977a, 326), which may well have the function of masking what might be considered a disadvantage: 'male domination is a very special kind, a domination that can be carried right into the gentlest, most loving moment without apparently causing strain – indeed, these moments can hardly be conceived of apart from these asymmetries' (Goffman 1979, 9).

To the extent that men benefit from the privileges of masculinity, they are complicit in reproducing oppression, while women, conforming to patriarchal norms of femininity, are complicit in their own subjection. Yet, the changing gender order further complicates the ambivalence which binds men and women together. In *Triangle of Sadness*, the *Palme d'Or* winning film in 2022 by Ruben Östlund, a heterosexual couple dines at the restaurant, and it is the woman who expects her reluctant boyfriend to pay for the dinner, generating a quarrel which precisely deals with how the genders must behave to carry out femininity and masculinity, unpacking the traditional ritualistic forms of subordination or domination that go with them.

Gender-related interactional asymmetry is clearly seen in the communication licence that may be taken towards women. In his last book, Goffman (1981) concentrates on forms of speech through which we play the identity game, making many references to men/women distinctions. The discussion of changes in footing, that is, changes in the position we take vis-à-vis ourselves and vis-à-vis others in our utterances, is introduced in fact with a gender-related example. President Nixon – in the Oval Room with a number of government officials and journalists after signing an important document – 'jokes' with a well-known woman journalist; he breaks off the discourse to pay her a compliment on her appearance, and even asks her to turn around to show herself off better. The president's badinage causes a change of register ('footing') – from earnest politics in the Oval Room to the micropolitics of the sexes; this drags the journalist inexorably down from her professional status to a merely decorative role anchored to her gender identity. As Goffman writes (ibid., 125):

> This incident points to the power of the president to force an individual who is female from her occupational capacity into a sexual, domestic one during an occasion in which she (and the many women who could accord her the role of symbolic representative) might well be very concerned that she be given her full professional due, and that due only. And of course [... there] is something much more significant: the contemporary social definition that women must always be ready to receive comments on their 'appearance', the chief constraints being that the remarks should be favorable, delivered by someone with whom they are acquainted, and not interpretable as sarcasm. Implicit, structurally, is that a woman must ever be ready to change ground, or rather, have the ground changed for her, by virtue of being subject to becoming momentarily an object of approving attention, not – or not merely – a participant in it.

This example tells us something general about communication, illuminating the jigsaw puzzle structure of our ways of talking, how they continually shuffle forms and contents taken from different contexts as well as our ability to slot a fleeting reference to one role into the broader context of another. Still, the example shows us something important about women's place in the world. It is significant that, to draw a serious event to a conclusion and show how sporting he is, Nixon should adroitly make use of a woman, playing with her public demeanour. This example demonstrates the inextricability of masculinity and femininity, their embodied nature, and the fact that the feminine is to some extent 'more embodied' than the masculine. Similar scenes, although increasingly contested due to the spreading of feminist consciousness and shifts in the gender order, tend to reduce women's attributes to their gender and at the same time naturalize masculinity as dominant.

It is interaction that makes a woman a woman, and a man a man: i.e., it creates a gender meaning (West & Zimmermann 1987). The body plays a crucial role as a conveyor of gender identity in face-to-face interaction, but it is also an integral part of the gendered subjectivities thus realized. To return to Goffman's example, President Nixon both drew general attention to the fact of the journalist being a woman and reinforced the notion that a woman is first and foremost a body (see chapters 3 and 6).

2. Bodies, feelings and emotional life

As the American sociologist Arlie Russell Hochschild notes, Goffman shows us that we calculate more than we believe to be the case while interacting with others: we work with and on our bodies so as to make a suitable impression. And yet Goffman was well aware that we are not free in that process of handling impressions, as different embodied subjectivities respond to and are shaped through different cultural expectations. In her important essay on the 'capacity to feel', Hochschild (2003, 76) stresses that this game of expectations is closely bound up with the emotions: 'we *feel* in socially arranged ways (more) than we think we do'. Our body is implicated in its depth as a repository and a source of emotions: emotions are typically felt and transmitted through embodiment and we work on our body to manage, change and adapt emotions to social situations.

Picking up from Goffman and going further, Hochschild focuses on that dimension of living which some posit as lying midway between the biological body, individual identity and the social structure: the emotional sphere (Wetherell 2012). To Hochschild, the subject is a 'sentient self' that can and must work on the emotions, and 'is capable of feelings and is aware of doing so' (Hochschild 2003, 77). The emotions are firmly anchored in the body but are nonetheless a social fact. At the same time, they do not have just a normative character, 'something we have to feel', since there are times when we would prefer not to feel as we do. Rather, it is an encounter, or rather an inextricable intertwining, often full of contradictions, between different impulses, and a work on ourselves and on the models of feeling that are proposed to us since childhood. Thus, for example, there is growing evidence to show that the way facial expressions are interpreted and experienced depends on the context. The context may completely change what we perceive, feel or communicate

(Hassin, Aviezer & Bentin 2013; Von Scheve 2012). Sociologists of the emotions have developed a new lexicon for social analysis, ranging from 'emotional vocabularies' to 'emotional codes' and 'feeling rules', revealing the social nature of human emotions, and the emotional nature of social phenomena (Bericat 2016). When it comes to gender, the sociological approach to the emotions becomes more incisive, enabling us to cut through the taken-for-granted essentialism that forever surrounds the male/female divide, and to pave a new way of understanding gender differences and inequalities in emotional set-up and well-being (Simon 2014).[4]

Women are encouraged to feel and convey emotions such as fear and sadness, while men must suppress and conceal such emotions, instead feeling and conveying emotions such as anger and pride; children's emotional socialization is also influenced by the gender order and tends to follow a binary pattern (Brody 1999; 2000). Emotions may also be expressed in different ways. Women, for example, are more likely than men to express anger verbally, whereas men are more likely to express anger behaviourally while women are more likely to cope with emotions in general by talking about their feelings with friends and family (Simon & Nath 2004; see also chapter 5). Expression of emotions differs between the genders: as Robin Simon (2020) suggests, for example, women are more prone to display emotions, especially negative ones, which in turn reflects on their management of their bodies and minds. She suggests that

> (b)ecause feelings of depression signal emotional weakness to self and others, it is a socially acceptable emotion for females but a sanctioned emotion for males. Males' expression of emotional distress and response to stress vis-à-vis externalizing mental health problems reflects their tendency to manage by suppressing culturally inappropriate feelings of depression with mood-altering substances to avoid being labeled by self and others as emotionally weak. (Simon 2020, 104)

The dance of emotions is complex and often ambiguous, articulated as it is through gender and culture. Negative emotions are particularly troublesome in today's consumer culture. Hochschild (2003), in particular, has noticed that the more bureaucratic and commodified society is, the more inflated positive expressions of feeling become, for which reason they are taken less seriously. Thus, we don't take very seriously the broadly smiling characters of today's advertising as such display of joy and contentment appears instrumental and fake. But, as different emotions are more or less serious for different genders, gender socialization may render '(e)xpressions of anger … more "serious" and more likely to be sensed as "true" for women rather than for men' (ibid., 84); hence women are driven to smile more often than men, even when feeling anxious or frustrated. Embodying subjectivity in the feminine here often means having to justify and account for an emotion like anger, while embodying masculinity often means feeling awkward with fear. Not surprisingly, if we look at children's fairy tales, we find the female characters are often described as frightened, while the male ones are enraged.

The home, the market and emotional labour

A glance at the constitution of the embodied subject in everyday life shows that emotions can and must be considered sociologically, for they imply recognition (understanding what is felt), negotiation (working on the emotions), and toeing the line (fitting our feelings into the current rules). Hochschild lays down the key concepts of 'emotion work' and 'feeling rules'. Emotion work is the 'act of trying to change in degree or quality an emotion or feeling. To "work on" emotion or feeling is … the same as "to manage" an emotion or to do "deep acting"' in the attempt to embody feelings held to be more consistent with the relevant feeling rules and appropriate to our position or one we should like to achieve (Hochschild 2003, 94). Emotion work is deployed through a range of techniques, many of which have to do with embodiment: besides cognitive techniques (ideas and thoughts about feelings), we have bodily ones (addressing the bodily symptoms of a certain emotion) and expressive ones (gestures of the body, like smiling, which express a feeling).

If there is one terrain on which gender and emotions meet every day, intertwining masculinity and femininity, it is family and domestic life. In her work on gender, material culture and housework in Spanish and British families, Sarah Pink (2004) depicted the gender order as it unfolds in the domestic arena. The British women interviewed rejected the idea of being housewives and following a domestic routine; they got round to housework when 'in the right mood': it answered an 'emotional and bodily need' which had a 'therapeutic' purpose. Spanish women, on the other hand, found housework a structured routine, something that brought a 'natural balance' amid the various sides to their lives. The women in this study differed from the men: though the former rejected the traditional housewife identity, they saw housework as part of their womanhood, whereas the latter assigned it to the classic male category of a chore. But men do also negotiate with traditional manhood, revising the gender code. A study on the typically masculine parts of the home (garage, cellar, study – the so-called 'mancaves') (Moisio & Beruchashvili 2016) shows that these domestic areas are not just places of 'therapeutic consumption', exempting men from household and professional duties, but are places where they take a leaf out of women's book, reviving and negotiating their role as husbands and fathers.[5]

These are humdrum details, maybe, minutiae of daily life. Thus, the illuminating work edited by Elinor Ochs and Tamar Kremer-Sadlick, *Fast-forward Family* (2013), explores the tiny rituals of the various moments of middle-class family life in the United States in which gendered embodiment and emotions are implicated, from returning home, to dinnertime, from housework to leisure time. In this wide-ranging research with its wealth of ethnographic detail, the central place goes to the role of work on the emotions in producing, not exactly perfect, but 'good enough' families. As the editors write, 'the devil is in the details' – and the details connect with the 'reciprocity of practical assistance and emotional support' made up of little gestures like getting ready for school and work, learning to coordinate and respect time schedules, and also in the 'ability and willingness of family members to attune to the commitments and yearnings, as well as the disappointments, weaknesses, and transgressions, of one another and the family as a social and emotional enterprise' (ibid., 250). To form a family and be fathers and/or mothers entails considerable emotion work, constant renegotiation of the boundaries to one's own and others' gender identity, rethinking the texture of the couple, imagining a way not only of being gendered parents, but of having children with gender-coded identities, and combining all this with the attempt to come to terms with our gender ideologies and the embodied rules of feeling that underpin them.[6] As Bridget Byrne (2006) suggests in a study looking at white mothers from London, gender, class and race all intersect in everyday life, both in terms of perception and in terms of narratives of self and practices such as the choice of schools or activities with children, to define the kind of mothering that is realized and cherished and therefore the kind of socialization to gender, class and race that children experience.

One way or another we are always at work on our emotions, even when alone, and it may even form part of our paid work. Thus, it may ultimately change and take the form of proper 'emotional labour', toiling with occupational rules far more prescriptive, controlled and bureaucratized than the general daily emotion work. This is a concept that Hochschild (2012a [1983]) develops in *The Managed Heart*: air hostesses and debt collectors (the former usually female, the latter male) must learn to work on their emotions in various ways and must do so as part of their job: accommodating, welcoming, reassuring in the first case, hard and inflexible in the second. Clearly such emotional jobs are gender-coded and tend to reproduce the preponderant differences; at the same time, in constantly working out as they do, they ratify women's 'natural' propensity for listening and men's for sanctioning imperiousness. In other words, the gender order seems to ensure that men and women cultivate different emotional styles and find fulfilment in different professions.

Even in the very same profession we may find a gender division of emotional labour, such as can be found in nursing: while emotional labour is fundamental to the job for both male and female nurses, the former appear more detached and professional, and the latter more involved with patients and physically close to them (Gray 2010). Of course, emotional labour is done in interaction with the clients or the patients and has effects on the social identities of both the providers and the recipients. This may have significant effects if we consider disadvantaged groups, such as the physically disabled or mentally impaired and their interaction with caregivers (see chapter 6).

With the progressive expansion of the boundaries of the market, even our most intimate attachments and our bodies themselves seem called to follow the logic of commodities and personal gratification. According to Eva Illouz (2007, 89) this is coupled with shifts in gender attitudes:

> throughout the twentieth century, there has been an increased androgynization of men and women due to the fact that capitalism tapped into and mobilized the resources of service workers, and to the fact that concomitantly to their entry into the workforce, feminism called on women to become autonomous, self-reliant and conscious of their rights in the private sphere.

In a famous essay Hochschild shows how the commercialization spirit can turn even the ideas of feminism to its own advantage (Hochschild 2003). Considering self-help manuals aimed at women, she shows how, instead of devotion, individual choice is praised, encouraging emancipated women to respond only to desires and subjective gratification, which can be easily commercialized. The coldness of the market is mingling with the culture of private life, vampirizing feminism, no less, and 'instead of humanizing men, we are capitalizing women'[7] (see also chapter 3). Emotions have indeed become commodified in consumer capitalism in many different ways (Illouz 2018). For example, we have witnessed the constitution of 'relaxation' as a central emotional experience to be achieved in holiday-making centres often on the commercialization of services for the body, such as in Club Med seaside resorts which offer 'all-inclusive' experiences (Alaluf 2018).

However, this slide towards commodification of the emotions and one's own body often comes up short against the logic of the gift through which we typically manage the most intimate aspects of our lives. Thus, Hochschild (2012b) shows the continuous negotiation of emotions entailed in the very commoditization of private life, and with it our bodies. For example, the bounds of the market have extended to the female body and its reproductive power: couples, mainly from the rich Global North, are turning to the flourishing Indian industry of surrogacy at affordable prices, an international fertility economy quite distorting the meaning of pregnancy as a bodily experience. And yet both couples seeking offspring, and women going through pregnancy on others' behalf, do try to negotiate an area, alongside the commercial mentality, where they can preserve a sense of emotional involvement in the future child's welfare, and this to some extent maintains the idea of maternity as a gift.

3. From body projects to habitus

The transformation of the market and the mounting importance of consumer culture are central to our understanding of how we relate to the body in the late modern age, and how the body is fundamental to the constitution of subjectivity. The body is often understood as a fundamental asset to be controlled and managed to acquire status, happiness, self-realization. Practices of body modifications can be very different from one another, in terms of duration, invasiveness, safety, social meanings, spread, painfulness and expenditure (Crossley 2005; see chapter 6), but they are all deeply intertwined with the way we create and perceive our identity.

Body projects and compulsion to control the body

The work of Anthony Giddens (1991) has been especially influential in looking at the way the body is implicated in the modern ways of constructing a self. In late modernity, says Giddens, the body no longer indicates the place a subject occupies in the social structure, but above all their person, character, self, which is why it becomes an object of continual choice. Giddens argues that, as the social context grew complex, fragmentary and de-traditionalized, the embodied self turned into a 'reflexive project'. In this process of reflexive individualization, subjects organize their own narrative biography and manage the presentation and construction of their own body. In the words of Giddens (1991, 7–8):

> in the spheres of biologic reproduction, genetic engineering and medical interventions of many sorts, the body is becoming a phenomenon of choices and options. These do not affect the individual alone: there are close connections between personal aspects of bodily development and global factors. Reproductive technologies and genetic engineering, for example, are parts of more general processes of the transmutation of nature into a field of human action.

In this perspective, while boundaries of the natural and the social are continuously renegotiated and constructed, in late modern society bodies are less and less an 'extrinsic', natural given and become themselves 'reflexively mobilized' to respond to the requirement of society (Shilling 2012). We have become increasingly responsible for the design of our own bodies in ways consistent with our biographical narrative and this is a responsibility which can weigh heavily. The pursuit of physical health and mental well-being has, for example, become a highly valued goal in contemporary life, commanding enormous resources and generating professionalization and commercialization of countless goods and services. But it has also become a 'signifying practice' associated, in late modernity, with 'healthism' and a striking moralization of health, especially among the middle class (Crawford 2006). Bodies become the matter on which subjects can and must operate so as to fashion themselves in culturally approved ways, as well as to achieve gratification and a full sense of identity. Although physical conduct always occurs within the limits set by our social position, the peculiarity of the late-modern condition seems to be that it drives us to take up certain body projects reflexively in order to create and sustain our personal identity.

As we indicated in the first chapter, from the twentieth century, modern individuals are asked to work on their bodies, making them increasingly rich, modifiable and improvable tools for personal growth and realization. No longer subject to the perils of sin that the Victorian imagination so dwelt on, the body becomes the bulwark of the self in contemporary consumer culture. Consumer culture seeks to expand the role of the body, increasing the scope it may enjoy and enlarging its potential, enhancing its form, not for work's sake but for personal fulfilment (Bordo 2003 [1993]; Featherstone 1982; 1991; Sassatelli 2012, see also chapter 1). The market endlessly invents goods and services to make us live out the body. Time devoted to the body is quintessentially time for oneself since '(t)he only visible aspect of continuity and of the cumulative effects of self-constitutive efforts is offered by the human body' (Bauman 1992, 194). Modernity's rationalization of the body combines with increasing positive and expansive control of the body, in this case primarily linked to the subject as a consumer. As Michel Foucault wrote (1980a [1975], 57), we find 'a new mode of investment which presents itself no longer in the form of control by repression but that of control by stimulation. "Get undressed – but be slim, good-looking, tanned!"'. The body becomes 'the finest consumer object' (Baudrillard 1998 [1970], 129) (see also chapter 3):

> [in] the consumer package, there is one object finer, more precious and more dazzling than any other ... That object is the BODY. Its 'rediscovery', in a spirit of physical and sexual liberation, after a millennial age of puritanism; its omnipresence (specifically the omnipresence of the female body ...) in advertising, fashion and mass culture; the hygienic, dietetic, therapeutic cult which surrounds it, the obsession with youth, elegance, virility/femininity, treatments and regimes, and the sacrificial practices attaching to it all bear witness to the fact that the body has today become an object of salvation. It has literally taken over that moral and ideological function from the soul.

People are thus asked to work incessantly on their bodies, to make them feel more, do more and look better. Subjects are asked to work on their body in depth (on emotions, as we just saw) and on the surface (on appearance, see chapter 6). And new technologies, including new media technologies and video art, are rendering visibility increasingly reflexive, thereby augmenting the scope of body malleability and at the same time paving the way, through the relevance of a dialectic with personal experiences and feeling, for greater indeterminacy (Featherstone 2010).

The expansion of body control in practice emphasized a personal rather than a collective goal; it applied to leisure time which, by definition, serves the personal expression of individuals. Using one's body as a vehicle for gratification through the consumption of objects and leisure-time services thus became a kind of duty. As Giddens points out (1991; see also Bauman 1992; Beck 1992), late modernity confronts the individual with an anxiety-making welter of choices and little help as to what option to go for.[8] In her *Fear of Falling* (1989), Barbara Ehrenreich showed that it was above all middle- or upper-middle-class professionals who feared losing their place in the job market and sought to control their body by fitness activities designed to keep them young and good-looking. This was especially the case with women. As Jean Baudrillard (1998 [1970]) and Susan Bordo (2003 [1993]) were quick to observe, consumer culture incessantly demands that women make their life a plastic and mouldable potential. Even more than in men's case, leisure time stands as an opportunity for women to 'find themselves' through their bodies, and the market grows incessantly to provide goods and services to groom, manage and alter women's bodily appearance (see chapter 6).

The importance of reflexive and rationalized modes of body control geared to forming and enhancing individual subjectivity, in particular for middle and upper-middle classes, is today evident in the diffusion of portable technology such as apps for health and sport. This maps out an area where a 'quantified self' can be constructed and constantly monitored; with the data collected, new online communities are formed which contribute to the consolidation of a rationalized management of the body (Lupton 2016). Increased control and planning do not translate into simple liberation though: these technologies' modes of measurement, data interpretation and goal setting tend, in fact, to reproduce male visions of women's health and well-being and reposition women as subjects of a specifically male gaze (Sanders 2017).

Habitus and inequality carved in the body

Whatever the normative injunctions we are faced with, in everyday life indeed we often have to reckon with a body that resists our aspirations and reflexive projects. Our projects take shape upon the body in the form of tastes, habits and attitudes, processes which are often unreflexive. They may work well to differentiate tastes, habits and attitudes along the lines of our social position in terms of gender, race, generation, age, class, etc. But the body cannot become fully reflexive. Here Giddens's vision of the embodied self as a reflexive project comes into collision with the French tradition stemming from Marcel Mauss and Pierre Bourdieu.

In the sociology of the body, Bourdieu is often hailed as the scholar who tried to merge two important but divergent traditions: on the one hand, structuralism and post-structuralism that see the body as a situated and socially constituted object, and, on the other hand, the phenomenological tradition which views the body according to the category of experience (see Connell & Mears 2018; Crossley 2001; McNay 1999; Shilling 2012; Williams & Bendelow 1999). It is especially in his theory of practice, and in particular in *The Logic of Practice* (1992 [1980]), that Bourdieu proposes to understand human experience not according to cognitive and linguistic models, but in the terms of imitation and embodiment. He here calls upon the notion of 'habitus', which allows us to conceive of corporeality as prior to consciousness without, however, resorting to biologistic essentialism. For Bourdieu (ibid., 53), habitus is made of

> systems of durable, transposable dispositions, structured structures predisposed to function as structuring structures, that is, as principles which generate and organize practices and representations that can be objectively adapted to their outcomes without presupposing a conscious aiming at ends or an express mastery of the operations necessary in order to attain them. Objectively 'regulated' and 'regular' without being in any way the product of obedience to rules, they can be collectively orchestrated without being the product of the organizing action of a conductor.

Bourdieu's insistence on embodiment is important for thinking differently about action: our practical way of approaching the world 'is not a "state of mind", still less a kind of arbitrary adherence to a set of instituted dogmas and doctrines ("beliefs"), but rather a state of the body' (ibid., 68). The 'practical sense' through which human action unfolds is then configured as a 'social necessity turned into nature, converted into motor schemes and body automatisms' (ibid., 69). Habitus is inscribed in the body through past embodied experiences in everyday life, is standardized in the first years of life through imitation and is an unconscious but highly adaptive mechanism that defines the state of the body (*hexis*) as well as the actors' attitude towards their own bodies, others and objects. It is an embodied, actualized political 'mythology' that helps stabilize people's position in the social order. One clear example is lower classes' typically fatalistic attitude to illness, which derives from and tends to reproduce their disadvantaged position of shorter life expectancy and higher morbidity (Bourdieu 1984 [1979]; see Boltanski 1971). Access to dominant body projects thus irremediably goes on being socially differentiated.

This conception of the habitus has the merit of showing certain limits of theories of reflexive individualization. The performative stance towards one's own body is only partly reflexive – since it rests on social and historical patterns that in some sense precede performers and define their dispositions – and it is also unequally distributed among various social categories. The condition and practices of the body reflect tastes culturally stemming from the specific point in the social space in which they originate.[9] Imitation, embodiment, tastes are implicated in a set of classificatory systems in which social advantages and obligations are unevenly distributed, and thus they are far less tools of knowledge than tools of power (Bourdieu 1984 [1979]). Even 'in its most natural appearance ... volume, size, weight, etc.' the body is a social product: 'the unequal distribution among social classes of corporeal properties' is both realized concretely through 'working conditions' and 'consumption habits', and perceived through 'categories and classification systems which are not independent of such distribution' (Bourdieu 1977, 51). The mirror effect of this is that social inequalities are less the result of institutional discrimination and more the effect of how differences are inscribed in the body: a form of symbolic violence wrought upon social actors with their active complicity.

The body is thus the vector of inequality, of stratification systems that dictate differing access to economic, social and symbolic resources that have filtered down in the course of generations. Gender is indeed a fundamental stratification system. Inequality between men and women is the theme of a well-known book on masculine domination by Bourdieu (2001 [1998]), which is a key example – perhaps the clearest – of the habitus embodiment mechanism at work. Inequality is maintained by a range of modes of living, feeling and managing the body typical of men and women, which meanwhile define what is masculine and what is feminine. To Bourdieu, the structure of gender inequality is naturalized as a form of symbolic power that turns something arbitrary into a natural and obvious foregone conclusion. To critically denaturalize gender distinctions, he focuses on a society remote from Europe, the Berbers of Kabylia in contemporary Algeria. This androcentric society performs rituals of submission, exclusion, recognition and gratitude sorting men from women by patterns of male/female opposition linked to a dualist configuration upon which the world is organized: high/low, dry/wet, hard/soft, inside/outside, above/below, day/night, light/dark, active/passive, sun/moon, fire/water. Seen in this way, gender structures are in some sense prior to economic structures: they organize the world, time, space, the body, movement. Hence differentiation of masculine and feminine gender is an arbitrary social construction, perpetuated by the reproduction of patterns of thinking pitting masculine against feminine. Thus

[t]he social world constructs the body as a sexually defined reality and as the depository of sexually defining principles of vision and division. This embodied social programme of perception is applied to all the things of the world and firstly to *the body itself* in its biological reality. It is this programme which constructs the difference between the biological sexes in conformity with the principles of a mythic vision of the world rooted in the arbitrary relationship of domination of men over women, itself inscribed, with the division of labour, in the reality of the social order. (ibid., 11)

Bourdieu does recognize that the very fact of masculine domination having been made into an issue in contemporary Western society has partly curbed its naturalizing force. Yet awareness of it is not enough, for masculine domination thrives on an unreflexive process of embodiment passed on by basic institutions like schools, family and the State, as well as the social division of labour and daily interaction. That domination is also, and above all, reproduced via women's own relationship to their bodies. Here Bourdieu taps into an important feminist insight (see chapters 3 and 7): female embodiment is indeed deeply related to how a woman's body is being perceived by an exterior gaze which is predominantly connoted as male: '(e)verything in the genesis of the female habitus and in the social conditions of its actualization combines to make the female experience of the body the limiting case of the universal experience of the body-for-others, constantly exposed to the objectification performed by the gaze and the discourse of others' (ibid., 63). As a form of symbolic power, in short, male domination works via women's own desires, will, aspirations, emotions, classifications and minute body practices. To get away from such practices calls for constant work on the issue, since women often face a contradiction: 'if they behave as men, they risk losing the obligatory attributes of "femininity" and call into question the natural right of males to the position of power; if they behave as women, they seem incapable and unfit for the job' (ibid., 67–8).

In this chapter we have considered the way body and subjectivity are interrelated, pointing firstly at the importance of interaction for the constitution of embodied subjectivity. Our notion of being human – independent, self-contained, respectable – is only understandable in relation to the ceremonial distance we can, and must, maintain as we interact via minute bodily signals bidding us to keep our distance, greet just so, feign polite indifference and so on. Such self-respect and consideration for others is primarily expressed through the body: gesture, look, the way we occupy space, the stance we adopt. Subjectivity is indissoluble from embodiment, and embodiment is realized starting from interaction in gendered ways, which bear witness and contribute to gender inequality. Our capacity to manage emotions appropriately in interactions is fundamental to our sense of self and this capacity is itself socially constructed. Women and men are often asked to play out different emotions; the gender order ensures that men and women cultivate different emotional styles which makes them differently suited for a variety of roles and professions. Despite the pressure in the Western late modern world to transform the body into a project that everyone can cultivate, we can only partially control our bodies. Bodies are a fundamental point of application of the social, and thus they partly escape us being invested by power. Hierarchy and power are implicated in the constitution of the gendered body. The gendered body, the embodied connotations of masculinity and femininity, become a fundamental terrain of politics, and around this politics the boundaries of the natural and the artificial, of the normal and the deviant, also come to be constituted. Still, power does sometimes meet with resistance, practice being unpredictable and the stuff of bodies not so docile. In the next chapter we shall look at the way bodies and power are intertwined.

3

Body Politics

After months of meticulous preparation and diplomatic effort, on 6 April 2021, two of the European Union's top leaders, the President of the European Council Charles Michel, and the President of the European Commission, Ursula von der Leyen, visited the Turkish President Recep Tayyip Erdoğan in Ankara. As the three gathered for talks there were only two chairs present in the middle of the room. The two men went right to the seats and sat down taking centre stage, while von der Leyen was left standing without somewhere to sit. She made her displeasure clear with an audible 'Ahem', until she was offered a seat on a sofa in the same room with the Turkish Foreign Minister.

This turned out to be a diplomatic scandal: von der Leyen and Michel commented on the meeting on social media and the incident appeared on the front pages of newspapers across the world. In previous years, EU and Turkish leaders were seated in equal rank, so the protocol was clearly being broken that day. This is no surprise, if we connect the incident with Erdoğan's political views on women's rights and feminist advances of recent decades. Just fifteen days earlier, Erdoğan had announced the country's withdrawal from the Istanbul Convention, a treaty aimed at preventing and combating violence against women – ironically the Turkish city was the location where it had first been opened for signature, so it keeps its name.

'Sofagate', as it was called afterwards, is insightful from a socio-logical point of view not just in relation to the Turkish president and his administration's overt sexism. The point is that, instead of being placed in equal standing as the protocol would have suggested, the European Commission President had been placed on a sofa just because the President's body was female. Ursula von der Leyen, in the very moment she was invited to sit down in a second-rank place, was not just a politician: she was reminded that she was a body, because she was a woman. As a woman, she does not only *have* a body, she *is* a body. Even in the public sphere.

The philosopher Jean-Jacques Rousseau in his masterpiece *Émile ou de l'éducation* wrote 'The male is male only at certain moments. The female is female her whole life or at least during her whole youth. Everything constantly recalls her sex to her' (2010 [1762], 535). In Western thought, since the times of ancient Greece, masculine nature was considered the seat of reason – *logos* – while feminine nature was conceived as governed by instinct and emotions, and women were deemed close to materiality and animality. Because of their nature, they did not fit in the public sphere.

This conception can still be found behind differentiated body use and norms, which might at first appear insignificant: widespread tacit rules which involve power relations that perpetuate inequality and exclusion. Body politics – the topic of this chapter – refers to both society's ways of regulating the use of the body (or making body parts and their capacities work in certain ways) and the conflicts over the degree of social and individual control over the body, its processes and expressions by individuals or social groups. In other words, body politics covers the two sides to the body/power relation: the power to control the body, and the resistance to such power.

In the past, analysis of body politics largely concerned the sover-eign's body, incarnating power *par excellence* as in the famous notion of 'The King's Two Bodies' in mediaeval times, which Kantorowicz described (2016 [1957]): one body subject to decay and physical death, the other more political, incorruptible, not subject to ageing, disease or death. In the modern era, studies into the link between power and the body have focused on the political quality of the bodies of the whole population. This has drawn attention to the gradual tension forming between different ways of being (in) the body that claim equal recognition in the public domain, often involving latent conflict: male and female, young and old, white and black, thin and fat, healthy and sick, able-bodied and disabled. As we shall see, along with this process, there gradually took root the idea that the body figures as a plastic entity both as to meaning and as to matter, something which we are individually and collectively responsible for.

The gender perspective we are proposing serves as a compass by which to draw a selective map within the broad issue of body politics. Clearly this is an exercise in reducing complexity. Here in particular we choose to follow the coordinates laid down by two major theoretical turning points: Michel Foucault's work and contemporary feminist thought. And, indeed, the body is a crucial junction between the French philosopher's thinking and a long reflection on the subordination of women which reached its peak in twentieth-century feminism. Contemporary gendered body politics is one of the most fertile outcomes of that dialogue.

In this chapter, we illustrate the major contributions of the work of Michel Foucault to an understanding of power, bodies and biopower. We will thereby discuss some of the major theorization of feminist thinking about sex and gender and we shall see how the French philosopher's accounts have played a crucial part in the postmodern turn of such theorization. We shall then turn to how gendered bodies have been discursively defined for centuries, accounting for the female body as inferior; we shall see how feminist thinking deals with such awareness in the need to refer to female bodies' specificity to resist biopower. To that aim, we shall illustrate some examples of important fields of theorization and research.

1. Power and the gendering of bodies

Most of Foucault's work is an attempt to illustrate how power works in the modern era via processes where knowledge and the body play a central role in producing subjectivity. Despite the many criticisms made of it (also for not taking the specificity of women's bodily experience into account), Foucault's work has been fundamental in recognizing how the body is directly implicated in the political field. In modern society, power operates in subtle ways: as we shall see, it is embodied in subjects, rather than merely exercised *over* them.

Biopolitics, discipline and power

According to the French philosopher, power relations do not simply 'repress' the body; they produce it, taking 'an immediate hold on it;

they invest it, mark it, train it, torture it, force it to carry out tasks, to perform ceremonies, to emit signs' (Foucault 1977 [1975], 25). In other words, power does not just punish, coerce or restrain bodies, but makes them behave and function in certain ways. Let's think of the norms of conduct and everyday practices in special environments such as school – where pupils are required to sit down correctly, stand up or move in the space of the class, or even go to the toilet only according to the prescriptions of the institution. Teachers and other adults have the power to prescribe these acts, how to perform them and to punish in case of transgression. Power essentially works upon the bodies as a 'microphysics', passing down the slenderest ambiguous channels that pervade everyday action. In the long term it can be interiorized and circulate via the perceptions and desires of the individuals themselves. But power is exercised also internally to the subjected groups: just think of some pupils being praised or ridiculed by older schoolmates or being subjugated to the peer group's norms. This is an example of what happens in society as a whole, in Foucault's approach: power is not a property of a specific group, as it was conceived traditionally, but it is relational, dispersed and pervasive. More generally, in its being *productive* and not just *repressive*, power does not simply 'mask' reality: it creates it since it produces (and is allowed by) 'regimes of truth', thus remaining mostly unseen and uncontested. Complex networks of power and knowledge work to make bodies fit to society's expectations.

In *Discipline and Punish*, Foucault (1977 [1975]) focuses on the modern transformation of the body into a docile instrument within organizations like schools, hospitals, the army, factories and prisons. He presents these as disciplinary institutions which bolster the practical functioning of power through surveillance. He gives as an example the *Panopticon* – a prison design whereby one guard (or guards in one centrally located tower) can observe all prisoners at once. Every inmate is under constant potential observation, though they can never be sure if they are currently being watched, just as we too are daily under video surveillance systems of which we are aware. The chief effect of the *Panopticon* is that it produces in the individual 'a conscious and permanent state of visibility that assures the automatic functioning of power' (ibid., 201) and thus controls them.

As a form of social organization, the modern prison epitomizes some features of disciplinary power. The mechanized organization and routine training foreseen by Marx and Weber, for instance, as discussed in the first chapter, are systematically analysed by Foucault's description of discipline. Discipline is a minute series of instructions (e.g., governing prisoners' movements inside a prison, workers in a factory or, as we shall see in greater detail in the sixth chapter, women's daily use of cosmetics and make-up practices) coordinating body movement and function in space and time. Unlike Weber, Foucault seems to take the body, instead of the individual, as the point where control is applied. To use his words, the modern idea of sovereignty coincides with a shift from the right *of death* to the power *over life*: that is, where once the sovereign's power extended only so far as putting someone to death (or allowing them to live), nowadays sovereignty claims power over the way people live their lives. In every society, the body has been the point of application of a network of power, obligations, constraints and prohibitions, but only in the modern era did a specific kind of power latch onto the body's docility and controllability (1977 [1975], 136–7):

> What was so new in these projects of docility that interested the eighteenth century so much? It was certainly not the first time that the body had become the object of such imperious and pressing investments; in every society, the body was in the grip of very strict powers, which imposed upon it constraints, prohibitions or obligations. However, there were several new things in these techniques. To begin with, there was the scale of the control; it was a question of treating the body, *en masse*, wholesale, as if it were an indissociable unity, but of working it 'retail', individually; of exercising upon it a subtle coercion, of obtaining holds upon it at the level of the mechanism itself – movements, gestures, attitudes, rapidity: an infinitesimal power over the active body. Then there was the object of the control: it was not or was no longer the signifying elements of behavior or the language of the body, but the economy, the efficiency of movements, their internal organization; ... Lastly, there is the modality: it implies an uninterrupted, constant coercion, supervising the processes of the activity rather than its results and it is exercised according to a codification that partitions as closely as possible time, space, movement.

This *anatomo-politics* of the human body which has just been described is aimed at disciplining the body as a machine, to integrate it and make it useful in the economic system of industrialized societies. It is one of the two forms in which power over life ('biopower', as *bios* means life in ancient Greek) has evolved in modern times, according to Foucault. The other one is the *biopolitics of the population* and deals not with the single human body but with the population as a whole. It acts through techniques of measuring, controlling and managing bodily experiences like birth, death, reproduction, health, etc. Nation states gain strength by encouraging life to grow in prescribed forms, but also by the development of welfare provision and the open-ended expansion of the conduct of government. This increasing role of public authorities in administering how we live our lives is referred to by Foucault as 'governmentality', and its effects can be easily detected today (in many ways, the management of social distancing during the Covid-19 pandemic could be the most explicit example of that). The point is that such measures work as forms of *normalization* – defining the boundaries of the 'normal': from insurance schemes establishing degrees of risk for different bodies (Defert 1991) to widespread, localized and internalized techniques regulating private consumption of potentially dangerous products such as alcohol (Valverde 1998).

Even if he did not mention gender explicitly, Foucault's notion of biopower can be used to understand a number of gendered practices, such as abortion services, reproductive and genetic technologies, affecting women's control of their bodies and their reproductive choices; prenatal care, consisting in lifestyle monitoring of pregnant women; medical classification deciding the pathways and candidates for assisted reproduction; surgical intervention on intersex children to make them fit into dichotomic classification of bodies; medical transition for transgender people seeking it (see chapter 4). These bodily experiences allow the power to be exercised and contribute to the creation of 'normal' bodies as opposed to deviant ones, in an endless mutual reinforcing of power and knowledge, and of practices, discourses and imagery.[1]

Foucault also theorized that, along with its objectifying tendency in modern times, the shift in the notion of sovereignty implied a shift in subjectivity. From subjects with an ascribed identity, individuals became free citizens who were expected to produce themselves. The body became the object of a concern with discovering one's 'true self', an aspiration deriving from mind–body dualism and hence historically determined. In *The History of Sexuality*, Foucault studied the steps by which individuals were led to recognize themselves as 'subjects of desire', where the 'desire' situated in the body contains 'the truth of their being, be it natural or fallen' (Foucault 1990 [1984], 5). In the modern age the 'truth' of individuals no longer rested on the position they occupied in the universal order of things but was built around a normalizing notion of inner responsibility interpreted through the body.

What emerges from his analysis of developing modern sexuality is how power creates more or less 'normal' or 'deviant' subjective stances around the sexual domain (Foucault 1978 [1976]; 1990

[1984]). A web of practical scientific intervention on the body came to produce a *scientia sexualis* which construed sexuality as a field for empirical enquiry as well as the secret essence of the individual. Once again, truth proves to be a historically specific category: the body has no intrinsic truth, but truths are constructed on the body by a variety of categorizing strategies that power relations latch onto. Therein lies a political approach to bodies. Discourses and practices, norms and expectations around the human bodies are the achievement of power in both its repressive and productive side, but they are different according to the sex of those bodies: we cannot overlook the fact that women's bodies are (constructed as) 'docile' in a different way from men's, and that the notions of 'woman' and 'man' are created in a set of power relations that favours one term over the other. Some feminist authors maintain Foucault was guilty of silence on this topic,[2] and it is to their development of these ideas that we now turn.

Sex and gender in feminist thinking

Let us imagine a body. A human body. Can we do so without giving it a specific sex? Probably not. And probably the very fact of calling it 'human' will have conjured up a *male* body, whatever our own may be. This mental process is no accident but stems from an age-old history of thinking. From its origins, Western thought has represented the female body as a variant, possibly imperfect, on the classic human body, its 'other than'. This basic consideration led feminist critics to the demonstration that not only is our conception of the body male-centred, designed for men without regard to the female experience of 'otherness', but that the body was actually a key arena in the material oppression of women.

At the time when Foucault wrote his masterpieces, in the second half of the 1970s, in Western societies the very phrase 'body politics' began to spread (as the vocabulary of the feminist movement used in pro-abortion campaigns in the 1970s in the United States can confirm). Women's movements[3] protested against objectification, violence and subordination meted out to women via their bodies. In academia, theoretical and empirical research began to more explicitly reappraise the body, how it is represented and how it is managed politically. There was a consensus that male domination manifested through acts of oppression on the female body: for example, by rejecting birth control, repressing sexuality or banning it from the public sphere in the name of its reproductive function. But positions on the relationship between femininity and the materiality of the body were extremely divergent.

Many feminist movements and theoreticians deemed it crucial we acknowledge the different experience of the female body compared to the male and turned the recognition of the difference between the sexes into a political objective. Hitherto, what had been written was *his*tory, allegedly the history of humanity; the time had come to write *her*story, as it was called, that is from *her* viewpoint, which was situated in a material 'Otherness' still untold. An example of this approach is the thinking of the Belgian-born French philosopher and psychoanalyst Luce Irigaray (1985), who analysed how much women had been excluded from the production of discourse and knowledge in Western thought, and saw in sexual difference a site from which a feminine language could eventuate.

At the same time, many positions focused on women's lib and emancipation, concentrating on gender construction processes, beginning with the sexual differentiation of bodies, and on how this entails the more or less free acquisition of stereotyped roles from early infancy (virtually boiling down to a reproductive function for her and a productive one for him and the material and symbolic subordination that follows). Decades of research focusing on *difference* rather than *similarities* between boys and girls, and tons of empirical studies demonstrating a large overlap in their attitudes and skills (Maccoby & Jacklin 1974) in fact suggested that the major role in creating the difference was played by socialization in childhood and the internalization of social dictates: consequently, it would have been enough to change these to overcome the problem of gender (Connell 2021). The optimistic assumption underlying such visions was that correct body and identity politics might work collectively on gender precisely in being detached from sex (which thus remained impermeable to historical change), towards a fairer distribution of power and opportunities between men and women. The term 'gender', which became mainstream in the 1980s, was then made famous by the anthropologist Gayle Rubin (1975) with the intent of taking apart the 'sex/gender system' that grounded the difference in a biological substrate, though in actual fact making women the object of an exchange in the kinship links among men.[4] Notwithstanding this original formulation, most subsequent studies (overtly 'gender studies') took the term in the broad sense of how the sex difference is expressed socially, particularly in the learning of social roles. On this view, which is still mainstream in many academic fields, gender was only the result of the process by which sex (the set of so-called biological and anatomical features by which people are placed in distinct categories, see chapter 4) is taken by society to denote a complex of expectations surrounding culturally settled personal attributes.

Producing gendered bodies

In many respects all these positions were challenged by post-structuralist feminist thinking inspired by Foucault's writings from the late 1980s onwards. As we have seen, Foucault was silent on the specificity of biopower over female bodies, so the dialogue with feminist thinking was far from smooth and unquestioned. Nevertheless, many authors began to see the French philosopher's theorization of how power both represses and constructs subjec-tivities through bodies as useful to understand the female condition in a patriarchal society. The body was a site of power and, as such, it could be also a site for resistance (Haber 1996, 139):

> But if in Western cultures the meaning of a woman's body has been constructed by phallocentric desire as Other to that desire, and women wish to refuse this role, then Foucault's writings on the body and power challenge us to fight back with our bodies, to find new ways of meaning our bodies, and hence new ways of understanding ourselves and shaping our culture.

Indeed, the body had been recognized as a site of resistance for both Foucault and feminists, but in a very different way until then. While feminism had long seen the body as a site of *repressive* power, Foucault added a new light on power relations, deemed to be *productive* as well as repressive. Thus, Foucauldian post-structuralism allowed feminist thinking to translate a *perspective on the gendered body* into a new *gendered perspective on the body*: it was not just a matter of denouncing the different social conditions which characterized male and female bodies, but of seeing how much those different conditions contributed to *create* male and female bodies, infusing those entities with social meanings and expectations. Querying the nature/culture divide and analysing both the theoretical side to bodies and the material side to disciplines, this new perspective revolutionized the idea that gender is the outcome of a more or less linear and consistent process whereby society was organized around the difference between male and female bodies. They also threw new light on the material reality of the *embodiment* of differences (as in Guillaumin's fabri-cation of the sexed body, seen in chapter 1).

More specifically, many feminist theorists began to challenge the traditional idea of autonomous subjectivity behind political agency. They aimed to show that the 'linear' approach from body to gender (or from 'nature' to 'nurture') had serious limits insofar as it assumed that the bodily sex difference was an unvarying, incontestable, basic dichotomy. By taking gender as a social construct built upon the taken-for-granted biological substrate, this view contributed to essentializing sex difference, i.e., fixing it as a natural, pre-ordained, unchangeable fact. In the words of historian Joan Scott (1988, 2):

> gender is the social organization of sexual difference. But this does not mean that gender reflects or implements fixed and natural physical differences between women and men; rather gender is the knowledge that establishes meaning for bodily differences. These meanings vary across cultures, social groups, and time since nothing about the body, including women's reproductive organs, determines univocally how social divisions will be shaped. ... Sexual difference is not, then, the originary cause from which social organization ultimately can be derived. It is instead a variable social organization that itself must be explained.

In short, this perspective suggested that gender creates sex, rather than the other way round, and in many respects, this recognition owed much to postmodern thought (and to Foucault's works in particular). Power was called into the scene by the very fact that the construction of gender identities is marked by hierarchies. According to Scott, 'gender is a constitutive element of social relationships based on perceived differences between the sexes, and gender is a primary way to signifying relationships of power' (1986, 1067). As has been noted (Locher & Prügl 2001), the first part of this definition 'asserts a reality of social construction: gender creates social forms based on a binary construction of masculinity and femininity', while the second part 'infuses power into social constructions: messages of gender always also express messages of super- and subordination' (p. 116).

This perspective was further refined in the following decades. The definition of male and female bodies was strictly interwoven with sexuality, since it was established in a context of 'compulsory hetero-sexuality', as Adrienne Rich had already argued (1980). The idea is that the gendering of the bodies is linked to power and hierarchies in the sphere of sexuality (see chapter 4): two and only two bodies, male and female, were constructed and set inside a relationship geared necessarily to reproduction; any departure from that pattern was deviant, pathological and 'unnatural'. Starting from this view, in 1990 the US philosopher Judith Butler wrote a book destined to become seminal: *Gender Trouble: Feminism and the Subversion of Identity* (2006 [1990]). It is one of the most important fruits also of the application of (some of) Foucault's insights on bodies as the results of *productive* applications of power. More precisely, it examines how femininity and masculinity are socially produced as emanating from an allegedly pre-social and pre-discursive reality. Again, gender is linked to sexuality, since bodies are defined as male or female in a 'heterosexual matrix', a cultural norm which takes heterosexuality for granted until proved differently. *Gender Trouble* not only challenges the idea that sex is biological while gender is cultural, stating that sex and gender are both constructed and sexed bodies cannot signify without gender. According to Butler, we cannot experience human bodies without the cultural lenses of language and discourse, that is without gender. The assumption that there exists a precise subjectivity named 'woman' requiring representation, regardless of all the variety of experiences behind this label, is itself but an outcome of gender. Rather, gender is *performative*: no stable identity exists outside of the acts that supposedly 'express' it, but these acts produce (the illusion of) it.

Besides Butler, whose masterpiece represents one of the most influential books in feminist thought in the twentieth century and is foundational to *Queer theory*, other authors, from Carol Gilligan to Rosi Braidotti, have elaborated on the idea that identity always entails differentiation and hence exclusion, and how what made male identity universal was, historically, the exclusion of women. Their aim was not just adding the female component when reconstructing the historical facts, powers and areas of knowledge: rethinking history also involves rethinking the concept of subjectivity as such.

In general, one may say that postmodern feminism deconstructs the categories of 'woman' and 'man' more or less explicitly starting from the mechanism (*dispositif*) that links sex and truth, which Foucault was the first to challenge. Gender *is* sex, since the sexual distinction of bodies itself does not derive from a biological reality subsequently given a social connotation, but from a discursive creation of the sexed body simultaneous with the moment of its being perceived socially. In this new perspective it became possible, on the one hand, to revolutionize the traditional nature/culture dichotomy that claims to distinguish sex in its naturalness from gender as a social construct; and, on the other hand, to understand how the biological bodies have been constructed not just as different and opposite, but also hierarchically ordered. Let's now see what this means and its implications in terms of possibility of resistance.

2. Constructing bodies as distinct and unequal

> Where is she? Activity/passivity. Sun/Moon. Culture/Nature. Day/
> Night. Father/Mother. Head/Heart. Intelligible/Palpable. Logos/
> Pathos. Form, convex, step, advance, semen, progress. Matter,
> concave, ground – where steps are taken, holding- and dumping-
> ground. Man | Woman. Always the same metaphor: we follow it, it
> carries us, beneath all its figures, wherever discourse is organized.
> If we read or speak, the same thread or double braid is leading
> us through literature, philosophy, criticism, centuries of represen-
> tation and reflection.

So mused the writers Hélène Cixous and Catherine Clement (1986
[1975], 63) in the 1970s. And, indeed, if we think of Western tradition
and its dichotomies deriving from the basis nature/culture (mind/
body; reason/instinct; public/private; outside/inside; aggression/
mildness; science/art; independence/dependency; relation/perfor-
mance; production/consumption; and many others), we are bound to
associate man with the first term of each pair and woman with the
second. It would appear to be a symbolic differentiation supporting
the idea of complementarity between the sexes which, in itself,
would not spell inequality in terms of opportunity, skill or power
and might carry no consequences whatsoever. The point is that if we
invert the attributions in our mind's eye (associating woman with
mind, reason, public, independence, science and so on, and man with
body, instinct, dependency, private, etc.), we soon see that the two
terms of each pair are not on a par. In most cases, inverting the order
takes the man down in status and promotes the woman. Therefore,
difference reveals to be inequality, when put to the test, as it arranges
the attributes of gender and the genders themselves in a hierarchy.
Even today, a boy who gives way to emotion and tears may well be
mocked by his peers, while a girl who shows assertiveness may be
esteemed for it, or criticized as aggressive at the most. Cixous and
Clement's quotation went on this way (1986 [1975], 63):

> Thought has always worked through opposition, through dual,
> hierarchical oppositions. Superior / Inferior. Myths, legends, books.
> Philosophical systems. Everywhere (where) ordering intervenes,
> where a law organizes what is thinkable by oppositions (dual,
> irreconcilable; or sublatable, dialectical). And all these pairs of
> opposites are couples. Does this mean something? Is the fact the
> Logocentrism subjects thought – all concepts, codes and values – to
> a binary system, related to 'the' couple, man/woman?

In short, the distinction between mind and body, nature and culture, is far from neutral: it hooks the male and female up to a series of dualities and hence, in being gendered, proves to be charged with power. If, as suggested, woman is body, and if body is less valuable and subordinate to mind, then woman equals subordination. In defining femininity as close to animal immediacy, male thought has contrived to rank itself as rational and political subjectivity, divorced from its own corporal materiality.

As Elisabeth Grosz pointed out (1994), much of twentieth-century theory of the body, from psychoanalysis to philosophy, postulates a human body that is actually male – for which reason Grosz proposes a brand of feminism that reinstates the material body, in that it contains some purely female experiences, like menstruation, pregnancy, childbirth, breast-feeding and the menopause. Bourgeois individualism in the modern age further elaborated on the male-biased view (see chapter 1), promoting the idea of an active body, plastic but impermeable, to be used instrumentally vis-à-vis other people and the environment, hence male. By contrast, women were essentially shown as receptive and passive. As Morag MacSween summarizes (2013 [1993], 63):

> The dominant conception of the self as a self-contained entity organized around a care of needs/desires which are satisfied through the exploitation of an environment composed of objects is masculine and bourgeois, rather than gender-neutral and universal. Further, this construction relies upon, and is constructed in apposition to, a conception of woman as fundamentally 'un-separate', as, indeed, part of the environment of objects through which the masculine subject expresses itself.

Where the reigning conception of individuality hinges on bodily and psychological separateness and wholeness, receptiveness means weakness, vulnerability, incompleteness, and is viewed with a mixture of fear, fascination and disgust. The generative body of woman, in the terminology of Julia Kristeva (1982), becomes 'abject', an object opposed to the true subject, which the subject must reject despite being attracted to it.

In a social system in which positions of privilege and dominance are primarily held by men, knowledge and power reinforce and legitimate each other. Science and medicine, for example, had long been a tool of patriarchal power over female bodies. Many studies showed that these disciplines had played their part in constructing a female body that is 'naturally' defective. It is not surprising, then, that for centuries the containment of women's bodies through the grip of a corset was explained in orthopaedics by the idea that it was their only way of making their body trim, upright and more beautiful, as well as redounding to their health (Vigarello 1978).

Analysis of the oppression of women via the definitions and practices revolving around their bodies is by no means new. What marks the work of post-structuralist feminism, especially inspired by Foucault's work, is showing how biological difference is constructed in various fields of scientific knowledge, thus robbing individuals of the very ability to understand themselves outside the categories of male and female. In such thinking, sexual dimorphism is itself, in short, a historically determined construction of thought (Lorber 1994; see also chapter 4).

Nineteenth-century psychology and neurology long tried to show that social dimorphism depended on biological dimorphism, but their efforts yielded scanty results (Maccoby & Jacklin 1974). Yet such studies somehow legitimated the widespread belief that men had a stronger sexual impulse, were 'naturally' more aggressive and competitive, more rational and taciturn than women, while women were better at delicate jobs, more patient, more intuitive, more receptive and more garrulous. Endocrinology itself could be used for understanding male/female-differentiated social practices as dependent upon hormonal components, thus justifying, for example, male infidelity and the debarring of women from politics and economics. Although hormone levels vary between people of the same sex and even in the same person over the course of their life, there is still a strong tendency to skate over this complexity and use hormones as evidence that men and women are discrete and opposite beings. Research conducted on sex hormones revealed that it is the activity of scientists, rather than nature, which has done most to consolidate many claims made of the male and female bodies (Oudshoorn 1994). In her prized book *Testosterone Rex: Myths of Sex, Science, and Society* (2017), the psychologist Cordelia Fine, drawing on evolutionary science, psychology, neuroscience, endocrinology and philosophy, has shown that modalities of sexual selection, sex effects on brain and behaviour *are not* so markedly different for males and females, nor so testosterone-dependent as we are usually led to think. The book thus shows that many characteristics usually associated with femininity or masculinity in a complementary perspective are surprisingly dynamic and unrelated to sex – not even when it comes to risk taking or competitiveness in the workplace or in the dating market, usually considered as strongly dependent upon the masculine biology.

The reproductive needs of the species had long been used to explain woman's physical inferiority: she had no need of greater faculties since reproduction demanded of her mere instinct and less reason (this was argued by the German neurologist Möbius in 1900 in an eloquently entitled essay, *On the Physiological Idiocy of Women*). Indeed, reproduction has proved a fertile field of study from a gendered biopolitical standpoint. By virtue of a (presumed) bodily inferiority, marked by instinct, mood swings, lack of logic and moral sense, dependence on other people's opinions or a myopic view of one's private interests (all qualities defined as 'feminine' and justified with the biological destiny of protecting offspring), women for centuries were denied the vote, to sit in a courtroom, to testify or judge, to study, to exercise a free profession, and even to have equal rights over children with respect to their husbands, fathers or brothers.

Thus, the acquisitions in some fields of knowledge could be transferred to another, so from science or medicine could pass to philosophy, arts, jurisprudence or politics, providing a justification for denying women political, social and civil rights. And, of course, they could be fuelled and confirmed by them in turn: literature, arts, even common sense contributed to the reproduction of the female body as inferior, instinctive and devoted to the care of offspring in the Western imagery. This is even truer for marginalized and subjugated female bodies (Gilroy 1993; Stoler 1995), such as Black women whose story has been documented by Sabrina Strings in *Fearing the Black Body* (2019). Through the study of literature and arts, from portraiture by late European Renaissance artists like Albrecht Dürer and Raphael to women's magazines, Strings explains that the imagery of Black women's bodies was linked to fatness and that process was part of the willingness of making whiteness and slimness signals of national identity. This is well illustrated, for example, in the emergence of the thin American beauty ideal during the nineteenth century in women's periodicals, such as *Godey's Lady's Book or Harper's Bazar* (initially spelled with a single 'a' at the end). Many articles argued that true American beauty went hand in hand with slimness and appetite control; and while acknowledging that the ideals of beauty varied among populations, they did not fail to give superiority, even moral, to the white and lean elegance of well-mannered and wealthy American women. The point is that this (alleged) superiority in beauty also became the means to support a moral superiority of the race and social hierarchy. This is clear when the magazines of the time established, for example, that 'There are two points in which it is seldom equaled, never excelled – the classic chasteness and delicacy of the features, and the smallness and exquisite symmetry of the extremities. In the latter respect, particularly, the American ladies are singularly fortunate' (ibid., 138), while other articles informed readers that 'it is idle to say that the laws of beauty are not fixed; that because the Turk sees beauty only in the obese and certain of the savages in the deformed, that therefore the laws of beauty are arbitrary' (ibid., 142). Others stated that women among 'African savages' 'stuff' themselves till they are 'rolling in folds of fat' so they could not understand the cultured beauty prized by the elevated races. According to the overtly hierarchical view of beauty and race at the time, 'what is held to be beauty by the most refined and intellectual of the world must be nearer the real than any thing accepted only by a lower order of beings' (ibid., 143). In her analysis of texts by English writers and French intellectuals in the eighteenth century describing the so-called nature of races, Strings shows how much Black people were described as lazy, overfed, with an unbridled desire to meet the demands of the flesh at the expense of cultivating higher pursuits. But for Black women, physicality was considered as 'excessive', immoral and unhealthy. The case of the exhibition of a presumed archetype of Hottentot female beauty in England at the beginning of the nineteenth century is helpful to understand this logic. She was born on a farm of a colonist in Cape Town and as a slave she was displayed for British soldiers' titillation. As her body was her master's property, she was brought to London and exhibited as a scientific and erotic freak show. As Strings notes (ibid., 89):

> Her presence as a symbol of black femininity helped transform the image of the Hottentot from thin to fat. It also helped make fatness an intrinsically black, and implicitly off-putting, form of feminine embodiment in the European scientific and popular imagination.

3. The (dis)empowering of female experience

Gendered bodies are discursively produced. Nonetheless, they are material: they generate, suffer, please and die, albeit in social contexts imbued with gendered meanings. How can we access those bodies in terms of resistance to power? To better answer to this question, let's now turn to how feminist thinking accounts for women's bodily agency in a context of domination with some examples of theorization of gendered body politics: reproduction and pregnancy, the management of female sexuality, gender violence and the politics of the veil.

Reproduction and pregnancy

Though starting from a shared recognition that female fertility has been a prime site in which dominant male power/knowledge has been imposed, feminist authors have generated a variety of responses to the experience of pregnancy. Some have espoused the view that oppression of women was directly due to reproductive biology which hence needed to be challenged. Classic feminist writers like Simone de Beauvoir (1989 [1949]) or Adrienne Rich (1976) proposed that women be released from the biological state of affairs. Radical feminist Shulamith Firestone (2015 [1970]) extolled the advantages of artificial means of reproduction to liberate women from the yoke of procreation.

Others reappraised the bodily experience of maternity, claiming that it offers a unique way of experiencing the world and enjoying freedom from male-regulated forms of knowledge. For example, Mary O'Brien (1981) developed the idea that experience correlates with knowing the world, arguing that the ability to reproduce and the experience of maternity gave women an irreducibly different perception of the world which has hitherto not been sufficiently appreciated. Iris Marion Young made an important contribution to these studies when she analysed the tensions and contradictions aroused by the idea and actual experience of the body that a pregnant woman undergoes. During pregnancy the woman literally loses the clear sense of where her body ends and where the world begins, notes Young (2005, 49):

> The first movements of the fetus produce this sense of the splitting subject; the fetus's movements are wholly mine, completely within me, condition my experience and space. Only I have access to these movements from their origin, as it were. For months only I can witness this life within me, and it is only under my direction of where to put their hands that others can feel these movements. I have a privileged relation to this other life, not unlike that which I have to my dreams and thoughts, which I can tell someone but which cannot be an object for both of us in the same way. Adrienne Rich reports this sense of the movements within me as mine, even though they are another's. … Pregnancy challenges the integration of my body experience by rendering fluid the boundary between what is within, myself, and what is outside, separate. I experience my insides as the space of another, yet my own body.

Unlike ordinary experience where we are only aware of our body when it hurts or it is damaged, the experience of pregnancy entails discomfort but also interest and sometimes pleasure. Young thinks it alienating to call pregnancy a 'time of waiting': it is a time charged with meaning in its own right. Pregnancy is often seen as a disease, and discourses on pregnancy usually omit women's subjective experience, and so it will be until the idea of 'taking care' of the body is distinguished from 'healing it' (for an anthropological approach to this debate, spelling out its limits in ethnocentric terms, see Strathern 1988).

Feminist studies converge, however, in emphasizing that women have been the main targets in the expansion of medicine and in placing the medicalization of pregnancy and childbirth as a loss of power of (female) midwifery in favour of (male) professional health providers (for a critical perspective on this historical account, see Riessman 1983). Over time childbirth has become a male-dominated medical specialization, and this has affected the management of the female body. Barbara Ehrenreich and Deirdre English (2005 [1978]) showed how, over the centuries, the idea arose that pregnancy was a pathological condition; from the seventeenth century onward, childbirth began to be viewed as an event requiring the presence of an expert in disease, typically a man. Emily Martin (1987) and Ann Oakley (2018 [1980]) likewise studied how the experience of pregnancy and birth was set aside and how, in the post-industrial age, the expert in that field became masculinized, while non-scientific forms of female wisdom were discarded as the fruit of ignorance or superstition. The advent of foetal photography and scans in the second half of the twentieth century, in a context of increasing iconic power of the visual, led to a profound change in the theory and interpretation of pregnancy, resulting in the female body becoming invisible or left out of consideration – literally out of the frame – a mere environment for the foetus (Duden 1993). Nevertheless, the new male-dominated technologies increasingly alienated women from the experience of childbirth, starting from technocratic definitions of obstetrics to instructions for the powerless role of women treated like patients, supine on a hospital bed, passive, delegating any choice and responsibility to the doctor.

By virtue of these studies and this awareness, also fuelled by *feminist praxis*, medical practice today is much more attentive to restoring agency to pregnant women, even in medicalized contexts. In an increasingly complex and global society, however, this implies taking into consideration the different cultural meanings that can be attributed to the experience of pregnancy and childbirth. New strands of ethnographic research are now addressing the challenges of migrant women's access to and experiences within the healthcare system with regard to pregnancy, childbirth and maternity care, but also non-maternity and the politics of management of reproduction, which is revealed to be strongly racialized in many contexts (for a review of reproduction studies, see Almeling 2015).

The management of female sexuality

Female sexuality has always been the object of strict social norms and pressures. Female pleasure has often been seen as wildly irrepressible, as well as immoral, which called for women's sexuality to be held in constant check. In some contemporary societies, female genital mutilations,[5] from clitoridectomy to excision (removal of the clitoris and part or all of the inner vaginal lips) and infibulation (removal of the external genitalia and stitching of the vaginal opening) or other forms of pricking, piercing, cauterization by burning or cutting, are still seen as signs of women's modesty and performed on girls during infancy up to the age of around 15. Especially in countries such as Somalia, Egypt, Ethiopia, Kenya, Nigeria and Sudan, traditional cultures in patriarchal communities define a woman as unfit to marry if such mutilations are not performed, as they prove her virginity, so social pressures are very high. This is not to say that a feminist-informed research shouldn't try to detect the spaces of agency within these patriarchal contexts, assuming opposite dichotomic ethno-centric claims that we should condemn those practices unreflexively, nor accept them naively, in the name of cultural relativism, by stating that they are the outcome of monolithic (premodern) cultures. As the anthropologist Ellen Gruenbaum (2001, 26) argues, after years of ethnographic research in Sudan,

> A sound analysis requires looking at female circumcision from many angles, listening to what women who do it have said about it, and trying to understand the reasons for resistance to change. Doing that does not make us advocates for the practices. It simply recognizes that without a more sympathetic 'listen' we miss the fundamental causes and the concrete obstacles to change.

As surprising as it may be, cases of mutilation of female genitals have also been reported in the West. As some authors show (Ehrenreich & English 2005 [1978]; Wolf 2002 [1990]), in the Victorian age the clitoris could be cut in order to 'cure' women for 'excessive masturbation', 'nymphomania', 'hysteria', 'epilepsy', 'melancholia' or 'marital intercourse distaste'. Although already controversial in its time, this example shows us that, across countries and ages, women's sexuality has been the focus of application of power and knowledge. Women as sexual bodies were represented and governed as objects, insofar as they have been depersonalized and conceived as a collection of separate parts. But how is it possible to restore their agency in sociological accounts of a patriarchal domain from a feminist point of view? Where is it possible to see the space of resistance to the patriarchal technologies of power and knowledge that define them as (nothing more than) sexual subjectivities?

A good example of such a dilemma is mainstream pornography. Here, too, feminist thinking has gone in different directions. On the one hand, we have authors and activists in the 1980s and 1990s, like Andrea Dworkin (1981) and Catharine MacKinnon (1993), who inveighed against pornography as a form of production of violence (by filmmakers) and the consumption of it (by the voyeur). It degrades and humiliates the women who interpret it, as well as cramping the complexity of heterosexual male desire (see chapter 4). As MacKinnon puts it (1993, 15):

> What pornography does, it does in the real world, not only in the mind. As an initial matter, it should be observed that it is the pornography industry, not the ideas in the materials, that forces, threatens, blackmails, pressures, tricks, and cajoles women into sex for pictures. In pornography, women are gang raped so they can be filmed. They are not gang raped by the idea of a gang rape. It is for pornography, and not by the ideas in it, that women are hurt and penetrated, tied and gagged, undressed and genitally spread and sprayed with lacquer and water so sex pictures can be made. Only for pornography are women killed to make a sex movie, and it is not the idea of a sex killing that kills them. It is unnecessary to do any of these things to express, as ideas, the ideas pornography expresses. It is essential to do them to make pornography. Similarly, on the consumption end, it is not the ideas in pornography that assault women: men do, men who are made, changed, and impelled by it.

On the other hand, one feminist stream has read pornography as a (potential) outlet for free expression of sexuality, including queer and antisexist. It has been pointed out, for instance, how ambivalent the alliance is between progressive feminists and conservative critics of pornography who fail to see how pornography can be an efficacious communication of otherwise unexpressed needs, so bolstering the idea of 'good' and 'bad' sexuality (Strossen 1995). Pornography has also been seen as an explosion of vitality, furthering the sexual liberation of the 1970s, and as a visual depiction of our culture's deepest desires, fears and anxieties (Kipnis 1996).

More recently, the collection of essays edited by Linda Williams (2004) and the studies by Rebecca Sullivan and Alan McKee (2015) have given a more detailed picture of pornography, production and consumption, past and present. Other authors see pornography's potential as a progressive force and have argued that gay porn contributes to legitimate a non-homophobic alternative world, a gay utopia. 'Gay porn asserts homosexual desire ... it has made life bearable for countless millions of gay men', Richard Dyer observes (1985, 27). In turn, the development of 'post-porn' represents a critique of the commodification of pornified male and female bodies in mainstream pornography, mobilizing the cultural and political potential of queer and feminist sex positivity (Rehberg 2022).

A similar approach has been taken to sex work (especially prostitution) more generally, which has also given rise to a heated debate.[6] As Ronald Weitzer (2009) summarizes, sex work has been considered according to three paradigms: the oppression paradigm, which considers it as the quintessential expression of patriarchal gender relations and female bodies' exploitation; the empowerment paradigm, focusing on the ways in which sexual commerce qualifies as work, involves human agency, and may be potentially empowering for workers; and the polymorphous paradigm, which holds that there is a constellation of occupational arrangements, power relations and complex structural conditions shaping agency, subordination and job satisfaction.

More generally speaking, field research suggests depicting sex workers not just as pure victims of male domination but as persons who chose a lifestyle from a (limited) range of options. But it suggests seeing the variety of situations in depth (e.g., letting the difference between street and indoor sex work emerge). According to Elizabeth Bernstein (2007), we should take into account what sexual services actually mean in the broader context of contemporary transformation of culture and sexuality, distinguishing among various forms of commercial sex, such as bounded intimate encounter, brief sexual liaisons, being served, etc. In a more theoretical vein, anthropologist Paola Tabet includes sex work within a broader sexual-economic exchange continuum, or in other words 'the relations between men and women involving some kind of compensation given by the man for the sexual services of a woman' (2012, 39): a range beginning with socially allowed sexual-economic exchanges, like marriage, which themselves entail some form of work (at home, as child-bearers, as moral support, and so on) to prostitution. While assuming, Tabet suggests, that there is no universally accepted definition of what a prostitute or a 'whore' is, in any case, there are services systematically offered by women as a gift or exchange in an asymmetrical balance of power with men. Again, resistance to patriarchal conditions of power and knowledge about female sexuality and subjectivity is far from simple since it calls into question broader structures and social institutions that define gender relations and individual identities.

Gender violence and rape

Feminist movements first denounced that family and intimate relations were the main stage for violence against women, and that it is largely covered up and goes unpunished. The origin of that silence is said to be structural, since again it related to asymmetry of power between men and women, both economically and culturally based. Qualitative research and feminist practices show how important it is to analyse the topic in depth, trying to go beyond the simple perpetrator/victim dichotomies (which can end up blaming the victim who does not rebel against the violent relationship or identifying her as a passive actor with no agency), and failing to grasp the connection between the subject's identity, construction of the dependent relationship and a broader vision of gender relations. This led studies with a feminist approach to find the link between the violent individual relationship and the dominant gender meanings in a society, again in the connection of power and knowledge. The very fact that the female body is loaded with sexual symbolic meanings in our collective imagination – argued Susan Brownmiller in the 1970s (1986 [1975]) – results in the widespread prevalence of sexual violence and rape in society.

In feminist body politics, battering and rape, once seen as private and aberrational, have been largely recognized as part of a broad-scale system of domination that affects women, connected with asymmetry of power between the genders. Today, sexist culture no longer blames women for asserting their independence and challenging male authority, but continues to naturalize and hence justify male aggression, for example by defining the male impulse as irrepressible and naturally aggressive and appropriative, or by blaming women for making themselves sexually attractive, thus confirming a 'hydraulic' and 'sex-machine' notion of male sexuality and predatory sexual scripts (Ferrero Camoletto & Bertone 2012; see chapter 4). No doubt values like independence are being loudly proclaimed on all fronts, and few today would openly support the idea that women should be subordinate to men. Yet the fact remains that many social scenarios, including in the media and advertisements, are riddled with symbols of female passivity and with beautiful women doing nothing but smile or looking to the camera sensually. As many authors have pointed out, this teaches women to be first and foremost desirable, that is to *be* an erotic body, above all (Tseëlon 1995).

Despite this recurrent dynamic, we must recognize that bodies are immersed in networks of power relations and women are never 'just women'. Each of them is at the intersection of multiple factors of privilege and oppression, according to their social class, race, age, sexual orientation and so on (see chapter 5). So, when referring to gender violence, Crenshaw (1991) suggested, we must take all these relations into the frame, to understand it and intervene accordingly. Otherwise, we will not grasp all the patterns of subordination which intersect in women's experience of domestic violence. For example, policies might be largely defined according to standards of need experienced by white, native-born and middle-class women, and thus not be appropriate for vulnerable (largely non-white, migrant, poor) women. This could entail secondary administrative violence from institutions which are meant to protect them: 'The fact that minority women suffer from the effects of multiple subordination, coupled with institutional expectations based on inappropriate non-intersectional contexts, shapes and ultimately limits the opportunities for meaningful intervention on their behalf', states Crenshaw (1991, 1251). Again, from a Foucauldian perspective, their bodies are at the intersection of multiple layers of domination, and power circulates, creating the 'good' violence victim who satisfies the institutional expectations, but excluding the others (Gribaldo 2020).

Challenging the veil, the veil as a challenge

Few other items of clothing are so steeped in cultural significance as the veil, that icon for the practice of covering up women in various Muslim cultures round the globe. *Hijab, chador, burqa* and *bui bui* cover heads and bodies to varying degrees and with varying degrees of obligatoriness. To the Western world they are the emblem of Muslim identity, and to their critics they are a classic symbol of women's subordination. Though revealing that this is not a prerogative of Islam, the academic and theoretical positions vary in their interpretation: it may stand for the symbol of oppression, liberation, piety, cultural authenticity, heresy or opposition to Westernization and Western values (Charrad 2011), while the recent debate within feminism over the burkini merely confirms the age-old wrangle over choice and imposition. By referring to Seyla Benhabib's (2002) concept of women's bodies as symbolic battlegrounds where societies impose their moral values, social research reveals the range of meanings the veil actually stretches to: wearing it may be a sign of conformism with the going rules; it may also express dissent and alignment with an Islamic political party; among second- or third-generation immigrants in Western countries it may be an identity statement. Discarding the veil was a political statement during the anti-colonial movements or in early twentieth-century campaigns for women's rights. Again, as Fadwa El Guindi (1999) shows in a long-term comparative historical study, especially after the Iranian revolution, the veil became the object and symbol of Islamic activism in places like contemporary Egypt, where it has been adopted once more by middle- and upper-class women as a modern urban style. The same author argues that if the first feminist gesture of unveiling the face signified emancipation from exclusion, resuming the *hijab* since the mid-1970s was rather to do with liberation from imposed and often imported identities, as well as from consumerism. Others, on the contrary, see it as a purely illusory emancipation, a way to come to terms with both the impositions of religion and patriarchy and a sense of self as autonomous woman. Today, we are witnessing different regulations regarding the use of women's headscarves. In some Western contexts, it can be banned in public institutions such as schools, while in other contexts, it may be mandatory in order to attend school and public spaces in general. Based on Benhabib's observations regarding women's bodies as symbolic battlegrounds where societies impose their moral values, Ángeles Ramírez (2015, 681) observes:

(b)oth laws that prohibit or mandate the wearing of headscarves are imposed on individuals who are considered inferior and subordinate, and it is seen as acceptable to regulate them. By enacting such laws, societies are expressing and strengthening the subordinate position of women in the social hierarchy.

The headscarf and the embodiment of Islam and Muslim female aesthetics have been on the increase in recent decades in the process of globalization of Islamic religion, so that scholars speak of 'Islamic gentrification', 'market Islam' and even *'hijabization'* (ibid.). The point here is that, even when wearing the veil is voluntary and responds to government's control of Muslim populations, from the Western point of view the headscarf is mostly explained as a symbol of backwardness and subordination to patriarchy, thus reinforcing the colonizer point of view, Leila Ahmed (1992) noted (see also Ramírez 2015). The picture is further enriched by ethnographic works weighing gender, religious belonging and life course. A series of studies show that many girls assume the veil in late adolescence or adulthood as an expression of their religious identity, while younger girls wear the veil for a specific purpose: for instance, so that their parents will let them go out (for an overview, see Voas & Fleischman 2012). Dwyer's (1999) interviews with young British Muslim women in two Hertfordshire schools in the United Kingdom reveal a postcolonial, albeit contradictory, production of 'new femininities' (see also Nayak & Kehily 2013). The choice of specific appearance, such as wearing the *hijab* and the loose-fitting *shalwar kameez* trouser suit, contributes to the ascription of an 'appropriate' femininity, but it also varies for the same person according to different spatial contexts. Respondents reveal a variety of scenarios, such as young Muslim women being judged negatively for wearing 'English' clothing; wearing the *hijab* to feel free to date boys; asserting their independence in relation to loosely headscarfed mothers through the *hijab* so as to claim their own moral superiority; asserting their rights to wear skirts and other Western fashions while remaining covered; using a headscarf strategically to negotiate with parents the right to attend potentially threatening public environments. Interestingly, as a 'safe space' from the family, the school reveals itself to be a place where Muslim girls can experiment not only with wearing make-up but also with wearing the *hijab*. Overall, young women are fashioning a new, ethnically assertive British Muslim identity that is as traditional as it is modern through a culturally hybrid 'pick-and-mix' approach to clothing.

More recently, Rhys Williams and Gira Vashi (2007) interviewed schoolgirls in the United States, for example, and showed that second- and third-generation girls adopted the veil in full awareness, after negotiation between contradictory values. Once again, then, as with cases of sexual and racial hybridization, practices and bodies situated between categories, contexts and representations, and eluding normalizing or categorizing judgement, throw into relief those taken-for-granted dynamics of meaning upon which differences are constructed. Once again, differences prove to be inequalities amid the stranglehold of power.

Recent protests in some countries like Iran show even further how much the body still is a battleground for women against patriarchal power. In the Islamic Republic of Iran, women are forced to cover their hair in the *hijab* and their bodies in loose clothing; they cannot dance publicly, cannot drive motorcycles and cannot travel without parental or spousal approval. These rules were set by the Islamic revolution, as described by Marjane Satrapi in the autobiographical comic novel *Persepolis* (2003): before that, they could display in public with no veil. In September 2022, during what seemed a typical detention over an inadequate *hijab*, Mahsa Amini, a young Kurdish woman visiting Tehran, was arrested and beaten. She subsequently died in custody. The country erupted in widespread protests, led by women and girls, not seen since the Green Revolution of 2009, demanding justice for Mahsa and freedom and civil rights for all women. And one of the major ways to adhere to protest is publicly removing their veils. Indeed, the body is still crucial in setting gendered biopolitics as well as in the resistance to it.

In this chapter, we have seen that by focusing on bodies as social constructs related to power, feminist thinking produced important accounts of how deep power can mould both the materiality and the notion of gendered subjects. We have argued that the postmodern turn in feminist theory, profoundly inspired by Foucault's work shedding light on power as a productive rather than merely repressive force, allowed seeing how power limits male and female bodies, making them function and act in different ways, but also creates male and female bodies as such, positing them in hierarchical order. In being both a product of discourse (we can access our bodies only through the lenses of our culture and language) and material entities (we feel, heal, suffer and enjoy as embodied subjects), our bodies can be the space for oppression, as well as of resistance. Confronting specific female experiences (including pregnancy and childbirth, pornography and sex work, rape and gender violence, the use of the veil), feminist research has shown how complex but fundamental body politics is, and how ambivalent it is to define a practice as empowering or disempowering. 'Personal is political', a slogan stated in the 1970s. And nothing is probably more personal than sexuality: we shall now see how much gender, sex and sexuality are indeed related to power.

4

Gender, Sex and Sexuality

In 2014 the Europe-wide pop music competition *Eurovision Song Contest* was won for Austria by Conchita Wurst. Long black hair, a dress of glittering sequins with a long train, nails perfectly painted – and a dark bushy beard. Whether the Wurst sensation indicates that mainstream is now fully accepting of *queer*, or whether her transgressive impact has been neutralized by cosy glamourization, the fact indubitably remains that for several decades everyday life and the media world have been witnessing more and more overt contestation of the traditional patterns of sex, gender and sexuality based on a complementary binary of man/woman, masculinity/femininity, etc. The media coverage of transgender issues is nowadays confronting the mass public with a narrative message that is markedly reflexive in a dual sense: trans stories are embodied in concrete subjectivities and experiences, and, in being told, such stories protest against the rigid gender divide.

The sexually hybrid body is to be found in much art and literature. Literature gives us, for instance, the transgender Hijra protagonist of Arundhati Roy's *The Ministry of Utmost Happiness*. Japanese manga has explored gender fluidity in series such as *Lady Oscar*, *Ranma* and *F-Compo*. Examples in cinema range from the classic *The*

Rocky Horror Picture Show, to *Boys Don't Cry*, *The Soldier's Wife* or *The Danish Girl*, while cult American television series (such as *Ellen*, *Friends* and *Game of Thrones*) have increasingly featured gay, lesbian and transgender characters, who have also become subjects in their own right of successful shows like *Transparent*. In this way we seem to witness the spreading and, as it were, normalizing of possibilities that were once found on very restricted occasions in contemporary Western society. 'Transgender' itself, broadly understood, stands as a warning against simplistic ideas about gender: it has become an abundantly used category of gender in its own right, embracing a wide-ranging constellation of more and more vocal sexual cultures. Famous drag queens like RuPaul have gained a high media profile, their personal lives the subject of successful, often ironic biographies attempting to carve out a space for them among the genders. Descriptions of self can rest on ambiguity and ambivalence. As RuPaul argues, gender isn't everything – 'You can call me he. You can call me she. You can call me Regis and Kathie Lee; I don't care! Just as long as you call me'.

Of course, the glamour of successful drag performers like RuPaul or the sexual ambiguity of many icons of youth culture should not obscure the marginal state in which many transgender people live outside the limelight, like the Brazilian *viados* who adopt feminine physical attributes but often profess a male homosexual identity (Kulick 1998). In this case irony, ambiguity and ambivalence take a step back: in the story of those lives, distinctions of sex, gender and sexuality are complicated but deadly earnest. Others still hit the limelight despite themselves for being located in between genders, such as trans men who become pregnant and have children. Indeed, media representation of male gestation allows for increasing social recognition of transgender people while, at the same time, fostering cisnormative views of reproduction by portraying transgender reproduction as new and different. Indeed, the media representation also creates a new 'transnormative reproductive subject', establishing a new socially sanctioned script for what it means to be transgender and what types of transgender experience may be recognized or accepted in mainstream society (Lampe, Carter & Sumerau 2019).

Such stories are living instances of body frameworks in action which incline us to distinguish people according to physical attributes that are slotted into a schema of contrasts, analogies and oppositions. Representations often continue to facilitate social patterns of gender inequality within such new frames. In the pages that follow we shall explore the construction of differences between bodies, pondering how gender, sex and sexuality interact and come up with differing positions in the social hierarchy. We will look at people who do not accommodate easily to gender norms, both noticing how their varied experiences reveal the power of the gender order and have contributed to shift it in many ways. Considering the experience of transgender and intersex people, we will explore the different ways in which the body can be constructed as *plastic* and how the gender order impinges on the way sex is constructed. Gendered bodies are also constructed in relation to sexuality. Although increasingly challenged, heterosexuality is fundamental to the gender binary and the fabrication of two distinct, different and complementary genders. We shall thereby examine how sexuality is organized and sexual desire constructed as a fundamental aspect of embodied subjectivities which spans across a spectrum of cultural variation and embodied difference.

1. Disarticulating sex and gender: from Agnes to Herculine

To understand how sexual differences are carved into bodies, and how they are institutionally sustained by our societies, sociology has often turned to those hybrid figures, intermediate between the sexes, who seem to reject the hard and fast dividing line of culture. A famous essay on the subject was Harold Garfinkel's on Agnes (Garfinkel 1999 [1967]). This was the first essay in which a history of sexual 'passing' was used to highlight the gender order. Working in close liaison with the well-known psychiatrist Robert Stoller, Garfinkel reconstructs the experience of Agnes, a young Californian transgender woman who was one of the first, in the late 1950s, to undergo surgery to amputate the penis and in its place construct a vagina. During their conversation Agnes made her gender identity clear and convinced the psychiatrist that she was to all effects a female trapped in a body with male sexual organs. Garfinkel departed from the biologistic paradigm in that he did not seek to explain her wish to change sexual status according to some alleged biological or psychological normality or abnormality, but tried to portray the cultural assumptions upon which Agnes' needs and requests were organized and negotiated, her rights to having an operation granted.

Agnes' tale provides a highly explicit portrait of the principles upon which gender identity is usually legitimated according to bodily endowment, behaviour, feelings, appearance and sexual orientation. From that viewpoint, Agnes' history highlights what gets taken for granted about gender, sex and sexual orientation. Garfinkel describes

Agnes as an attractive 19-year-old white girl, with a 'convincingly female appearance', with long hair, a soft voice, thin shoulders, ample breasts and a narrow waist. She feminized her gender according to the standard of the time by adopting what used to be called (and still partly are) stereotyped womanly traits, playing 'the coy, sexually innocent, fun-loving, passive, receptive "young thing"'. The wealth of details provided by Garfinkel and the relevance he grants to Agnes' accounts was criticized by sociologists at the time (Sassatelli 2007b), but the position he adopts is one of the reasons why his work on Agnes has become a milestone in gender studies and continues to raise attention and debate (Chu & Drager 2019; Connell 2009; Lorber 2021; Rogers 1992; Schilt 2016; West & Zimmerman 1987).

The story Garfinkel tells of Agnes helped provide a reading of the gender order that anticipated many insights from contemporary feminism: '(w)hen we view gender as an accomplishment, an achieved property of situated conduct, our attention shifts from matters internal to the individual and focuses on interactional and, ultimately, institutional arenas' (West & Zimmerman 1987, 126; see also Kessler & McKenna 1978; West & Zimmerman 2009; and chapters 1 and 2). Gender is seen as something performative, a 'doing' that gets stably implanted in everyday life by what people say and do to confirm, time and again, that they are 'real' men and 'real' women. For Garfinkel, the transgender woman had something of the same function as Alfred Schütz's stranger: having to develop great skill and forethought in order to cope with (to her) new situations, Agnes 'treated sexed persons as cultural events that members make happen' and was 'self-consciously equipped' to reveal how gender and sexuality happen in everyday life as 'an obvious, familiar, recognizable, natural and serious matter of fact' (Garfinkel 1999 [1967], 180–1). Agnes is both like and unlike cisgender people, i.e., those who feel they fit the sex they were given at birth. On the one hand, she too is good at acting within the meshes of appropriateness underpinning femininity (and masculinity). On the other hand, she is far more aware of playing that part. So, while most adults tend to take gender and sexuality as ordinary resources while they go about other business – as well as 'essential impressions' that get conveyed while one is engaged in doing something else (see also Goffman 1979; chapter 2) – Garfinkel stresses that to a transgender person like Agnes, mustering gender skills is a constant problem and remains as such.

Like the other trans people that the Los Angeles team studied, Agnes shared the binary view of the sexes, and included herself in it. She is accordingly on her guard against the risk of debasement, in her everyday life and in her bid for gender-affirming surgery, if ever she gets classified as outside the two-way divide. But that is not to say Agnes is literally playing a part; she is not detached or scheming in handling the impressions she arouses. More than most people, she is aware of the routines that forge gender and assign us to our sexual category, but she too subscribes to the social conventions. She is forever learning to be a woman, fully engrossed, using every occasion as a learning opportunity for what is the 'appropriate', 'right' or 'natural' way for a woman to behave.

From the standpoint of gender studies and the sociology of the body, Garfinkel's conclusions partly align with post-structuralist feminist theory which was in turn inspired by Michel Foucault's seminal work on the history of sexuality and on the disciplining role of medical science in the construction and transformation of sexual identities (see chapter 3).[1] Editing an integral version of the *mémoires* of Herculine Barbin who lived in nineteenth-century France, Foucault (1980b) raised a number of points relevant to the issue of how we are assigned to our sexual category.

Herculine was designated as a girl at birth but, coming to the threshold of adulthood and following a series of genital inspections, was declared to be a man and forced to live as such, relinquishing all female trappings despite her life story and mixed anatomy. Rounding out the memoirs with medical evidence, Foucault sets out to show how science got its teeth into the Herculine affair which it treated as a puzzle for pathology and an easily corrected error for the registry office. In the end, given the prevailing trends in sexual categorization – binary (male/female), essentialist (biologistic) and metonymic (prioritizing the genitals in defining sex category) – Herculine was in fact acknowledged to be a 'hermaphrodite', but with a 'predominance of male sex'.

This history is a pillar of the Foucauldian theory, whereby the very perception of sex presupposes a regulatory framework that alters over time: the way it categorized bodies was constantly evolving and, in the modern age, became enshrined in medicine. Foucault's combination of history and theory influenced many studies which charted the evolution of a scientific theory of sex. In his famous study on sex and gender, the historian Thomas Laqueur (1992) showed how premodern Europe conceived of there being two genders but only one sex, male sex, which was 'inverted' in the female form, the vagina being seen as a penis turned inside out. As the scientific discipline of pathology developed, the gender binary found biological support: the sexes became two in number, rigidly distinguished by the conformation of the genitals. More recently, as we saw in the previous chapter, developments in endocrinology added another idea to the anatomical either/or: that the crucial factor is hormones (Fine 2017; Hausman 1995; Oudshoorn 1994; Roberts 2002), chemical substances differing only in quantity from the male to the female body.[2]

In comparing Agnes and Herculine in this historical and institutional light, we soon see that they differ in scope. The rise of endocrinology questioned the primary focus on genitals, though not to the point of ousting it. Thus, in our own day the body is still seen more as a mouldable datum – but a datum nonetheless – when it comes to sexual categorization. Highly specific protocols of surgical reassignment have become consolidated: they are practised on infants born with mixed sexual traits, and on adults who apply for gender-affirming surgery. However, access to these protocols differs markedly: for children born with mixed sexual features like Herculine, there is often no choice; for adults like Agnes who wish to pass from one sex to the other, access depends more on their likelihood of 'psychologically' adapting to the new gender identity and less on any official report on their genital, hormonal or physiological characteristics. The body's plasticity is thus viewed in different ways, to which there still corresponds a heavily binary normative view of gender and sexual morphology. As we shall see in the final section of this chapter, this continues to be heterosexually biased.

2. Between the genders, between the sexes

Trans and intersex identities may be seen as locating themselves between the genders and between the sexes. Yet, while on the one hand they appear to go beyond neat binaries, on the other hand there has been a constant pressure, especially from the medical profession, to reinforce the binaries. In the following pages we shall explore the role of medicine as well as the experiences of gender-variant people to consider how gender and sex are shaped in contemporary society, with the simultaneous reproduction of and challenge to binaries.

The role of medicine in defining and shaping sex

In his study, Garfinkel did not directly tackle the role of medical expertise or the impact of evolving medical practice, nor did he frame the power ratio between the doctors and Agnes as an issue, though he did include extracts from health reports in the footnotes.

But in present-day sociology, we really must consider the institutional arena and the scientific pressures that trans persons still need to cope with. It is a setting where various branches and interests of scientific knowledge mingle, not always harmoniously. The focus on this context has led some to believe that transgender desire for body modification is an expression of gender conformism, invented by medical science in collusion with the cultural imperative of the male/female divide (Szasz 1990). This, for example, was the reading of it given by feminist Janice Raymond (1979) in *The Transsexual Empire*. Provocatively branding it as a merger between the patriarchal system and medical power, she sees 'transsexuality' as simply reinforcing the gender binary, being based on personification of the old stereotypes about femininity and kowtowing to patriarchal norms. In their ethnographic study on doctors assessing candidates applying for genital surgery, Dwight Billings and Thomas Urban (1982, 266) came to the same conclusion: they argue that '(t)he legitimation, rationalization and commodification of sex-change operations has produced an identity category – transsexual – for a diverse group of sexual deviants and victims of severe gender role distress'.

Through such lenses, as with cosmetic surgery (see chapter 6), we again seem faced with patients who are unaware of their 'real needs' and like to think they can change their lives by a change of body, instead of plumping for an androgynous body-identity in collision with convention. However, Garfinkel's lesson shows that it is not a question of individual choice; it is rather the binary gender order which, working as a normative principle, permeates social practices and the options available to self-identity/self-creation. Agnes ends up adopting a certain style of femininity since it is that femininity which seems to work for all practical purposes, allowing her to pass for a woman without question. In the first instance, then, her story can be read subversively as minutely dissecting the alignment between gender, sexuality and sex, not to mention pressure impinging on female identity.

In *Framing Agnes*, a documentary first released in 2018, the story of Garfinkel's study and of Agnes' experience is retrieved showing precisely the strictures she had to face in order to be granted the full status of a woman.[3] What Goffman (2010 [1971]) called 'normal appearances', as we have seen, were in fact fundamental for her. By her ability to play the female gender as the society of her day cast it, and by bolstering it with a hint of heterosexual experience and leanings, Agnes in practice managed to secure the sexual belonging that she wanted. Her first problem was 'not so much living up to some prototype of essential femininity but preserving her categorization as a female' (West & Zimmerman 1987, 132). She had to embody that categorization: corporeality is not an attribute of the individual but, as Merleau-Ponty (1962 [1945]) puts it, it's human beings' 'being-in-the-world', their starting point from which to experience it. Agnes didn't just want to be publicly cast as a woman – something she could anyway achieve fairly easily without any operation since the public process of sexual categorization is not based on the genitals which tend not to be on show, as we pointed out in the first chapter. The visual signs of gender attribution replace and work on behalf of sex, being a kind of 'cultural genitals' in Kessler and McKenna's definition (Schilt & Lagos 2017). Indeed, the fact that by her appearance, gestures and demeanour, moving, talking and describing herself, she could pass for a woman shows the 'routinized nature' of the basic expectations associated with femininity. Still, Agnes applied for surgical realignment because she shared the view that sex – as primary sexual characteristics – was of the essence for gender identity.

The biologistic, metonymic view of gender taking root in the modern era meant that the conformation of the genitals could not be something marginal for Agnes, however good she was at being a woman. It was, to her, a need for bodily experience, based on a wish to develop 'normal' sexual relations with her fiancé who had begun to insist on 'going all the way'. But her ambition was destined to be disappointed: her vagina would always be artificial; her intimate experience would be different from that of a woman recognized as such from birth. Trans people were confronted with a medical profession that normalized them according to its own medicalized frameworks, keeping them in a marginal position.

In her study on the experiences of people with mixed sexual traits who have undergone surgery, Suzanne Kessler (1998) reveals that the surgeons are themselves sure that a reconstructed vagina, let alone a penis, can never compare with the 'natural' article. It is a 'prop' helping to avoid jarring embarrassment and, at the same time, a sign of medical progress. One thus glimpses a tacit conflict between medical know-how and the person undergoing gender-affirming surgery. The hope of full gender embodiment founders upon the medical constructivist mentality which simultaneously supports both the plasticity of the body and the superiority of certain 'natural' forms.

There has been increasing attention to intersex identities, of which Herculine represents an early studied example. The notion of 'intersex' is an umbrella term covering a wide range of conditions to do with sex chromosomes, the genital apparatus and secondary sexual characteristics. Until the nineteenth century, intersex was the province of law, politics and religion, but in time it moved more under the wing of medical knowledge and practice, based on indexes like hormones, sex chromosomes and genetic markers (Fausto-Sterling 2000).[4] In her influential analysis of such kinds of treatment, spanning from the nineteenth century to our own day, Alice Domurat Dreger (1998, 6) observed:

> [h]ermaphroditism causes a great deal of confusion, more than one might at first appreciate, because ... the discovery of a 'hermaph-roditic' body raises doubts not just about the particular body in question, but about all bodies. The questioned body forces us to ask what exactly it is – if anything – that makes the rest of us unquestionable. It forces the not-so-easy question of what it means to be a 'normal' male or a 'normal' female.

'Hermaphroditic' bodies (as they were called for centuries) are still a battlefield upon which the definition of 'natural' maleness and femaleness is being reviewed. That terrain is governed by medical science which, expressing as it does a wider cultural mentality, has sought to reconstruct bodies with mixed-sex characteristics in order to 'reinforce primarily what they threatened most: the idea that there was a single, knowable, male or female "true" sex in every human body' (Dreger 1998, 44; see also Fausto-Sterling 2000; Kessler 1998; Malatino 2019; Meyerowitz 2002). In short, following dynamics we have already noted (see chapter 3), medical science has gradually taken possession of a cultural icon, the hermaphrodite, which used to arouse attraction and disgust, and turned it into a 'scientific' fact, a 'sick organism'.

As orthodox medicine has progressed, the gonads, hormones, chromosomes, etc., have become complex and not always harmonious indexes of sexual categorization and at the same time a field for medical intervention (surgical, hormonal, genetic) to re-establish the clearest possible dividing line between male and female as early as possible in infancy. The male/female classificatory principle has thus prevailed over the actual existence of hybrid bodies whose 'indeterminate' sex needs surgical correction. Surgical intervention aimed at making intersex children conform to sex binaries is also linked to the erasure of intersex at legal and cultural levels (Travis 2015). Small wonder that the growing activism of associations and groups of people born with mixed sexual traits that were surgically realigned in earliest infancy has tackled that. One of the policy objectives of the

Intersex Society of North America (ISNA), the first to be created in the mid-1990s, was the right for newborns not to undergo surgical assignment. The association has proved that, by reason of a purely size-based rule whereby any sex organ longer than 2.5 cm is ranked as a penis, and any shorter one as a clitoris (Hird 2000), the tendency has been for over-large clitorises above all to be removed, often leading to disorientation and loss of sexual sensation.

Sharon Preves (2003) studied over thirty cases of American intersex people, emphasizing the importance of personal experience beyond the strictures of medical categorization and the role of political action and consolidation of public visibility in the construction of intersex identity. Rather than focusing on what intersex people 'medically' are, therefore, a growing body of work has examined the challenges that intersex people face, which include normalization according to binarism, marginalization and human rights violations (Crocetti, Arfini, Monro & Yeadon-Lee 2020).

Challenging the gender and sex binary outside medicine

Reviewing these practices and the pushback against them, it becomes clear how phallocentric assumptions are embedded in medical and surgical know-how. Reconstructing a vagina is apparently simple: it seems to fit a literal definition bound up with its passive capacity (depth, width) to accommodate a penis, and not its active potential (sensation, movement) for sharing orgasm. Even today this fact, together with a more general hierarchy among the genders, explains the very prevalence of male-to-female over female-to-male transitions (Hird 2000).[5] All in all, especially in the last twenty years, thanks in particular to queer studies and movements, trans people are less constrained in a straitjacket, and this is often related to recognition within intimate life and personal relations. Tey Meadow (2018) has shown how gender non-conformity may be facilitated in children, with transition occurring early in life and children being supported by parents in their challenge to their birth-ascribed gender.

Looking at partners' experiences of trans men's changing bodies, Katelynn Bishop (2006, 84) has defied popular and medical understandings of trans bodies which reduce them to parts: 'the materiality of trans men's bodies, as experienced by their intimate partners, goes far beyond the presence or absence of particular body parts, and is inseparable from partners' understanding of who trans men are as people'. Pregnancy among trans men is also a phenomenon which stretches the binary construction of gender. Still, for both trans women and trans men, transforming the body and its presentation to trade one gender for the other is central (Dozier 2005; Schrock, Reid & Boyd 2005). Going beyond the binary is not simple, as Catherine Connell (2010) has found in her study of trans men and women at work: trans people who tried to mix male and female presentations often felt they were gender policed and constantly read through conventional gender norms. Race, class and geographical location are also implicated in transition and in the obstacles and possibilities encountered in the accomplishment of trans identities, impinging on the way they may be experienced and realized in everyday life (Abelson 2019; Doan & Johnston 2022; Hines & Sanger 2010).

Given such tensions, some have argued that cross-dressing is a more consistent form of protest against the ideology of sexual dimorphism since it does not entail the aligning of sex and gender via surgery. Judith Butler (2006 [1990]) points out that dress change is a performance, an ironic leg-pull, and opens our eyes to the performative nature of all genders, including those aligned with sex. Femininity and masculinity are ways of behaviour and presentation based on imitation and learning, rather than immutable qualities imprinted in the body at birth once and for all. Butler's work points out the coercive power of the gender order. As we saw in the third chapter, she explains that the effect of gender is dissimulatory: it encourages certain kinds of behaviour while obscuring the fact that there is no essential biological fact serving us as a starting datum. On that view, the male and female morphology by which gender differences are naturalized are always ideal constructs, measured against which we all somehow feel inadequate, given the great range of human physical endowment. It pays here to remember the difference not just between passing (when someone, typically a transgender person, is perceived as cisgender) and cross-dressing (wearing items of clothing not commonly associated with one's sex), but also between 'transgender' and 'transsexual', the latter causing some people greater perplexity than the former because of its connection to medicalization and the focus it can put on surgical transition.

Cross-dressing actually has an age-old history and comprises famous figures such as the eighteenth-century Chevalier d'Éon who lived part of his life disguised as a man, and part as a woman (Bullough & Bullough 1993). In such cases, though, the dressing up did not turn into a political manifesto or a collective stand but was often an expedient enabling homoerotic relations. Only during the 1980s in the United States and Europe did overtly transgender communities and associations come to the fore. Anne Bolin (1994;

see also Hird 2000; Prosser 1998), for example, talked of these movements as protesting against the two-gender system by mixing masculine with feminine traits or undertaking only some of the surgical operations available for reassigning one's sexual category. Famous trans scholars like Kate Bornstein (1994), Leslie Feinberg (1996) and Sandy Stone (1991) called not for full identification with the female gender but an intermediate position, proudly relating their own stories and challenging the gender/sex binary.

The guiding principle behind many transgender groups today seems to be the idea that every individual should be free to change the sex assigned at birth; this may be a permanent or just a temporary change, either way shaking free of the either/or straitjacket of sex, gender and sexuality. More and more we are witnessing a tension between those wishing to pass for 'genitally corrected' women or men, and the growing number of trans people whose aim is to overthrow the binary gender order. Drawing upon in-depth interviews with trans people in Portugal and in the United Kingdom, Ana Cristina Marques (2019) considers how they recreate their gender displays, particularly in terms of gender embodiment and aesthetics. She finds a number of strategies, which are not mutually exclusive, through which display and subjectivity are articulated in everyday life: 'blending in', 'masking', 'naturalizing' and 'subverting'. Such strategies are multiple and dependent on context and the life course and may be used in different and varying combinations on different occasions.

Queer theory insistently uses trans identities to epitomize a challenge to the unbending sexual binary and build up its transgressive potential (Elliot 2010). What is more, as Genny Beemyn and Susan Rankin note in *The Lives of Transgender People* (2011), a survey of trans people in the United States, gender-non-conforming people are increasingly diversified and often adopting queering definitions of themselves that reflexively confront gender binaries and stereotypes. Utilizing interviews with women from the United States, Canada and Australia, who recounted relationships with transgender men, Carla Pfeffer (2014) considers how the experiences of these queer social actors hold the potential to crash normative binaries, highlighting the more and more blurred intersections and overlaps between sex, gender and sexual orientation.

The multiplication of gender identities is becoming visible and the number of people who identify as non-binary or fluid has grown. Helana Darwin, in her online ethnography on Reddit, observes that, in the genderqueer subgroup, there is now a variety of gender identifications: '"genderqueer" is but one of the several popular nonbinary categories/labels; others that members invoke include agender, aliagender, androgynous, bigender, demigirl/demiguy, genderfluid, genderflux, genderfuck, gender variant, intergender, neutrois, polygender and pangender' (2017, 324). Interviewing an assorted group of non-binary individuals in a further study, Darwin (2020) points to the significant ambivalence among them regarding transgender identification. There were also considerable differences as to which model of transgender identification defines group membership: the 'binary and medicalized' model or the 'umbrella' model. The responses were varied and diverse, with people often questioning their belonging and a simple yes/no categorization. The range of responses showed the extent to which the diverse gender identities that non-binary people claim for themselves cannot simply be sorted into either a man/woman or a cisgender/transgender binary.

Asexuality and agender subjectivities play an even more subtle game of resistance against dominant gender and sexuality norms. A recent study conducted in Scotland and England (Cuthbert 2019) found that agender subjectivities can be understood as arising from an embodied meaning-making process where gender is understood to be fundamentally about sexuality. Agender subjectivity may be felt as a necessity to come to terms with asexuality and a way to manage the pressures of heteropatriarchy for those who had been assigned female at birth while a variety of responses to gender remains prevalent among them.

The plastic body and the persistent power of the binary

The comparison between transgender people who seek gender-affirming surgery as adults and intersex people who are typically operated on very early in childhood clearly highlights the force of the cultural imperative to distinguish the sexes even when gender and the body are seen as socially constructed facts. The urge to categorize is at its most evident when the 'patient' is a transgender adult (regardless of their original physical endowment), or a child newly born with mixed sexual features.

Today, private health schemes (and the public service in several European countries) cover gender-affirming therapies and/or surgery for such adults who feel an obligation to choose to become what they already are. But the same institutions leave no such choice in the case of mixed-sex newborns. The assumption behind this still transpires from the protocols circulated by American sexologist John Money who established the Johns Hopkins Gender Identity Clinic in the 1960s: that one learns to be a woman or man from the very first days of life; that proper genital apparatus is fundamental if one is to learn correctly; and that surgeons must simply provide the right genitals so that proper gender socialization may go ahead (Hird 2000; Kessler 1998). Nevertheless, as Georgiann Davis (2015) notes, intersex people tend to respond differently to medicalization, and while some accept strict binary realignment, many now embrace an intersex identity which tries to go beyond the binary of gender and heterosexuality.

However, there seem to be differences among health providers when it comes to trans and intersex subjectivities. In a further study of health providers specializing in intersex and trans medicine, Davis and her colleagues (Davis, Dewey & Murphy 2016) show that, while both sets of providers hold essentialist ideology about sex, gender and sexuality, providers for intersex people are inclined to approach intersex as an emergency that necessitates medical attention, whereas providers for trans people attempt to slow down their patients' urgent requests for transitioning services. In the accounts of most providers, successful medical interventions are achieved when a person adheres to heteronormative gender practices.

It appears, then, that body plasticity can be construed in various ways, though they do tend in one dominant direction. Thus, whilst medical practice seems to challenge the idea that biological sex is incontrovertible, it firmly espouses the dualistic view of sex/gender. In other words, doctors and medical providers are more prepared to interfere with sex than with gender. In fact, they seem to provide a sex for the accomplishment of heteronormative gender.[6] The fact that it is possible and legitimate to operate and change a body, even radically, does not mean that this is easily granted in all situations. Even today, any bodily identity that falls outside the parameters set for gender identity seems to come up against a wall of discipline, therapeutic protocol and a naturalizing tendency geared to re-establishing the binary order.

3. Sexuality and gender identities

Heterosexuality is the central factor in our daily production of two distinct, different and complementary genders – the way we normally see male and female – and one which Davis and colleagues found to underlie the attitudes of health providers in trans and intersex medicine (Davis, Dewey & Murphy 2016). To resume our previous example, Agnes' battle to change sex was partly intended to satisfy

Bill, the man with whom she had started a relationship and who was beginning to demand sexual relations. Bill plays an important part in her process of feminization. To feel a convincing woman, Agnes needed a 'normal' man who, she explained, 'would not be interested in me if I weren't normal' (Garfinkel 1999 [1967]). She had learnt by now to handle her sexuality like a 'normal woman', feminizing her libido on a model that feminist thinking traces back to the patriarchal system; that is, she had managed to derive gratification from being leered at by men. In interviews she also alluded to the female rivalry her looks aroused; above all, she talked of playing the submissive role with her fiancé. To complete the transition, she needed to be able to have 'normal' sex with him.

Heterosexuality, biological determinism and gender inequality

The root of that need is the idea of two complementary sexes in a relationship of mutual attraction, and that this plays an important part in constructing and projecting sexual status. Dividing people into just two distinct sexes serves to prevent any challenging of what Judith Butler (2006 [1990]) calls the 'heterosexual matrix'. Butler (ibid., 208) suggests that this works as a

> grid of cultural intelligibility through which bodies, genders, and desires are naturalized. ... that assumes that for bodies to cohere and make sense there must be a stable sex expressed through a stable gender (masculine expresses male, feminine expresses female) that is oppositionally and hierarchically defined through the compulsory practice of heterosexuality.

Male hegemony over women rests on the same basis as does the hegemony of heterosexuality over other sexualities. The matrix is a symbolic apparatus which sets up sexual distinction as the norm, and in so doing creates a hierarchy among the sexes, as well as decreeing the relations allowed between same-sex persons, and the outcast or abject status of homosexuality and all practices not contemplated by the matrix. The space for the outcast is beyond the pale (see chapter 3), and that is where feminists, gay people and other minorities have to live politically, according to Butler.[7]

Agnes' mention of competition with other women (a cousin, for example) to gain a man's attention shows us how pervasive the heterosexual model is in steering relations between individuals, and likewise how individuals play their part in bolstering the model by their ways of relating. Construction of sexuality and construction of gender are thus mutually implicating and mutually reinforcing processes.

In a seminal work on masculinity, Raewyn Connell (1987) puts forward a model of gender hierarchy construction in which a series of asymmetrical standpoints view the threesome: gender, identity and sexuality. In top place is masculinity ('hegemonic masculinity' in the Gramscian sense), the dominant form of male in the typical patriarchal system which guarantees it will be socially accepted and legitimated. Although that is only one way of being a man, and not necessarily the commonest one, it stands distinct from others by posing as the winning model, the socially most desirable manner of being men. In Western capitalist society, the hegemonic ideal is represented by the competitive, career-oriented, aggressive, cynical, emotionally numb and, of course, heterosexual male. Other forms of heterosexual masculinity take a lower place, though they too enjoy the 'patriarchal dividend': the social advantages accruing from being men rather than women in various walks of public and private life. The counterpart to hegemonic masculinity is 'emphasized femininity', a form of heterosexual femininity that is based on compliance to patriarchy and is legitimated by the principle of complementarity. As Connell (1987, 184–5) defines it:

> One form [of femininity] is defined around compliance with this subordination and is oriented to accommodating the interests and desires of men. I will call this 'emphasized femininity'. Others are defined centrally by strategies of resistance or forms of non-compliance. Others again are defined by complex strategic combinations of compliance, resistance, and co-operation.

In subordinate and fringe positions we have a great range of 'other' subjective states, like homosexual masculinities and femininities, or hybrid forms of sex, gender and sexuality which have less social power as being 'abject' but pack a strong subversive punch (take bisexuality and its divisive potential vis-à-vis the hetero/homo dichotomy). This scheme was subsequently refined (Connell & Messerschmidt 2005; Messerschmidt 2018) to allow also for antagonism and resistance from subordinate men and for the fact that gay men have acquired social status and have come to be more accepted by heterosexual men.

Another no less famous feminist approach to constructing identity upon sex, gender and sexuality comes from the American law scholar, Catharine MacKinnon. To MacKinnon, the way heterosexual desire is constructed in our society is influenced by the sex industry and is humiliating to women. Pornography (MacKinnon 1993) is both a form of violence and a representation of it, presented and perceived as being agreeable to the women who undergo it. It is therefore the clearest example of the misleading way in which heterosexual desire is presented: heterosexuality is defined by pornography and not vice versa, but in defining what is sexual and what is not, pornography cloaks the real violence that it reproduces. This contributes to the meaning of masculinity and femininity (women in this configuration of sexual desire are defined as 'sex', whilst being deprived of their sexuality), and likewise that of desire, which becomes male desire *par excellence*. MacKinnon (1987, 49) comments that

> The molding, direction, and expression of sexuality organize society into two sexes, women and men. This division underlies the totality of social relations; it is as structural and pervasive as class is in Marxist theory, although of course its structure and quality of pervasion are different. Sexuality is the social process that creates, organizes, expresses, and directs desire. Desire here is parallel to value in Marxist theory, not the same, though it occupies an analogous theoretical location. It is taken for a natural essence or presocial impetus but is actually *created by* the social relations, the hierarchical relations, in question. This process creates the social beings we know as women and men, as their relations create society. Sexuality to feminism is, like work to Marxism, socially constructed and at the same time constructing.

MacKinnon's thoughts on pornography have been challenged by feminist authors, as we saw in chapter 3, for being close to traditional patriarchal moralism, not acknowledging the multiple forms of masculinity and heterosexual desire, and above all denying any form of agency on the part of the women creating and consuming pornography. Yet her views do have the merit of tracing the historical course of sexual desire and its connection with sexuality and gender as they get reciprocally constructed.

This connection was shown by one of the founders of the Chicago School, Ernest Burgess, in the late 1940s: 'the ideal of masculinity becomes associated with toughness, with physical exploits, with profane and obscene language, and with unrestrained sex behavior' (Burgess 1949 in Plummer 2002, 137). For decades now, the sociological literature has been urging us to distinguish analytically and theoretically among sexual drive, desire and sexuality (Plummer 2002). There was long a tendency, in fact, to separate sexual drive from its cultural results, thus setting the former up as a biologically based universal factor. That biological model of sex owed much to the theory of evolution and, although distinguishing between sexuality and reproduction, gave primacy to penetration, thereby tacitly rebooting the idea that sex had to have a reproductive function.

Social interaction and sexual roles

By contrast, more recent studies concentrate on how desire itself is constructed – quite another thing from an approach that simply examined its various outlets in different cultural contexts. From the 1960s and 1970s on, society has been seen to play an active role in giving form to sexual desire via social learning and everyday inter-action; and it became clear that there was no need to repress an (alleged) natural impulse in order to explain how sexual desire became domesticated: it was more a question of giving form to desire itself along pathways serving the developing social order, and gender in particular. Interactionist sociology made a fundamental contribution here, shifting the accent from sexual roles onto a broader concept of sexual identity; '(i)nteractionists shifted the research emphasis from sexual roles to the looser notion of sexual identity – from showing how social norms constrain and shape the sexual impulse, to showing how individuals, as active agents, negotiate sexual conduct through social interaction' (Stein 1989, 7).

A crucial factor in this shift of perspective was John Gagnon and William Simon's theory of sexual scripts. Developed fifty years ago, it is now recognized as among the most important social research on sexuality (Wiederman 2015). Even before Foucault formulated his thoughts on the repressive hypothesis of sexuality (Foucault 1978 [1976]; see chapter 3), Gagnon and Simon broke away from all naturalizing ideas on human sexuality based on representing the sex drive as a biological imperative upon which society is supposed to act by censorship or repression. As a force, sexuality is not independent of the social, but rather is defined and moulded by society.

On their view, people learn the meanings culturally ascribed to certain events and situations which they dub sexual; they learn an ability to define situations as sexual or to act in a sexual manner: '[s]cripts are involved in learning the meaning of internal states, organizing the sequences of specifically sexual acts, decoding novel situations, setting limits on sexual responses and linking meanings from non-sexual aspects of life to specifically sexual experience' (Gagnon & Simon 1973, 17). Applying symbolic interactionism and the lesson of the Chicago School, they distinguish between different (interrelated) levels of social management of desire: cultural scenarios (general guidelines to defining what is sexual, generating frames that make sense of individual experience, and defining sexual roles); intra-psychic scripts (such as fantasies and memories that cause arousal); and interpersonal scripts (instructions on how to behave).

Gender comes into it on all levels: for instance, men and women learn in adolescence the acceptable timing of engagement in active sex, forms of socio-sexual behaviour, the frequency of masturbation, the number of partners and so on. Such learning takes place in highly gender-differentiated settings. Within male groups – Gagnon and Simon relate – one finds a public validation, promotion and regulation of orgasm, masturbation and heterosexual experience, and the number of girlfriends serve as mediators of social standing among the boys. Girls, by contrast, live in a girl-dominated world which is nonetheless geared to future heterosexuality, romanticism, attachment, and in some cases a slight degree of masochism. In both boys and girls, heterosexual scripts are to the fore throughout sociali-zation and into adult life; they assume males are always up for sex, as justified by certain basic facts (hormones, penis). Any young man who opts out of a predatory attitude is cast by his peers as a loser or even a non-man. For their part, young women are urged to sit on their desires unless they have formed a steady couple (Sakaluk et al. 2014). Studies of heterosexual sex have in fact revealed a gendered double standard in which women are more likely to be derogated for pursuing casual sexual pleasure (Sagebin Bordini & Sperb 2013). It is often the men who feel they should initiate sexual activity, talk about having honed their amatory prowess, and go into physical details, while women fall more often into the part of the prey. The same authors claim that when women talk in sexual terms, even today this is very likely to be demeaning to them, which is far from the case with men.

Simply put, Gagnon and Simon's idea of the hyper-socialized individual has been criticized by later perspectives for placing too much importance on symbolic factors and disregarding material factors. Following Bourdieu, attention has been drawn to the various forces at play in the 'sexual field' that exposes individuals to constraints of a material, economic and social kind (Green 2008). Meanings of masculinity and femininity, as well as their relationship with sexual practices, are different from one culture to another, and should be reported with reference to their specific material conditions.

Thus, cultural situations give us an opportunity to understand and paint ourselves as sexual subjects even when that does not square with personal experience. In any case, the sexual scripts approach has been immensely useful for sociological studies on sexuality, since it enables desire to be set in historical context and connected with social forms that organize it. Nowadays, to act and feel sexually is increasingly seen as the outcome of a reflexive, interpretive, inter-actional process, not a hard-to-control instinctive impulse as the socio-evolutionist schools saw it, applying a 'hydraulic' dynamic to (usually male) sexuality. The contemporary sociology of sexuality hence argues against reducing sexual drive to a mere fact of biology, and proposes we enrich the picture to include a range of dimensions.

As a recent work on the sex industry demonstrates (Jones 2020), erotic pleasure itself is not a mere physiological response but a social experience that shapes social action, reflects our identities and intersects with gender. A distinction is made between desire and pleasure (Halperin 1995) and, as Eve Sedgwick (2008) writes, the power to describe and name one's sexual desire is unevenly distributed, especially between the sexes. One well-known work edited by Edward Laumann and colleagues on sexuality in the United States (Laumann, Gagnon, Michael & Michaels 1994) distinguishes between attraction (including both desire and affect), behaviour (erotic activity and practices) and identity (the set of meanings one attributes to what one feels or does), showing that the coincidence of all three is far from commonplace, and there are no set sequences in an individual's life for passing from one to another: someone, for example, may wish for intercourse with a person of their own sex without considering themselves gay or wishing to put it into practice.[8] Likewise, the fact of sexual relations between men in the ancient world did not equate to the performance of homosexual desire as we understand it today, nor greater social tolerance of it. It was a question of taste and relationship under rules of age, function and obligation. The distinction between hetero- and homosexual desire itself has a history of its own (Halperin 2002). A biologistic approach cannot explain social or individual change, or the presence of multiple and divergent impulses in sexual desire, and also finds it difficult to come to terms with the continuous negotiation of sexual practices, gender and emotions which is now taking place among gay and queer couples, aiming to transcend the conventional dichotomy between male and female which has defined heteronormative sexual relations (Zamantakis 2022).

One cannot deny, as many have pointed out, that there have been some major changes in men and women's sexual behaviour during the last few decades, there being a levelling, for example, in the number of sexual partners or pre-marital relations, both in the United States and in other countries, to the point where the sexual gap between boys and girls has gradually closed. But in this convergence, the meanings attached to such practices may still be affected by gender.

Michael Kimmel and Rebecca Plante (2004) collected student accounts of their own sexual fantasies, which were found to differ. The boys gave a more detailed account: the sex act was described more directly and included a greater variety of practices; the girls mentioned their partners' physical traits less and referred to real love partners more than ideal ones, giving more details of the setting. This result was clearly conditioned by the gendered construction of sexuality.

More generally, recent critical reviews of heterosexuality have pointed out how multidimensional it is, and how complex the intersection between sexuality and gender is (Richardson 2007). There has been new empirical investigation of how men and women experience and practise heterosexuality in everyday life, proving to have a wide range of stances on it and on sexual desire as well. Jenny Hockey, Angela Meah and Victoria Robinson, for example, in their book *Mundane Heterosexualities* (2007), investigate the cross-generational, intrafamilial, cultural transmission of heterosexuality. Through life-course interviews with members of different generations within extended families, the authors explore the socialization to heterosexuality and the gendering of the bodies in a heterosexual culture, and what individuals perceive as heterosexual 'failures'. The authors argue that heterosexuality transcends the domain of sexuality but shapes our identities as well as our daily existence. As they state, 'for our interviewees and their families, "being" heterosexual equated to "doing what comes naturally" – and so could be left unsaid' (ibid., 10). The idea is to shed light on heterosexual life 'from managing menstruation to struggling with disappointment, from finding a home to going weak-kneed at a first kiss' so as to scrutinize 'how heterosexuality might operate, as a system of power relations which pervade(s) the organization of everyday life' (ibid., 13). Studies on life-course sexuality have also shown how moments of rupture or major transition in life may cause people to resume old manners of negotiating their sex life, though also to adopt new ones (Carpenter 2015). In a quantitative study on life relationship dissolution, stage transitions and sexual choices, Lisa Wade and John DeLamater (2002), for example, show that considering phases such as being single, being recently divorced, or being long time divorced helps understand the diversity in sexual attitudes and behaviours, even more than individual characteristics.

Given that in most walks of society men and women are encouraged to follow different sexual scripts, 'insofar as the scripts individuals enact at one stage of life partly govern what scripts are accessible and appealing to them at later stages, sexual scripting is a gendered process that tends to produce distinctive cumulative dynamics for men and women' (Carpenter 2015, 72). For example, men who adopt scripts identifying masculinity with an uncontrollable sex urge will be more likely to have extramarital affairs. The interaction of sexual scripts, gendered interpretation of sexual drive and phase of life may thus lead to differentiated sex practices. Indeed, the change in gendered meanings attributed to sexuality over the life course has been studied since as early as the 1960s. One frequent topic of research, for example, was how boys and girls reacted to first intercourse, with a common finding that boys experienced more satisfaction and pleasure, and women more guilt, more negative and less pleasant sensations. Similar gender differences in emotional reactions to first sexual intercourse were reported in more recent studies, confirming the persistent influence of a double standard (DeLamater 1987; Peragine, Skorska, Maxwell, Impett & VanderLaan 2022).

The way in which desire and gender identity are constructed explains why, for instance, the 'real man' is still construed as one who, by definition, wants penetration as part of his sex. Masculinity is still produced and reproduced via repertoires of performance and meaning that are shared within 'communities of practice' (Paechter 2003) and are later narrated largely according to recognizable scripts (from the traditional predatory, to the romantic – duly negotiated – to the problematic, recounted with ironical detachment). Heterosexual masculinity especially demands a shying away from homosexuality. This is not the case with femininity. In other words, being female does not mean 'not being lesbian', whereas being male does often mean 'not being gay'. If the spectre of homosexuality is an essential part of gender definition, as we have seen, detachment from it is acutely important for the profile of the hegemonic male, whereas lesbianism is not its counterpart in the construction of femininity. So, growing up to become a man often still means making sure one steers away from homosexuality, which is a decisive influence on gender socialization among adolescents.

In this chapter we have looked at the way gender, sex and sexuality intersect. As we saw earlier in this book, gender is socially constructed in interaction, institutions and culture and the continuous work of making the body sexed is a fundamental part of this. If the gender binary is still a powerful resource for the work of making the body sexed, bodies that situate themselves between the genders and the sexes have become likewise powerful resources for the destabilization of the gender binary. The gender binary is also upheld by heterosexuality. The masculine and the feminine have typically been constructed not only as 'naturally' complementary in their features, but also 'naturally' reciprocally attracted. This has often implied the development of sexual scripts that tend to subordinate women. However, heterosexual experiences and narratives are proving to be more complex and they articulate a variety of visions of gender. As research on sex and sexuality shows, age, race, disability and other bodily features interact in multiple ways in shaping our gendered experiences and identities: sometimes reinforcing, sometimes contradicting one another. As has been noted, 'much of research on sexualities – whether behaviour, identity desire or sexual politics – has focused on how sexual identity and/or sexual behaviour may reproduce additional social hierarchies' (Harris & Bartlow 2015, 266). In the next chapter we shall see that gendered bodies are indeed prismatic entities; they live at the intersection of many social forces which impinge on bodies and gender.

5

Intersectional Experiences and Identities

When Covid-19 began to spread, with hundreds of thousands of people being infected every day, and the authorities trying to limit it through social distancing, quarantine and community containment measures, it became suddenly clear that the pandemic was not the 'great equalizer' that it had at first been depicted as. From a biological standpoint, the virus could infect all human bodies regardless of their sex, race, age or social status. But the consequences of the contagion and liability to come into contact with it could vary enormously, precisely according to differences in those. In the United States, African Americans were more affected by the virus than whites, because of the entrenched inequalities they had experienced for decades: higher morbidity, lower health insurance access, over-representation in essential work, greater health risk factors, poor health service coverage in certain geographical areas, and even unconscious bias among health providers. Overcrowded housing in vulnerable areas and the impossibility of social distancing increased the risk of being infected and dying of Covid. Low income, disability, age and being a migrant in irregular situations were further elements that differentially exposed people to risk of being hospitalized and dying of Covid-19.

The analysis of these factors and their mutual interrelation provides the potential for understanding the impacts of Covid-19. It is a matter not just of collecting data on features like gender, age, race, economic status and other factors of disadvantage. Rather, when referring to the pandemic, we need to challenge 'narratives about communities being homogenous and (seek) to critically situate people's experiences in a systemic analysis of power' (Lokot & Avakyan 2020, 42). Indeed, Covid-19 has been branded a 'syndemic' (the whole of disease interactions and the social, environmental and economic factors that promote such interactions and ultimately their worst outcomes), which can only be understood considering the synergic influences of health disparities as related to the intersection of a variety of factors such as age, ethnicity, socioeconomic position or underlying comorbidities.

In fact, our body is a point at the crossroads of social influences that place it in a network of power relations and inequalities. For analytical purposes, we could argue that human bodies differ along two axes, one *vertical* and one *horizontal*. The former is to do with the phases of a lifetime and moments of transition in growing old and ageing: milestones that we pass in common with our peers, which means being able to share associated experiences, culture and symbols, often from a similar standpoint. The second is to do with, for example, gender, race, ethnicity, social class, ethnic background, sexual orientation and disability. All these frames for categorizing and identifying individuals leave a deep mark on a variety of material bodily experiences and attitudes such as life expectancy, health conditions, physical appearance, bodily display, perception of risk and so on.

First, in dealing with differences on the vertical axis of categorization, we shall see that the various stages of life – childhood, adolescence, adulthood and old age – are deeply gendered and socially constructed. Indeed, we could think that life stages are somehow 'less constructed' than other features of our identity. But the way we experience and deal with our bodies as they grow old is necessarily mediated by culture. Ageing itself (the way we live it, experience it, conceive it, 'see' it) is the result of our being in society: we take it to be biological, but it is also a social construct, insofar as we can access our own body only through the lenses of language, meanings, values and our interaction with others and with social institutions. We shall see how a gendered sociological approach to lifespan stages helps denaturalize it.

Second, based on research on the horizontal axis about how bodily differences along lines of race, class, sexuality, ability and ethnic group tend once again to translate into inequality, we shall refer to an intersectional approach to bodies. 'Intersectionality' is an analytical framework which considers multiple factors of advantages and disadvantages (such as gender, race, class, sexual orientation, age, religion, disability, ethnicity, BMI, physical appearance, etc.) and look at how their various ways of combining place individuals at different points in systems of oppression and privilege (Crenshaw 1989). These systems are overlapping and inter-dependent, insofar as these factors of exclusion create and reinforce one another, so the effects on people's embodied experience can be multiplicative.

So, we cannot experience our body growing old regardless of our gender, our social class, our race, etc., because these factors affect the cultural meanings and the social limitations attached to the stage of life we are currently living. At the same time, the way we experience our infant, teenage or adult embodiment is affected by the culture of our peer group and our generation, as well as by other features of social identity, from race, to class, to disability. Eating disorders will be one example of how all factors along both axes of differentiation, vertical and horizontal, can be brought into the analysis of a bodily experience. The final part of the chapter will be dedicated to examples of intersectional research on a specific field: sexual health in various stages of life and for multi-marginalized people. We will thus see how the application of interconnected categorizations like race, sexual orientation or disability can affect sensibly even the (allegedly) most intimate and individual bodily experience.

1. Gender and the body across the life course

When we talk of the body and its ageing, we seem to refer to a bodily condition common to all human beings, though it may manifest differently at certain times and depending on the geographical area. Anthropology, history and sociology have long challenged such a view of things, arguing that it naturalizes culturally and socially defined conditions. Thus, we are accustomed to plotting out a lifetime – defining bodily characteristics according to biographical age – as roughly divided into three phases: childhood, adulthood and old age. These phases are traditionally determined by their relation to the reproductive cycle, and each of them corresponds to a different degree of individual responsibility and awareness.

Denaturalizing the lifespan: the social construction of
generations and identity

We are inclined to think that this sequence of phases applies universally, unvarying in space and time. At the beginning of the twentieth
century, thinkers like Sigmund Freud, Lev Semënovič Vygotskij and
Jean Piaget conducted a fundamental study of the psychological and
moral development of the child and, come the 1950s, their thoughts
were enriched by studies on adult development too, those of Erik
Erikson, Robert Havighurst and Daniel Levinson, for example. The
underlying idea is that the life cycle is divided into hierarchically
arranged stages and that passing from one to the next requires the
achievement of certain developmental tasks. A similar view has long
lain behind our interpretation of phases during which individual life
stories develop (being born, acquiring a school education, attaining
economic independence, getting married, having children, retiring
from the productive sphere and growing old).

However, much contemporary research has shown the limits
of such a view to account not just for the complex trajectories of
modern life cycles and the ever less standardized sequences and
transitions from one stage to the next, but also for the ways in
which the biological body and the cultural construct impinge on one
another in a process that is by no means always linear. This is not
new within the social sciences. One of the earliest sociologists, Karl
Mannheim, underlined the need to study the life course with due
attention to the whole interaction among individuals, age groups and
settings. In his essay 'The problem of generations' (1952 [1927/28]),
Mannheim eschews the idea that sociological phenomena can be
deduced from natural facts: '(a)nthropology and biology only help us
explain the phenomena of life and death, the limited span of life, and
the mental, spiritual, and physical changes accompanying ageing as
such; they offer no explanation of the relevance these primary factors
have for the shaping of social interrelationships in their historic flux'
(ibid., 290).

If we stratify society simply by the rigid boundaries of people's
age, presupposing one single process of development, we shall fail
to explain how a set of individuals from one particular generation
share a specific cultural and historical experience. Indeed, Mannheim
is known for having introduced the notion of 'generation' to understand what it means to be 'contemporaries'. One may share with
one's contemporaries nothing but being born in the same socio-
historical slot. Alternatively, one's placement may, so to speak, turn

'active' through the sharing of experiences and orientation, giving rise to a 'collective subject' among members of one and the same generation. Let's think of Boomers, X, Millennials and Z generations in relation to media technology, for example: the first, born in the two decades following the Second World War, when there was a large increase in the number of babies born (the 'baby boom') and in general all those saw the dramatic expansion of TV; the second, born between the second half of the 1960s and the beginning of the 1980s, grew up as the computer revolution was taking hold; the third, born between the early 1980s and the end of the 1990s, came of age during the internet explosion; the fourth, instead, grew up in an 'always on' technological environment, connected with the web through mobile devices, WiFi and high-bandwidth cellular service. All these changes had implications for behaviours, attitudes and lifestyles. This holds true even around body practices and (dis)embodied social inter- actions: the gendered display of their body in the social media by teenagers of the Z generation is completely different from their peers in previous times (see chapter 7) and couldn't be fully grasped unless considering both age and generation.

Childhood, adolescent bodies and the formation of gendered identities

Focusing on the way age groups and generations are conditioned by the cultural background they belong to, and at the same time on how they contribute to changing or consolidating that culture, is one more instance of denaturalizing the bodily experience. Philip Ariès's (1962 [1960]) well-known study on family relations in mediaeval and modern Europe was one of the first to show how childhood is a social construction: the evidence being that only in the modern era is it seen as a life stage distinct from adulthood. Ariès argues that this occurred in response to broader phenomena, such as the rise of the market and industrial production, which consolidated the family as a sphere of intimacy and relative independence from social constric- tions. Childhood thus began to have external trappings – style of dress, play, schooling, everyday ways of relating to others – which marked it off from adulthood.

Until a few decades ago, as Barrie Thorne noted (1987), little attention was paid to childhood in social theory, which focused on adulthood and viewed children basically as 'what they were not yet', namely from the standpoint of 'socialization' and 'development', rather than as a specific reality. In her ethnography in two primary schools (1993), Thorne vividly showed how active children can be in elaborating, reproducing, but sometimes challenging, the social meanings (especially of gender). Nowadays, though, a growing number of studies reveal the depth and complexity of children's experience, aiming to restore children to full social agency on a par with their elders. However, this is not to deny the existence of conventions and rules regulating children's lives. For example, unlike adults, they generally undergo a highly rationalized bureaucratic system of education; they are debarred from paid labour; their sexuality is strictly monitored; participation in politics comes relatively late; and the law sees them by and large as not fully responsible (Prout 2000; James, Jenks & Prout 1998). This occurs in a heavily gender-based way. We know, for example, that toys are important tools of social introduction to the male or female role, and that from early on children tend to negotiate their gender identity by playing with toys that embody the dominant views of femininity, masculinity and relations between the sexes (Kline 2005). What is more, the development of ultrasound scanning technology has meant not just a change in how we relate to the foetus as a gendered being even before birth, but that today's newborns are more likely to be surrounded by objects, furniture and clothing bought by their parents during pregnancy and heavily coded according to a male/female binary (Barnes 2015). A series of sociological studies under this heading are showing how young girls and boys are actually competent individuals able to manipulate and take on board both cultural meanings and the practices and commodities surrounding them, which they renegotiate with adults and peers and accordingly alter, as the ethnography by William Corsaro showed (Corsaro 2003; see also Corsaro 2015).

Nevertheless, socialization is still imbued with gender norms. In a study based on interviews with boys aged 11–14 in the United Kingdom, Rob Pattman shows how boys' relationships with each other are structured around the link between masculinity and toughness, which makes it hard for them to verbalize feelings of intimacy (Frosh, Phoenix & Pattman 2002; see Nayak & Kehily 2013) (see also chapter 2). Despite the many changes that occurred in the last decade, often stimulated by initiatives for addressing stereotypes and sexist harmful practices through edutainment and education fuelled by non-governmental organizations (NGOs) and international institutions (as exemplified by UNICEF's commitment to promoting gender equality), meanings and values linked to hierarchized visions of femininity and masculinity persist in children and younger generations in general. Extensive qualitative research has recently shown how much such norms are linked to the way bodies are narrated and experienced. For example, in a study based on interviews with children in a Colombian primary school, meaningfully entitled 'Girls do not sweat', researchers have illustrated how much 8–10-year-old children still frame abilities and interest in physical education through a wide range of gender stereotypes (Cárcamo, Moreno & del Barrio 2021). It is not just a matter of perceiving football as a men's sport, and skating, handball and volleyball as women's sports, but of inserting visions of sporting bodies into a dominant gender narrative that makes femininity subordinated to masculinity. 'The boys, they like running, they like sweating a lot, they really like playing football, getting dirty', a girl argues in the interviews. Thereby, a girl's sweat and dirty body is less feminine, while the same features make a boy's body fully perform masculinity. And this view ends up legitimizing the occupation of more space and the performance of more dynamic and competitive activities by boys, who are more likely to be praised for their physical success by girls. Girls, in turn, prefer to play passive roles as cheerleaders and spectators of the masculine teams.

The biographical stage from late childhood to early adulthood, known as adolescence, is itself a twentieth-century construct (Demos & Demos 1969). Such a stage is marked by a particular form of relationship to self and the world, centring on learning to be responsible, form an independent self of one's own and become independent. We could view adolescence as a special phase in the life trajectory since youths of that age feel as if they are on the fringe, like an outsider coming afresh upon a cultural repertoire. In this process, the embodied identity plays a central role.

Let us take the example of gender studies on teenagers' sexuality. Although sexual socialization is increasingly similar for boys and girls, the latter are still targeted by a greater range of information sources and models: their peer group, parents, teachers, counsellors, courses at school, other relatives like sisters and aunts. Boys commonly find sexual content in magazines, websites and other media, and take it more as entertainment than information sources. Even among the latest generations of adolescents, many boys are reluctant to talk about their own puberty and find it hard to admit their ignorance about sex. They are more concerned with 'being normal' than gaining proper knowledge; their awareness of changes is due more to others' comments than to pursued information. For girls, instead, puberty corresponds with greater control by the family and less independence. Generally speaking, while research shows that adolescent girls' behaviour in the sexual domain has moved closer to their boy peers, the meaning of it still differs from boys to girls, as does the universe of values underpinning it. Thus, ideas remain based on a double standard: for girls, sexuality is meant to be linked to romantic involvement, and this is maintained also for many adult women. Jean-Claude Kaufmann's book *The Single Woman and the Fairytale Prince* (2008) shows, by studying letters to the magazine *Marie-Claire*, that many independent single women were torn between their own sexual freedom and their romantic dreams. For boys, instead, sexuality is meant to be bound up with physical pleasure (and this understanding makes it more legitimate to experiment with sexuality without the restraints of affection). The upshot of the double standard is that girls who go in for sexual experiment are more likely to be deemed immoral, and boys who seek emotional involvement could be thought to lack virility.

Adolescence is commonly the time when sexual identity is forming and not simply being manifested. Socialization allows sexual differences to emerge and at the same time produces and organizes them. In media coverage such issue is often linked to a growing public concern over the premature sexualization of pre-teen girls, their exposure to increased sexualized contents and the subtle encouragement to embody a sexualized look through clothes and products. But ethnographic research allows us to go deeper into the matter, by documenting how girls and boys actually feel about their own sexuality. In *Puberty, Sexuality and the Self*, Karin Martin (2018) explores how experiences like menarche, breast development, masturbation, voice change, shaving and weight gain, along with first sexual intercourse, differently affect girls' and boys' self-worth. Through interviews with 14–19-year-old teenagers, Martin shows how girls' self-esteem drops during adolescence more than boys', as they are more likely to feel guilty and ashamed of such changes.

But the relevance and the contents of gender meanings surrounding the adolescent vary according to their sociocultural status, background and patterns of cultural and media consumption. Thus, for instance, a growing number of studies shows the effect of consumer patterns on gender meanings of teenagers dealing with sexual identities sold as a desirable packet dressed up by the media and commercial marketing. In their ethnographic study, for example, Anoop Nayak and Mary Jane Kehily (2013) show the importance, among other consumer practices, of the reading of teenager magazines in girls' and boys' peer groups. Many girls spoke of regular collective practice among friends that provided a springboard for discussions about parents, boyfriends and friendships – but magazines are also full of advice on fashion, sex, intimate relationships, body care and so on. Such reading practices were fundamental for the adolescent female peer groups in collectively establishing acceptable and unacceptable behaviours, while they were looked at with suspicion by the male peers. To the question: 'Do you wish there was a boys' magazine?' a boy answered: 'Nah, you'd get called a sissy wouldn't you?' (ibid., 147). Nevertheless, global communications (especially the social media) and interaction with different gender orders further multiply the masculinities and femininities as well as the sexual behaviour patterns available to youngsters of today.

In today's consumer culture as prevalent in the West, more or less permanent or invasive modification of one's body is quite common in adolescence (Ghigi & Sassatelli 2018; see chapter 6). This is a stage of life when doing something to one's own outward appearance may hold crucial meaningfulness, as part of a bid for identity and control over the changes that are typical of puberty. At no other time in our lifespan do we both love and hate our own body so passionately, nor take such loving trouble to render it a place in which to fashion a feeling of our own identity. Teenagers manipulate their body with a mix of challenge and devotion to tell the world at large about their self-representation as it begins to come into focus. They can spend huge amounts of time and effort on their body, changing it, adorning it and reshaping it, largely to gain others' respect and esteem, and to gauge to what extent they can exert control over their life.

The body in its outward appearance is charged with a deliberate expressive task. Yet the present generation of youngsters seems more bound up in making appropriative body and image statements than those before them. One important example is the increasingly frequent and early occurrence of adolescent gender transitions and gender fluidity. This topic is at the centre of many debated medical, legal, political and ethical issues, such as the minimum age to obtain hormone therapies or to obtain surgical reassignment, and practices are far from smooth.

Kinnon Ross MacKinnon and colleagues (2021) conducted an institutional ethnography of gender-affirming medical care assessment practices in Canada, where there is no standard legal age for medical decision-making but in most provinces or regions, youths 16 and older are capable of giving and refusing consent in connection with their own care. Institutional ethnography, developed by Canadian sociologist Dorothy Smith, involves the study of a system through an analysis of how work practices are mediated by discursive ruling relations, for instance how people work with, and activate, institutional texts. In this case, 'preventing regret' was identified as a prominent discursive theme in gender-affirming care policy, practice and medical research. The analysis of clinicians' and patients' interviews and health policy texts showed that possibilities of regret and detransitioning (despite their low prevalence) were used as a rationale to heavily restrict gender-affirming care for young trans people. According to the authors, this gatekeeping model of 'strict assessment practices designed to identify only those who "truly" meet eligibility criteria may create unethical, paternalistic, and dehumanizing practice conditions' (ibid., 3). What the research uncovered was how much the assessment practices treated trans patients as different from other patients, namely as persons who aren't capable of medical decision-making. In this case, being young was an additional factor inducing such a paternalistic attitude from clinicians.

Indeed, gender-affirming surgeries are just one (radical) form of voluntary body modification. Body art, like piercing and tattooing, is a much more common practice, now running right across genders and social classes. It is no longer a sign that one belongs to a subculture (Pitts 2003) and is much more common among teenagers than in the past. Though it is true that both genders are exposed to a manipulative, standardizing body culture, and appropriative practices like tattooing and piercing are popular among both genders, it is also the case that – other factors being equal, such as social class and race – being a young woman rather than a young man in the Western world continues to count when it comes to satisfaction with one's own body image, perceiving one's body as a set of individual parts that can be changed, and wanting to do so by invasive and definitive practices such as cosmetic surgery (see chapter 6).

All in all, then, among white Western middle- to upper-middle-class youngsters, adolescence and early youth typically are phases of life with a corresponding structure of expectations marking it as the prime moment when individuals can 'choose' who they want to be, experimenting though not altogether freely, since there is a great deal at stake – and the body is central to this in relation to the discovery of sexuality, the shaping of one's own appearance, the development of sports skills and so on (Furlong & Cartmel 1997). Adolescents and youths find themselves in a contradictory position: they come across as seeking freedom and spontaneity by way of resistance to the bureaucratic power weighing on them, yet at the same time they yearn for a sense of belonging. They feel a pressure to make a statement as original independent beings expressing a style in their bodily aspect; this may be subcultural or generational and tends to be channelled through objects and decorations that can be bought on the market: yet it feels like a personal style. This attitude may be taken as a consequence of the fact that, in contemporary Western society, everyone is expected to build, and at the same time discover, their true 'self', starting from an ability to define themselves and organize their experience according to a proper project played out on their body (see chapter 2). Not surprisingly, just as happens with certain extreme forms of diet or with body art, one of the main recurrent motivations is to modify the body in order to 'feel unique' or 'independent'. During this phase any part of the body may become 'phobogenic' (i.e., can generate intense negative feeling), channelling feelings of insecurity at a phase when the sexual identity is being structured. 'It's my body, I'm free to do what I want with it' is a common cry by youngsters quoted in studies on the topic. Fashions and youth subcultures are used by the individual adolescent in carrying out their tasks of development: they mark a break with childhood, independence of the family and appropriation of the body.

To understand why, and especially how, ever-new youth cultures are spawned, we should not just define adolescence as a phase of impulsive rebellion and hormonal instability but observe the structure of expectations sketched above. Teenagers and young adults may be a reservoir of cultural change, but it is their structural position, above all with the mass economic development and social mobility that took off in the post-war years, that activates that reservoir and translates it into a host of varying cultural or subcultural forms.

Old age and death as failures of the individual body project

Compared to the increasing visibility of teens, old age appears marginal, despite its increasing importance from a demographic point of view. Of course, Western societies have a range of economic and social cushions (the pensions system, the health system) serving to make more bearable what appears as the physical degeneration bound up with growing old. But that just shows how a rather universalizing biomedical account of mental and bodily decline occupies a dominant position in how the ageing body is understood, something which is particularly difficult to manage in the context of a consumer culture where the body has become a site of self-identity and reflexivity.

The ageing body has thus been considered as living through a 'mask', as the 'cumulative effect of stigmatization' may well be 'an increased submissive response expressed in the tendency to conceal or mask expression of emotional and personal needs' (Featherstone & Hepworth 1991, 378). This is partly due to the way the modern era came to define illness. Medical techniques have persuaded us to snatch life from death day by day, robbing the so-called 'third age' of meaning, an insignificant accumulation of years given that the gaining of experience is no longer valued as something to be exchanged with the wider group (the opposite of traditional societies where old age held fundamental symbolic value for the group).

This is especially true for women, and feminist authors studying social gerontology struggle to find a space for resistance in either age denial or the rhetoric of natural ageing. Is it possible to consider hair dyes and face creams as cultural capitulations to the devaluation of being old in consumer capitalism without denying old women the pleasures and joy of self-fashioning? they ask. According to authors like Julia Twigg (2004), the answer must be reasserting subjectivity in relation to the body, and ethnographic observation and sociological research may help in giving due weight to the complexity of practices and meanings of elderly body experience.

But such dynamics need to be combined with other labels that define the individual. Considering ageing corporeality, Chris Gilleard and Paul Higgs (2013) stress the need to end the thought of ageing as a seamless, universal process. Indeed, an overview of studies conducted by Susan Venn, Kate Davidson and Sara Arber (2011) shows that our approach to old age should bear in mind how race, ethnic background, sexuality and gender change the significance and patterns of ageing, as does the influence of socio-economic circumstances on the experience of ageing and on the ways in which individuals negotiate changes in roles and relationships. Therefore, we should add other dimensions of inequality, like marital status or partnership status, as variables affecting ageing, especially in later life. This allows, for example, an emphasis on the disadvantaged position of older Black women in relation to their pensions, health status and access to care as compared to men and to white women. It also allows us to pay attention to the advantages faced by older women compared to some groups of older men, for example in social relationships with both friends or in the sense of autonomy first experienced in widowhood. At the same time, Susan Sontag's famous article (1977 [1972]) 'The double standard of ageing' remains true today, when it contended that '(g)etting older is less profoundly wounding for a man. ... Men are "allowed" to age, without penalty, in several ways that women are not' (ibid., 286). Today, there are higher pressures on women to keep young and 'look' young, which are less demanding for men as they age, despite some changes, especially among upper-class men. 'It is no surprise that women express greater dissatisfaction with their ageing bodies than do men', Venn, Davidson and Arber (2011, 77) conclude.

When the notion of a pathological condition getting into the body is replaced by the idea of the body itself turning into something sick, death transforms into disease and degeneration, a prolonged, piecemeal breakdown. This gives scope for medicalizing it, treating it as something dirty and impure: the institutionalizing of dying. Indeed, death is a universal of human existence, but what it means to die, how it feels, the events surrounding it, are historically and culturally shaped. How the moribund face up to death differs completely if, as so often in our society, life is seen as a secular, individualistic phenomenon and not, as in tribal or traditional societies, as part of a natural or spiritual cycle extending beyond the life of the body.

Tracing over a thousand years of attitudes towards death, from the Middle Ages down to the present day, Ariès (2008 [1977]) maintained that death is now seen as something repugnant and uncontrollable, to be ashamed of, a blameworthy failure, whereas in the past even children's deaths were taken as a normal fact, surrounded by densely significant ritual accompanying the dying and their closest family: a 'domestication' of dying. The Western model of death was greatly influenced by the rise of bourgeois society, the Enlightenment and the market, writes Ariès: it sought to protect the dying or invalid from their emotions, hiding from them the seriousness of their condition right to the end, and this 'has led society to be ashamed of death, more ashamed than afraid, to behave as if death did not exist' (ibid., 613) – except in films and news reportage, we might add, where it becomes tragic and heroic.

As modernity advanced, Ariès suggested, the development of science came to appear as the highway to happiness, so that disease and death were seen as failures of knowledge. The smells, the sounds, the sight of the decomposing body were treated with disgust, something hard to bear and better hidden away in places like hospitals. In the Middle Ages, by contrast, death was by no means a purely individual affair: it was an opportunity for the community to strengthen its bonds by wrapping the event in public ceremony (ibid.). One gathered around the deathbed; all were invited to share in expressing their distress at the threat to the community when a member was taken away. The rituals ended in a banquet or party event to celebrate the return of vigour and unity to the group. Death was once a collective event; now it is private, inside the family, hidden from view and especially from the youngest. As Norbert Elias wrote (1985, 23), 'Never before in the history of humanity have the dying been removed so hygienically behind the scenes of social life; never before have human corpses been expedited so odourlessly and with such technical perfection from the deathbed to the grave'. The pandemic of Covid-19 in many countries has temporarily changed this. Narratives on death returned to prominence on the public stage amid a re-evaluation of modern regimes of health, healing and care.[1]

Our argument so far has shown how even the phases most bound up with our biology, immutable and universal like the ages of humans, are steeped in culture, made concrete by interaction, institutions and social events that change as history unfolds. We have also seen how such categorizations connected to bodily development (child, adolescent, youth, adult, elder) return to that body by differing practices and representations. The analytical process of denaturalizing the elements on the vertical axis of differentiation may also be extended to other labels on the horizontal one, even though such labels appear to be stable, universal fixtures as being based on bodily matter. An intersectional approach reveals all the arbitrary and historical foundation of features on both axes, observing them as placed in a hierarchical order established by society.

2. The intersectionality of bodily labels

First defined by Kimberlé Crenshaw (1989), then enriched by Patricia Hill Collins (1990) and other authors, the term 'intersectionality' refers to the 'critical insight that race, class, gender, sexuality, ethnicity, nation, ability, and age operate not as unitary, mutually exclusive entities, but rather as reciprocally constructing phenomena that in turn shape complex social inequalities' (Collins 2015, 2). The concept was the development of a preview of Black feminist thought (like the one by the Combahee River Collective at the end of the 1970s; see also Anzaldúa 1987; Davis 1981; hooks 1981; Lorde 1984), which had acknowledged that the experience of gender was not the same for a white woman as it was for a Black woman. As Crenshaw put it, 'because the intersectional experience is greater than the sum of racism and sexism, any analysis that does not take intersectionality into account cannot sufficiently address the particular manner in which Black women are subordinated' (1989, 153). Gender alone cannot account for all disparities, nor does race or class, because people's conditions are affected by overlapping and interdependent systems of discrimination or disadvantage. Any analysis of women that leaves out race is incomplete and is only fit to set up white women's models, while models of racial inequality that do not include gender likewise fail to understand the lives of women of colour.

But intersectionality is also an analytical tool to see lines of privilege among marginalized people and lines of oppression among privileged people. For example, Collins (2015) notes that a generic statement that men oppress women misses the potential complexity of a relationship between certain groups of non-white men and white women. In many towns, she observes, white women enjoy greater well-being and power than Black men and Latinos. People can experience privilege and oppression simultaneously. In such a perspective our reference ought therefore to be 'systems of inter-connection of race, class and gender' as constituting a full-blown 'matrix of domination' (Collins 1990). In such a matrix an individual may simultaneously experience disadvantages and privileges through combined statuses of gender, race and class. However, the novelty of the intersectional approach lies in the idea that race and gender are not just categories influencing individual life stories each in its own right, but organizing principles of the social system constructing one another so as to produce and maintain the social hierarchy along intersecting axes of privilege and oppression. Irene Browne and Joya Misra (2003) point out, for instance, that we have long studied the condition of Black women in the job market, how they are discriminated against as women and as Black; but an intersectional approach suggests that their experiences reflect the way in which social constructions of gender are racialized and how social construc-tions of race are conditioned by gender, resulting in their particular experience. In other words, the accent on the intersection of race and gender is not confined to including race in gender research or gender in racial studies, but maintains that race is always 'gendered' and gender is always 'racialized'. As Lynn Weber (2001) suggests, there is no perception of gender that is blind to race, and there is no perception of race that is blind to gender.

Although its origins lay with Black feminist thought, decon-structing (supposed) universally shared women's attitudes and experiences (when the latter generally referred to white, heterosexual, able-bodied, middle- and upper-class women in Western countries), the dimensions considered central to intersectionality have since multiplied to include social class, age, sexual orientation, disability, ethnic origin and religion. Even if most of such literature is to do with race and gender, intersectionality offers a way to define social issues by considering all the different social positions of those who are involved. As legal scholar Mari J. Matsuda (quoted in Romero 2018, 167) explains,

The way I try to understand the interconnection of all forms of subordination is through a method I call 'ask the other question'. When I see something that looks racist, I ask, 'Where is the patriarchy in this? When I see something that looks sexist, I ask, 'Where is the heterosexism in this?' When I see something that looks homophobic, I ask, 'Where are the class interests in this?' Working in coalition forces us to look for both the obvious and nonobvious relationships of domination, helping us to realize that no form of subordination ever stands alone.

Like gender, race too (though the same might be said of disability) may be viewed as a frame for body definition that accords absolute priority to certain biological features. Thus, many European societies have contrived to bundle together all physical types different from the typically European-Caucasian and call them 'coloured' or 'Black', when their actual ethnic experiences may be totally different. It is also upon the basis of radical, embodied difference that the coloured body (especially the female one) has been denigrated by association with a whole range of sexual or mental pathologies, or else praised for its natural physical prowess or savage sensuality (Bordo 2003 [1993]; Nayak 1997). From the late seventeenth century on, over one hundred million Africans were enslaved in the New World by Europeans and the United States to provide cheap labour required by nascent capitalist forces. Even in early modern times slaves, like prostitutes, were branded with hot metal. But soon it was decided that 'natural' signs could be read on their bodies confirming the difference and inferiority, such signs being the colour of the skin, the hair, the shape of the skull and so on. But then, on closer inspection, the European states prove historically to have formed in opposition to so-called 'exotic' countries like China or their own colonies in Africa, for example. Indeed, several studies collected under the banner of 'whiteness studies', bringing together insights from sociology, history, legal studies and many other disciplines, have shown that the very categories of 'white' and 'whiteness' are part and parcel of the process of racialization (Nayak 2007).[2]

It was in order to overtly reject the idea that the body defined racial difference that the sociologist W.E.B. Du Bois began collecting a broad array of pictures of people with inter-racial features to include in his *Exposition des Nègres d'Amerique* at the 1900 Paris Exposition (Smith 2004).[3] Du Bois wanted to challenge skin colour as an aspect of racial difference. As well as powerfully evoking 'passing' (in terms of living and being accepted as part of a different race or ethnic origin) as a possibility open to many people formally classified as Black, the variety of skin tones and facial shapes he portrayed merged the Black-white distinction into an infinitesimal spectrum which challenged the very existence of white from a colour standpoint (along with other criteria serving at the time to classify race). Over a century later, those photos still powerfully challenge the idea that any detached, universal point of observation exists, and confirm again the naturalization of the social (in this case 'black' and 'white') in the body.

In this way, two bodily markers that are only apparently pre-social – sex and race – merged to create specific experiences and opportunities for everyone – and not just women of colour (Lorber 1994). Many beliefs and practices associated with gender are indeed inextricably interwoven with beliefs and practices associated with race: for example, the traditional definitions of femininity based on weakness and passivity described a social norm for the white middle-class woman, while Black femininity was constructed as the counterpart to that image. According to Collins (2015), stereotypes about Black women thus created a desexualized 'Mammy' or a brazen eroticized 'Jezebel', but castigated Black lesbian women as being neither one thing nor the other. As Browne and Misra explain (2003, 490):

> These images reinforce racial divisions by denigrating Black women in comparison with White women. At the same time, these images reinforce gender inequality among Whites by positing White women as weak and in need of White male protection. Thus, the experience of gender deeply reflects racial and ethnic meanings.

By the same token, as these authors point out, stereotypes of Black men circulating in the dominant culture include the notion of a 'hypersexualized Black man' as a potential threat to white women. In his essay about how the Black male body has been conceptualized over time, Anthony Brown (2021) recognizes a multiplicity of images (from the subhuman Black male body to the invisible one, to the damaged and powerless) circulating in social science and education scholarship from the 1930s to modern qualitative studies. The problem is, Brown observes, that all these accounts are normative constructs of Black masculinity that do not allow for complexity, nuances or contradictions. Allowing Black male voices to be at the centre of the sociological inquiry is thereby crucial to let their standpoint and positionality emerge and avoid such objectifications and simplifications. The literature on colonialism and postcolonialism abounds with discussion as to the sexualization or otherwise applied by colonial authorities to other 'exotics'. For instance, popular ideology has often 'desexualized' or 'feminized' Asian men, legitimizing the fact of casting them professionally, for instance, as house-servants, whose voice is far from taken seriously when protesting or resisting. Again, describing 'others' through their feminization always has a delegitimizing and trivializing effect.

At the intersection of axes: the case of eating disorders

Intersectional analysis helps us understand how various social categories, such as race, gender, class, sexual orientation and disability, intersect and influence individual experiences and outcomes. When applying this framework to the analysis of bodies, we consider how these factors shape embodiment, body image and bodily ideals and corporeal agency. This implies, for example, acknowledging that society has constructed certain ideals of beauty, health and ability that may be unattainable or exclusive for many people; but it also means understanding how individuals perceive their own bodies and the bodies of others, how they use their bodies and how their bodily experience relates to their subjectivity.

For instance, people's perceptions and attitudes towards their own bodies can be influenced by their race, as certain racial and ethnic groups may experience unique beauty standards and expectations, but also varying levels of control over their own bodies. Women, transgender individuals and people with disabilities may face unique challenges in asserting their bodily autonomy due to societal norms and discrimination (e.g., in barriers to accessing health care). But they could also experience a relative autonomy and agency in certain dimensions of their daily life (as in sexual intercourse), depending on the current social order of a specific domain. Any in-depth analysis of individual bodily experience should be open to embrace complexity.

Bodily labels on both the vertical axis (age, generation and life stages) and the horizontal (gender, social class, race, sexual orientation, etc.) can produce stigmatization. Agency, biographical path and cultural meanings, generational change and social order blend into each other. How can this be? Eating disorders – especially anorexia nervosa – is an interesting case study of bodily experience where such dynamics can be acknowledged.

In recent decades a bodily injunction (slimness, 'you must lose weight') has gained ever more stringent force in the global capitalist North. It is agreed that eating disorders have spread unprecedentedly as well. In his historical study of female ascetics in mediaeval times, Rudolph Bell (1987) showed how cases of self-imposed fasting in centuries past, especially among young girls who knew no other way of protesting at patriarchal restrictions, might be undiagnosed forms of anorexia nervosa. Others, like Walter Vandereycken and

Ron Van Deth (1994), distanced themselves from such retrospective diagnosis and called anorexia an epidemic-scale syndrome typical of our contemporary era. In any case, it deals with the meanings of femininity and patriarchal power in each era. Small wonder, however, that it fascinated not just psychologists and psychiatrists, for example Hilde Bruch's well-known studies, but also many social scientists, especially of the feminist school (Bordo 2003 [1993]; MacSween 2013 [1993]): 'Fat is a feminist issue', Susie Orbach (1978) was wont to say.

From a strictly sociological standpoint, eating disorders are a clear-cut example of how the body and body management are bound up with a range of individual and social conditions: factors recurring in the course of a lifetime (such as entering puberty, fear of reaching adulthood, managing a changing body) organized upon cultural constructs (having a commercially fostered aesthetic ideal in favour of slimness, sharing in a fatphobic/lipophobic culture) and differently processed according to one's position in social life (e.g., being a woman, white, middle-class, educationally qualified, living in a town of the Global North).

Eating disorders do, of course, depend on emotional factors (like difficulty in expressing one's emotions and sensations), psychological factors (i.e., low self-esteem or the sensation one can't control one's life at all) and interpersonal factors (such as family-related problems). But the way their incidence varies in space and time strongly suggests they also have a social side. Like the nineteenth-century wave of hysteria – the acid test, Vandereycken and Van Deth (1994) argue, for Victorian women's condition and repression of female sexuality – anorexia nervosa, for example, has been interpreted as the body's undocile protest against the present era with its cultural emphasis on slimness, its economy dominated by rigid self-control, and its anxiety-generating morality about female desires (Spitzack 1990). And indeed, how else could we understand, from a sociological point of view, present-day anorexia except in terms of the three cultures – that of gender, body and generation – at the intersection of which it stands?

We have already discussed the culture of the body: we live in a society which keeps fear private and is afraid of inadequacy; the body is private property to be invested in, but its health is perceived to be precarious, something to watch over and work on (as we saw in chapter 2). The mass media foster dreams of liberation *via* and *of* the body, seen as the individual's land of independence; individual subjects proclaim what they are and what they want via bodily transformation, while medical discourse supplies the tools and is the source of dominant power and knowledge (see chapter 3). This is the terrain for the mute protest that the anorexic body launches out upon; a protest that leads the willpower bent on controlling hunger and impulses to dire consequences (Bordo 2003 [1993]).

It is, meanwhile, a setting in which women essentially *are* bodies, rather than *having* them, and where in managing their corporeality, they are expected to embody their ideal self, internalizing how they are seen from the outside (see chapter 6): anorexia nervosa occurs nine times more often in women than in men. True, consumer culture has gradually involved men in increasingly sophisticated forms of body care and spurred increased male attention to aesthetic appearance. But the bulk of the literature confirms that even today girls are much more prone than boys (other things being equal) to having low bodily self-esteem, a propensity for surgical modification, distortion of the body image, dysmorphophobia syndrome and, it goes without saying, eating disorders. Far more than their male peers, girls are keenly aware of the gap between the form of their body and those ideal proportions said by the media to be attainable and will do fierce battle to bring their appearance up to scratch.

There is, besides, a generational propensity to lavish care on the body, transforming, embellishing and manipulating it, largely to gauge one's own ability to control reality. At a stage of life like adolescence, one's outward appearance may hold crucial significance, forming part of a bid for identity and control of changes, which makes it a classic time for anorexic syndrome, an extreme response to phobogenic feelings related to the structuring of identity. Fasting means shedding the body's sexual characterization but also a wish to self-eclipse – almost to disappear. Anorexia, and eating disorders in general, are thus the outcome of cultural processes in which age, generation and gender play a crucial role.

This is also true for obese women. As the autobiographical account of Roxane Gay (2017, 146) shows, being overweight is a form of undiscipline, but also of denial:

> Part of disciplining the body is denial. We want but we dare not have. We deny ourselves certain foods. We deny ourselves rest by working out. We deny ourselves peace of mind by remaining ever vigilant over our bodies. We withhold from ourselves until we achieve a goal and then we withhold from ourselves to maintain that goal. My body is wildly undisciplined, and yet I deny myself nearly everything I desire. I deny myself the right to space when I am public, trying to fold in on myself, to make my body invisible even though it is, in fact, grandly visible. ... as if I do not have the

right to such expression when my body does not follow society's dictates for what a woman's body should look like. I deny myself gentler kinds of affection – to touch or to be kindly touched – as if that is a pleasure a body like mine does not deserve. Punishment is, in fact, one of the few things I allow myself.

What we read in her biography is that Gay is not just overweight, she is also a Haitian American woman, who recognizes that Black women are rarely allowed their femininity. And she is also a lesbian woman who was raped at the age of twelve. The history of her body is the individual outcome of all these elements, which are inserted into a patriarchal and heteronormative culture, as well as the meanings we attach to them.

Comparative studies have shown that eating disorders are present in increasing strata of the population globally, but they differ in diffusion pattern, modes and meanings. For example, Black women are less likely than white women to engage in excessive dieting and are less fearful of fat, although they are more likely to be obese and experience compulsive overeating (Lovejoy 2001). By and large, researchers found indirect correlations between ethnicity (African American, Latinas, Asian American) and eating disorders, mediated by the sharing of Western ideals of beauty: those groups who identify with such ideals experience the same sociocultural risks as their Caucasian counterpart. This is far from univocal, though. How multi-stigmatized bodies could be related to eating disorders in general is a challenging object of research: on the one hand, girls and women at the intersection of multiple factors of oppression could be more likely to experience eating disorders as marginalized; on the other hand, they could develop community-specific and non-normative beauty ideals which could protect them from some damaging eating behaviours (Beccia et al. 2021).

3. Gender and sexuality through intersectional lenses

The intersectional approach enables us to scrutinize not only how gender, race and sexuality, in their complex intertwining, impinge on bodies, but also how bodies produce effects on the differing positioning of subjects. Physical sexual development, sexual health and sexual practices for people with disability are meaningful examples of how gendered embodiment can be located at the intersection of systems of oppression and privilege, sometimes reinforcing, sometimes contradicting one another.

Sexual development and maturity: from puberty to menopause

Along the vertical axis of body differentiation, life stages are experienced (even created) through the lenses of our social and cultural characterizations, which are marked by distinctions on the horizontal axis, as we have seen. Let's take body changes with puberty and their meaning.[4] For girls, arrival at sexual maturity coincides with the first menstrual period. Several authors, such as Germaine Greer (1992), have analysed the symbolic imagery revolving around the phases of girls' sexual development, from the idea of menstrual body abjection (the blood being seen as contaminant and contaminated as well as generative) down to construal of the menopause as a dreaded if not pathological event. This holds true for millions of women in Western society: nonetheless, we must consider a multiplicity of meanings and experiences related to menstrual periods or to the menopause, which are culturally and socially contextual.

The critical lenses through which we can consider the stigma of menstruation have been further enriched, for example, by looking beyond the limits of white, middle- and upper-class Western women's experiences and shedding light on the profound inequalities occurring among women of different sorts. Many of them, especially in the Global South, cannot afford menstrual products, education, hygiene facilities, waste management or a combination of these. This means that they cannot go to school or work or otherwise participate in daily life. This 'period poverty', as it is now called, causes further physical, mental and emotional challenges, making women feel ashamed for menstruating and emphasizing the stigma.

But adolescence and puberty for girls are marked by other changes and, once again, reveal themselves to be highly influenced by an adolescent's positioning along the axes of privilege and dominance. A common assumption is that girls have lower sexual desire compared to boys, while male desire is portrayed as omnipresent; but within these common frameworks, assumptions may be diverse. Some studies have shown, for instance, that black and urban Latina girls have to negotiate assumptions of hypersexuality and obesity, while suburban girls often have to contend with the assumption of lacking sexual desire and being anorexic (Fahs & Swank 2015). Other studies indicate that girls more readily experience sexual fluidity and performative bisexuality, exploring sexual practices outside of heterosexuality, but in many cases, this is also done to please their male peers (ibid.).

The study of intersecting cultural meanings of male sexual development is underdeveloped (as the male body has been conceived as 'universal' and not having a gendered dimension) but on the rise. Male pubescence, for example, is no longer a taken-for-granted process as it was in the past. Richard Mora studied how a group of sixth-grade Latino boys in a low-income working-class neighbourhood, who publicly acknowledged that they were experiencing puberty, employed their bodies at school to construct their masculine identities (Mora 2012). In their vision, puberty was a social accomplishment of masculinity, made of physical strength, allusions to genitalia, desire of muscles, and this understanding was informed by the dominant gendered expectations of peers at school and in their neighbourhoods, by commercial hip hop rappers, and by the gender orders in the United States and both Dominican and Puerto Rican communities.

Research on sexual development in adulthood focuses on topics such as sexual desire and satisfaction, body image, embodied practices. Many studies report women facing more pressures to contain and manage their bodies throughout adulthood: from hiding menstrual product and odours to body hair removal and contradictory pressures to embody a normative femininity. Some studies showed that, for example, women do not feel entitled to choose the degree to which they will remain hairy, while men do.[5] And, among women, those of colour face more severe penalties than white ones for choosing to have body hair, particularly in contexts where their 'respectability' is at stake (see also chapter 7). Compared to this bulk of research, studies on male embodiment (such as men's relationship with their sperm or practices around the management of ejaculation) are underdeveloped, especially heterosexual male embodiment (Fahs & Swank 2015).

In a review of literature about the cultural meanings of menopause and their consequences, Lisa Hall and colleagues (2007, 106) show that 'although women's cultural beliefs and practices related to menopause affect symptom distress and management, there is wide variance in the individual woman's personal perceptions of the experience'. As an example, immigrant women from societies where beliefs and customs are passed down from generation to generation may find the menopausal experience challenging because of the belief that family needs come first, rather than self-care. In the case of low-income families, financial concerns may keep them from accessing health care for menopausal symptoms, while high-class career women experience menopause as a time of loss of youth, beauty and control over bothersome symptoms. A study of Korean immigrant menopausal women reports that some felt energetic and healthy while living in Korea but felt that they aged quickly in the migration destination country, dealing with language barriers, financial challenges and isolation from their culture (Im & Meleis 2000).

Embodied sexual otherness

It is impossible to understand gender and sexuality simply through white, middle-class, Western lenses. The well-known works of Dubar Moodie (1994) on masculinity among workers in South African mines and of Gloria Wekker (2006) on women of the Afro-Surinamese diaspora and sexuality are clear examples of the importance of connecting individual interpretations and interactions with contexts and social institutions. Tomás Almaguer (1991), for example, explored sexual desire, practices and identities of gay men of Mexican origin living in the United States. He observed that, unlike Western countries, in Mexico and other Latin American countries the distinction of gender and sexuality was marked by an understanding of the (male) actors' positioning in sexual activity: a heterosexual man was still considered such in the event of having sex with another man if he was *activo*, relegating the homosexual stigma to be penetrated, as the *pasivo* person. This work was considered as ground-breaking, but is not exempt from criticism, as it did not account for material factors affecting Mexican men having sex with other men. This is what the research of Gonzáles-López (2006) did, for instance, when he explored the socially constructed hetero-sexuality of *jornaleros* (day labourers) and their exposure to sexual harassment and commercial sex with their employers, frequently white gay men. But this is also what Andrea Bolivar (2021) finds in her ethnographic research with transgender Latinas in Chicago, exploring the meanings attributed to money accessed through sexual labour. After financing basic needs like food and housing, the women used the money for medical and cosmetic interventions to feminize their appearances through surgical procedures to the face, breasts and hips, as well as hormone therapy, hair extensions and permanent and semi-permanent face and body hair removal. Here, gender, body and sex collapse in a mutual construction and recognition. But, above all, sexual practices and meaning are shown as fundamental arenas where systems of oppression and privilege based on social class and ethnicity are achieved, as an intersectional approach suggests.

Approaching sexuality from a different intersectional angle, for example, Joane Nagel (2000) shows how social group boundaries can also be sexual boundaries. The frontiers that divide racial, ethnic and national communities and identities are always 'ethno-sexual' frontiers, within which any mixed relationships are heavily controlled and penalized. Compulsory heterosexuality (to use Adrienne Rich's expression, see chapter 3) is another central component of racial, ethnic and nationalist definitions. A combination of these factors ensures that correct male and female heterosexual behaviour often establishes the gender regime in those ethnic cultures that distinguish between 'our' women (typically, pure virgins or mothers) and 'their' women (dirty, prostitutes), and 'our' men (virile, strong, brave) and 'their' men (degenerate, weak, cowardly). Such heteronormative and ethno-sexual stereotypes are common to many cultures and may greatly cramp the lives of those placed on the borderline, or even across it. Indeed, non-heterosexual sexuality is often invisible within ethnic communities. For instance, Sharmila Rudrappa (1999; quoted in Nagel 2000) studied the tensions experienced by young Indian American women as they try to square the two worlds of gender and sex in which they live: the more traditional expectations as to the freedom (including sexual freedom) of women in their families that are often immigrant families, as opposed to the broader culture of the United States. Meanwhile white women are described as weak or promiscuous, objects upon whom the members of some ethnic groups in the United States and elsewhere found their own sense of moral superiority.

Indeed, the interweaving of factors of inequality changes from one generation to another: as Dan Woodmann and Johanna Wyn (2015, 1408) argue, 'it is a mistake to predefine class, or gender and race, as processes that remain stable. Institutional arrangements adjust, politics is played, policies are changed, and people actively draw on unequal resources to maintain and recreate distinctions and advantages over others in the face of conditions that change over time'. Such awareness provides space for resistance, innovation and negotiation of course. But structural constraints also limit the resources they can rely upon.

The power to negotiate

Studies on AIDS/HIV are a fundamental testing ground for the intersectional approach. In a review of micro- and macro-sociology studies, Celeste Watkins-Hayes (2014) explicitly calls the topic 'an epidemic of intersectional inequalities', where the way of managing the disease and the risk of contracting it are heavily conditioned by the interweaving of racial, gender, class and sex inequalities. One example mentioned in the review is Jorge Fontdevila's research on the sexual accounts of gay and bisexual immigrant male Mexicans in San Diego (Fontdevila 2009). The author stresses the key role of interactions facilitating HIV transmission and points out the differing construction of frames for sexual encounters, sometimes based on protection and use of barriers against contagion, and other times on trust and partners' information about each other. The research shows a picture of individuals constantly moving between different frames during sexual encounters, reacting to the setting and taking impromptu decisions whether to use a condom or not. In a successive qualitative study, Fontdevila, with Héctor Carrillo, tried to go beyond monolithic views of sexualities in this population, showing that patterns of interpretation and practice of same-sex desires change during a lifespan and can be affected by contexts and life experiences. In that case, the experience of migration is illustrated as a factor that can strongly influence interpretations and practices. Drawing on in-depth interviews with eighty self-identified gay and bisexual Mexican immigrant men, the authors show that highly gendered understandings and styles of sexual interaction between men changed after migration and adapted to new sexual contexts, while some others resisted any changes (Carrillo & Fontdevila 2014). Other research shows that Black men engaging in sex with other men find it harder to call themselves 'gay' on that account, or to disclose their sex life with partners (of either sex), hence run a high risk of contracting the disease. Overall, the interaction of a migrant history, poverty, drugs, traditional notions of gender role and even a hierarchy of skin colour tones may strongly affect the likelihood of Black and Latino males taking precautions, as documented by the rate of new HIV infections in such groups. Similarly, 'sexualized racism' affects the chances and relative power of Black women taking decisions about their own sex life and protection from contagion (Watkins-Hayes 2014).

The expectations around certain groups, based on their race, may imply that non-heterosexual persons (such as lesbian, gay or trans people) find themselves stereotyped even within their own circle (e.g., the hypersexualization of Black masculinity by white gay men). Some research on transgender men of colour has shown that acquiring masculinity in social interaction also entails a greater risk of harassment and violent abuse, while transgender women of colour run a greater risk of being killed, discriminated against, assaulted and imprisoned than do white transgender men and women (Schilt & Lagos 2017). Such results are often confirmed by quantitative studies. Data collected on a large sample of mostly low-income

Latina women in the United States, for example, show that the ability to negotiate safer sexual practices is related to their power in the relationship, as defined by a scale both considering control (with items such as 'Most of the time, we do what my partner wants to do' or 'My partner won't let me wear certain things' or 'My partner always wants to know where I am') and decision-making in the couple (with items about who has more say about whether to have sex or about what to do together). Results show that the likelihood of consistent condom use is related to how much power women have in the couple (Pulerwitz, Amaro, De Jong, Gortmaker & Rudd 2002).

These are clear examples of how the intersectional approach boosts social research into bodies and identity. The decision to wear a condom is not simply a medical precaution, but an instance of negotiated behaviour dependent on power dynamics between sexual partners, codes of respectability, the degree of information, the way a situation is defined, and a person's freedom to assert a particular sexual identity. All these aspects are not just marked by social categorization – gender, race, class, age, sexual orientation – but also by the way they interact: they are performative and contribute to creating such categorization and giving it meaning in everyday life.

The challenges of disability

Cultural norms of acceptance of gender identity and sexuality can be even stricter when related to minorities. The experience of persons with disabilities is a clear example of that, as documented by a vast ethnographic literature on disability and sexuality. Social assumptions pertaining to appropriate 'gender performances' can result in rejection or stigmatization when a person with disabilities is unable to follow stereotypical performances of gender. For instance, a man with a physical disability, not able to work and financially support a family, may find his masculinity questioned (Gerschick 2000). Several studies have documented how hard it can be for men with disabilities to deal with the social expectations of competitiveness, strength, control and independence related to the ideal of hegemonic masculinity, especially in relation with potential partners. Similarly, the femininity of a woman with disabilities who does not meet social expectations around caregiving and appearance can be perceived as dubious.

This is reflected also in the domain of sexuality: research found that persons with visible and physical disabilities are often perceived as asexual, while those with cognitive disability are perceived as promiscuous (Cheng 2009) or 'hypersexual' (Whittle & Butler 2018). Similarly, queer identities from within the disability community may also be marginalized because of predominant notions of sexuality (see chapter 4). For instance, Lotta Löfgren-Mårtenson (2004) conducted an ethnographic study at dances geared towards youths with intellectual disability and interviewed youngsters, staff members and parents. She found that homosexual acts were often interpreted as friendships or 'misdirected' expressions and 'therefore adjusted' (ibid., 205).

Since they are sometimes perceived as asexual beings, some people with physical disabilities can find it difficult to openly express their needs regarding sexual pleasure, childbirth and body image with physicians and personal care attendants. This may happen in everyday interactions as well as in institutional policies and has been stressed by the provoking ethnography by Don Kulick and Jens Rydström (2015) entitled *Loneliness and Its Opposite: Sex, Disability, and the Ethics of Engagement*. The study was based on interviews with people with disabilities (who primarily lived in care homes and who had limited or no mobility in their limbs), their parents, experts, sex workers, personal assistants and care-home workers, and observations in care homes. The interviews were conducted in Denmark and Sweden, two liberal welfare states which are similar in many aspects, such as a generous Scandinavian model of welfare, but very different when it comes to sexuality and disability. Care homes represented safe and intimate spaces for people with disabilities who lived there, but they were also the workplace of caregivers. In Denmark, the erotic lives of people with disabilities were acknowledged and facilitated, so that their erotic lives were assisted by people who worked with and cared for them in the first case (e.g., in positioning them for sex with another person, procuring pornographic material or contraception, including putting on condoms, aiding in masturbation or in acquiring a sex worker). In Sweden, in contrast, the erotic lives, and the entitlement to sexuality, of adults with significant disabilities were denied, their sexuality was perceived as a potential (and even a likely) 'danger', and carers were instructed not to independently raise questions of sexuality. The book thus explores the complex boundaries between private and public, love and sex, work and intimacy, and affection and abuse.

Research on sex and disability often registers forms of active resistance to cultural norms about the sexual body. For instance, Anne Guldin (2000) interviewed men and women with congenital conditions (spina bifida and spinal muscular atrophy) and spinal cord injuries about their sexual practices. Participants recognized that their bodies did not fit cultural expectations, but this led them to focus on other qualities. She reported men who resisted dominant ideals of eroticism, sensuality or sexuality, who felt their disability gave them some advantage over men without disabilities in terms of sexual skills and sexual introspection, patience, sensitivity, willingness to go slowly and focus on the entire body of the (female) partner and on her pleasure. 'What is constructed – if not a sexy body – is nonetheless a sexy being' (ibid., 235).

However, the strength of social norms is not always so easily dismissed and the other's gaze can be also profoundly internalized. Russell Shuttleworth (2000) conducted life history interviews with men with cerebral palsy who live independently in the San Francisco Bay Area, focusing on the ways in which they attempted to establish intimacy and sexual relationships with others. The interviewees, often with no or little adolescent experience in the interpersonal etiquette of flirting, made implicit comparison to hegemonic ideals of attractiveness, showed an embodied sense of the others' negative resistance to seeing them in a sexual light, and all that affected their self-agency. Shuttleworth then concludes (ibid., 279–80):

> There does appear to be an increasingly constitutive role for sex in terms of identity and selfhood in the history of the West. In such a context, securing some kind of sexual intimacy, however defined by the individual, becomes a paramount project of self-constitution. From this perspective, the claiming of sexuality by disabled people against the cultural assumption of their asexuality, is thus also a bid for full subjectivity. This is one reason why the issue of disabled people's sexuality has assumed such political importance in recent years.

Thus, intersectionality allows us to see discrimination where we think we don't find it – even as performed by otherwise discriminated-against people – and to understand what factors are contingently relevant and what not. It should be noted that, differently from 'multiple discrimination' (Verloo 2006), which assumes that all factors of social exclusion are independent categories and that forms of discrimination an individual may be subjected to take place at the same time, intersectionality can see discrimination as related to place, time and surroundings. Those identities that place each of us along the axes of privilege and oppression may be sometimes relevant, sometimes not. They may even be subverted as factors of disadvantage in certain circumstances and contexts. As La Rivière-Zijdel's study (2009, 34) reports:

In the disability movement I have experienced discrimination on the intersecting identities of sex and sexual orientation. The disability movement tends to be quite homophobic as disabled people desire to belong as much as possible to the majority norm (i.e. heterosexual). They already deviate from this norm through their impairments and all negative connotations attached to it. Like all social and political movements (except for the women's movement) the disability movement is mostly run by (disabled) men, which has put the women's agenda on a secondary and often tertiary place (i.e. impairment specific first and men second). I discovered a similar process within the LGBT movement that has difficulty with the aspects of being disabled, as the norm is beauty, virility, independence and so on.

This example shows how central the body and its sexual role can be to gender and self-identity. Sexuality constitutes a fundamental aspect of gendered bodies: it contributes to the anchoring of gender differences on bodies and, simultaneously, plays on bodies to construct gender relations.

In this chapter, we have seen that the labels attached to our bodily experience are far from 'natural': indeed, they are the result of social processes. The different stages of life are limited and signified by cultural meanings and institutions, and by our position in the social order. Our identity is at the intersection of different labels, and each label expresses a certain position in an interlocked system of oppression and privileges. The intersectional approach enables us to account for the interwoven structural constraints that affect our bodily experience. Research on a variety of embodied practices (as the examples about sexuality have shown) informed by such an approach sheds light on our being at the crossroads of different systems of domination and lets us consider how it contributes to (and is affected by) our gendered experience of the body. More generally, such studies allow us to understand not just how the different combinations of labels that everybody carries give it a different ranking from others in the social hierarchy, but also how the labels themselves are merely the outcome of that self-same ranking: an outcome that is arbitrary, historical and relational. As such, it is strictly related to power. In the next chapter, we go further into the discussion of how power and agency run into individual embodiment with an insight into a specific field of sociological research: the gendered management of bodily appearances.

6

The Power of Appearances

'Start eating three meals and one snack daily. Plan to get 25 to 30 per cent of your total calories from each meal, with the rest from your snack. ... If you wake up without an appetite, give it an hour to develop. If you're still not hungry, eat anyway'. 'Shake up your routine and get some exercise at the same time by taking a walk and eating your lunch somewhere outside. You don't have to go far ... Also remember to take the stairs on your way back to the office. ... Dinner at a friend's? Walk there instead of driving. Relaxing at home? Try a 15-minute yoga video'. 'Park further away, use a standing desk, sit on an exercise ball'. 'Now, one of the universal truths about being a mum, is that there is always some chore pending. Washing to be put out, taken in, folded, etc. But we can stretch, tone and exercise while we do it!'

Periodicals, social media, personal trainers, blogs and websites devoted to body care often advise their (especially female) public how to spend time and energy each day attending to the slightest details of their outward appearance, the right diet to follow, what posture to adopt, what kind of movements. Weight loss technologies, from apps on smartphones to wearable devices to bodily implants intensify this further, within an increasing trend of deliberate observations of one's own body, monitoring, records and consequent actions addressed to specific goals. These digital self-tracking practices through technologies enable users to endlessly monitor their health – diet, exercise, sleep, calories, steps, blood pressure, heart rate and so on. This of course generates a new form of self-knowledge, but also turns personal data into a commodity ('digital biocapital') for the profit of corporations through profiling techniques or customer loyalty programmes, as Deborah Lupton's provocative book *The Quantified Self* (2016) illustrates.

From media content to the app messages, all these technologies serve as tools to gain an ideal beautiful body, ideal yet also personal. The body's qualities no longer lie in natural endowment, as in the past, but in being the visible manifestation of proper, regular training. Appearance is no longer a matter of destiny, but the result of bodily discipline. The basic rule is to leave no stone unturned: all one's energy must go into rational management of one's body, and the body is supposed to show this management off (Bauman 1992; Giddens 1991). The accent is on the individual and their ability to choose, conditioned by the commonly accepted canons of beauty. Such tasks are presented as gratifying and agreeable, as 'taking time for oneself'.

If we analyse the message of the beauty magazines through the Foucauldian lenses described in the third chapter, some points immediately spring to mind. First, we are talking here of a set of minute guidelines: how to get a result from one's body by rationalizing the use of time, by paying attention to functional body movement, channelling energy and above all internalizing an exacting outer eye of judgement. When it comes to it, such a political anatomy of detail is not so different from modern techniques for embodied surveillance of prisoners, soldiers and schoolchildren as described by Foucault in *Discipline and Punish* (1977 [1975]). The language is scientific sounding, urging us in terms verging on the pathological to analyse aspects that medicine once ignored, along the lines described in *The Birth of the Clinic* (2012 [1963]). At the same time, the tone is a confidential one, 'woman to woman' or 'man to man' (depending on whether the magazine targets a female or male audience), suggesting mutual acknowledgement of shared needs.

In other words, a copious production of performative discursive acts addressing *women as women* and *men as men* constructs the 'woman' or 'man' inasmuch as they refer to a subject whose needs and goals it takes for granted – and in so doing demarcates the socially accepted sphere of action. Aesthetic appearance, the surface dimension of the body, in short, is wholly political. It acts out dynamics of exclusion, conflict and social recognition impinging on our relationship to our own body and to other people's. What is more, from the early decades of the twentieth century it has been engulfed in a global market of goods and services whose turnover has spiralled.

In this chapter we shall explore the way in which dynamics of power, and of withstanding it, are worked out upon the outward form of bodies. In the second chapter, we touched on how the body is constructed in its depth by considering emotions, gender and inter-action; we shall now consider the surface of the body, considering it a fundamental aspect for the embodiment of gender, related, as it is, to the self-positioning of the subject in the social world as well as social categorization in institutions and culture. Picking up some of the analytical frameworks by classic sociologists together with important exponents of contemporary feminist thought, in the first section we shall see how the quest for beauty has been analysed in sociology, and how it ties up with social exclusion and inclusion, consumerism and the market. We will then see how ugliness has been patholo-gized over time, thus requiring an increasing scientific and rational intervention by consumers; cosmetic surgery is the clearest example of such discourse. The management and modification of the body, from fitness to tattoos and piercing, again is a terrain where social constraints and individual agency around embodiment and gender are continuously challenged and confirmed.

1. Gender, beauty and power

A welter of research based on psychology and economics dwells on the standardization of facial and body features that are universally deemed beautiful, and on the advantages that this beauty confers: better school performance, a better position on the labour and marriage markets, a more central role in one's social network, higher self-esteem (Amadieu 2002). On the other hand, history, anthro-pology and sociology studies have tended to stress the variability of aesthetic norms and their differing impact on different parts of the population. Beauty standards, it has been remarked, are closely dependent on the society's economic and social structure (a white skin is appreciated in multi-ethnic societies where whites occupy positions of power; slimness is sought after in the consumer society as a sign of inner discipline amid the temptations of plentiful food). Likewise, the threshold and implications of what is deemed ugly or sub-standard will vary accordingly. At the same time, beauty standards reinforce all forms of discrimination (racism, sexism, ableism, ageism and so on) in a subtle way, since they are rarely questioned: we usually deny the importance of aesthetic discrimination (Rhode 2010). As Bonnie Berry puts it: 'Unlike our dealings with other "isms" … (racism, and so on), the social awareness we have of appearance bias is shallow, infantile in its development, and mostly acceptable as a given and unchangeable form of inequality' (2016 [2008], 2). Beauty has always been imbued with virtue, but the other side of its coin is the social exclusion of those who cannot or don't want to achieve it. No surprise that from its birth, sociology has focused particularly on the practices and implications of different social group members adapting (or not adapting) their bodily appearance to the going norms.

Female beautification and status

Beauty care has received alternating moral interpretations over time, according to the changing threshold between nature and artifice (Rémaury 2000). The dominant approach to cosmetics has always appreciated the natural, but the idea of what counts as a 'natural-seeming' body and face has changed over the centuries, involving an ever-greater number of treatments. Ever since Renaissance times, self-beautification has figured as a way of completing femininity rather than masculinity, albeit differing between women of different social classes. In the nineteenth century the American bourgeoisie frowned on cosmetics as inappropriate and vulgar: the culture of sincerity and temperance only reinforced the natural fixed distinctions in the social pecking order (Peiss 1998). Over the nineteenth century the industrial production of cosmetics and the rise of professional beautician services spread the right/duty to look beautiful more and more democratically across the social scale: 'There are no ugly women', thundered Helena Rubinstein at the head of one of the first cosmetic industries to go global midway through the last century, 'there are only lazy women'. That is not to say that people have the same access to beauty products and the disciplining of their own body, as Luc Boltanski (1971) pointed out.

Besides, it has been argued that the difference between the quest for personal beauty and more generic forms of body care is that the former is much more likely to be described as an exciting creative transformation of the individual, a passing celebration of one's own difference 'over and above all other difference' (Bordo 2003 [1993]).

In any case, the connection between beauty and power has been widely analysed for centuries. 'Taught from their infancy that beauty is woman's sceptre, the mind shapes itself to the body, and, roaming round its gilt cage, only seeks to adorn its prison' – so wrote Mary Wollstonecraft back in 1792 in her celebrated *A Vindication of the Rights of Woman* (1995 [1792], 116). At one stroke she thus summed up a whole scholarly literature that in subsequent centuries would surround women's attention to their bodies, and the result thereof in terms of self-esteem and personal freedom. Years of experience in service with lady aristocrats gave Wollstonecraft a ringside seat on the teaching of 'feminine arts' to young ladies: embroidery, painting and, above all, close observation of fashion and self-adornment. But as Wollstonecraft pointed out, beauty brings only a passing success, paid for by lifelong exclusion from public affairs and economic production. Women sacrifice virtue 'to temporary gratifications, and the respectability of life to the triumph of an hour' (ibid., 111). Permanently obsessed with their outward appearance, women were thus relegated to the function of ornaments, something that could be exchanged on the marriage market, and which doomed them to live in their husbands' shadow.

The American economist and sociologist Thorstein Veblen would come to much the same conclusion a century later. In his *The Theory of the Leisure Class*, written at the close of the nineteenth century, Veblen observes how wealthy women appoint themselves supreme representatives of their husbands' affluence by ostentatious spending and beautification of their own person. From a detailed examination of female clothing and ornaments, of the kind that serve no practical purpose beyond decoration and basic personal needs, Veblen (1994 [1899]) concludes that such articles only confirm that the user cannot engage in any manual work or spend her time profitably: she is thus incapable of performing any menial function. The uselessness of the woman thus redounds to the credit of her husband, who is deemed capable of providing so abundantly that she need not work. An ostentatious waste of energy and substance serving, at least apparently, to mark the social distance between them and other people. That was the sole function of the affluent lady's attention to her own outward appearance. Which simply confirms the patriarchal system (ibid., 105ff.):

> The dress of women goes even farther than that of men in the way of demonstrating the wearer's abstinence from productive employment. It needs no argument to enforce the generalisation that the more elegant styles of feminine bonnets go even farther towards making work impossible than does the man's high hat. The woman's shoe adds the so-called French heel to the evidence of enforced leisure afforded by its polish; because this high heel

obviously makes any, even the simplest and most necessary manual work extremely difficult. ... The corset is, in economic theory, substantially a mutilation, undergone for the purpose of lowering the subject's vitality and rendering her permanently and obviously unfit for work. ... To apply this generalisation to women's dress, and put the matter in concrete terms: the high heel, the skirt, the impracticable bonnet, the corset, and the general disregard of the wearer's comfort which is an obvious feature of all civilised women's apparel, are so many items of evidence to the effect that in the modern civilised scheme of life the woman is still, in theory, the economic dependent of the man – that, perhaps in a highly idealised sense, she still is the man's chattel.

To be true, as Valerie Steele (2001) has noticed, the corset was an ambivalent item for women, which was not just imposed on them but actively appropriated to signal self-discipline, attractiveness and status; furthermore, in today's society the corset has, on the one hand, been replaced by various forms of exercise to shape the body and, on the other, it has become an outside garment expressing the eroticization of the female body.

Veblen is not alone in detecting the implications of beauty and appearance work in early sociology. For instance, the German sociologist Georg Simmel placed great emphasis on people's desire, and women's in particular, for pleasure and being envied by others. Simmel's essay 'Excursus on jewellery and adornment' (Simmel 2009 [1908]) investigates the contradiction between apparent altruism in dressing up for other people and the egoistic sense of power conferred by their aesthetic appreciation. The sensation of acquiring a distinct personality, he argues, comes from an extension of self onto the ornament. Adorned, the body augments the individual: the intrinsically superfluous ornamental object symbolically places its own impersonality at the service of the individual's personality, thus raising it above other people. Such a process underscores the essentially relational character of beauty, inasmuch as other people share in the radiance and actively reflect it back onto the adorned individual. An ornament somehow marks both a distance from, and a complicity with. In such a perspective Simmel sees the woman's position as closely dependent on fashion. Precisely the collective quality that fashion promises confers on the woman the security and exemption from individual aesthetic and ethical responsibility which those who have a weak social position so crave. In his studies on social differentiation and fashion, Simmel (1957 [1904]) interprets such phenomena as social forms designed to satisfy the individual need both to bond with and to stand out from other people. In a setting marked by constant fleeting and self-seeking contact among strangers, amid the anonymous hurly-burly of a modern metropolis, it is appearance that provides the basic clue to an individual's social niche. Failing other reference points, it is how you look that is often taken to express what you are, your 'authentic self' in the public sphere (Simmel 1950 [1903]; 1957 [1904]; see also Goffman 1959).

Such interpretation stood the test of time. Indeed, in Simmel's view, the more emancipated woman flaunted her indifference to her outward appearance, but both the production and the consumption of make-up and adornments played an ambivalent role in women's emancipation in contemporary times. For example, at the beginning of the twentieth century the cosmetics industry gave women a great opportunity of entering the ranks of paid work (Scranton 2001) and the public arena (Peiss 1998). Nevertheless, he was right in his account of the relationship among femininity, power and appearance, but also in the importance that the look and beauty care would have in contemporary times.

Feminist interpretations of beauty

Contemporary sociology of beauty studies falls into three basic strands. The first is largely feminist and sees the desire to be beautiful as stemming from cultural and social pressures on the individual, especially women, to conform to aesthetic ideals (Bartky 1990; Chapkis 1986; Morgan 1991; Wolf 2002 [1990]). On this view, the beauty-seeker is persuaded by various agencies that personalizing her (or his) own body answers to a spontaneous personal need, whereas in fact so doing bends it to norms that cannot be attained, and to standards decided by other people. In a popular critical essay towards the end of the twentieth century, *The Beauty Myth* (2002 [1990]), Naomi Wolf suggests, for example, that aesthetic competition among women is just a means through which the patriarchal system gets its own back on feminist conquests. It drives even the most emancipated to spend energy vying over something as frivolous as aesthetic appearance, suggesting that the system has undermined their sisterly solidarity and women's competitive presence at work, in the economy and in politics. The beauty myth fuelled by cosmetics sellers is a 'political weapon against women's advancement', aimed at depriving women of self-esteem through the creation of unattainable standards. Once again, recourse to beautification is a substitute for power providing ephemeral advantage not based on solidarity and collective awareness.

The second strand sees the quest for beauty as a rational way of turning one's body to actively account for and thus improve one's social standing just like any other consumer or occupational choice. The much-debated essay on erotic capital by sociologist Catherine Hakim (2010) should be included in this second perspective. In addition to the other forms of capital studied by Pierre Bourdieu (economic, social, cultural, symbolic and physical), Hakim defines erotic capital as a combination of beauty, sexual attractiveness, charm, liveliness, style of presentation and sexuality, which can be an asset in mating and marriage markets, in labour markets, the media, politics and in everyday social interaction. The positive outcome of using such capital may be seen in all areas of social life, argues Hakim, and women have the biggest share of it and are better able to build it up and try and preserve it in time. Alongside other resources, also outward appearance and the ability to attract others can be a source of power, according to this sociologist. However, it should be noted that such power is not independent from social class and education. Moreover, appreciating a woman's look is far from thinking highly of her. In the aforementioned study of VIP party circuits, Mears (2020) points out, as we have seen, that girls' bodily capital can generate enormous returns to wealthy men, as it serves as an asset in their search for status. Indeed, bodily and erotic capital gets women on the scene, allows them to be indulged with freebies of food and drink and with the compliment of being included in an exclusive world, as in Hakim's account. But, in fact, it secures no recognition to them as serious players once inside. They are spoken of as brainless and sexually loose by men, who are very aware that girls' bodily capital is short term and can be easily replaced by a new supply. In other words, the profits of girls' beauty are more in men's than girls' hands (ibid., 266).

In recent years sociology studies have got over the theoretical deadlock between subjective agency and social structure by focusing more on how individuals talk about, understand and experience beauty, as well as on the aesthetic discrimination potentially incurred (for a nuanced collection of readings on the effects of beauty norms on the bodies, see Liebelt et al., 2019). The empirical research forming part of this third strand largely based its approach on participant observation and interviews with people involved in embellishing their own or other people's bodies, from beauty parlours to gyms, from cosmetic surgery clinics to beauty contests (Gimlin 2002; Sassatelli 2010a). What emerges from such literature is the importance of listening to the reflexive narration of beauty, including experiences of embodiment, desires, emotions and values that may be mutually conflicting.

For sure, interest in looking good is not just a matter of manipulating one's own outside appearance. Beauty care is seen as a mixture of a calculating kind of discipline, self-interest and gratification. We are now facing an intensification of beauty pressures extending over new sites of the body (further increased by beauty apps). Body care practices are presented in the media as self-liberating, under the idea that they 'enhance natural beauty' and 'empower individuals to love and care for themselves', as an advertisement stated, making their 'inner beauty' align with outward appearance (Elias, Gill and Scharff 2017). Women are suggested to be confident, resilient, and love their bodies, but such discourse 'rather than representing a loosening of the grip of punishing appearance standards for women, it is an escalation – the additional move of beauty into the arena of subjectivity' (Gill 2021, 15). It's a further pressure to follow the appropriate feeling rules towards their body (see chapter 2). Individuals, especially women, are compelled to adhere to ideals of 'aesthetic entrepreneurship' to construct themselves as responsible subjects invested in self-beautification.

Body conforming and sense of self

All in all, such studies tend to show the social advantage of one's appearance conforming to the norm for everybody; but if one is a woman, the expectation that one conforms to the aesthetic norm is even higher. Susan Bordo (2003 [1993], 208) observes the career woman:

> From the standpoint of male anxiety, the lean body of the career businesswoman today may symbolize such a neutralization. With her body and her dress, she declares symbolic allegiance to the professional, white, male world along with her lack of intention to subvert that arena with alternative 'female values.' At the same time, insofar as she is clearly 'dressing up', *playing* male (almost always with a 'softening' fashion touch to establish traditional feminine decorativeness, and continually cautioned against the dire consequences of allotting success higher priority than her looks), she represents no serious competition (symbolically, that is) to the real men of the workplace.

Efrat Tseëlon's research also shows how one of the paradoxes dogging current definitions of femininity is the need to be seductive but modest with it too (1995). The women she interviewed relate how hard it is to avoid giving the wrong message at the workplace: for many of them, being a sex object when you don't want to means losing control, losing credibility and hence feeling humiliated. In turn, Joanne Entwistle (2023 [2000]) shows how entering the male work environment demands a 'compromise' between authority and sensuality which obliges women to maintain considerable awareness and calls for complex negotiation between male and female connotations: so-called 'power dressing' – adopting masculine dress code at work to convey an image of authority – has helped women to fit into the work scenario, retaining a note of femininity but downplaying the sexual overtones. A well-cut jacket and plain sober colours, combined with a skirt and high heels, creates a hybrid that hovers between male connotations (authority, detachment) and female (sexuality, emotionalism). Women can sometimes turn this unstable balance to their own advantage, but it needs continual vigilance and much more awareness than is demanded of their male colleagues.

Moreover, the conceptual overlap of beauty work and femininity can result in overlooking the social and individual costs of the former, as highlighted in Melissa Tyler and Pamela Abbott's study on the recruitment, training and management of flight attendants. The research illustrates how flight attendants' bodies are expected to embody the company, and as such they are routinely scrutinized by the managers. Female attendants are asked to lose weight if their weight-to-height ratio exceeds the required one and their make-up and appearance are strictly controlled (while male attendants are expected to be just clean and neat). To achieve the expected look, they sustained greater expenses for beauty services than their male colleagues and were not refunded for them. The interesting point here is that the skills deployed in performing and maintaining the expected look were not recognized nor remunerated, as the work for looking good is perceived as 'an aspect of just "being a woman", from which women are deemed to derive both pleasure and a sense of identity': the maintenance 'of an appropriate state of embodiment demands both time and resources', but is seen as 'being part of what women *are* rather than what women *do*' (Tyler & Abbott 1998, 434).

Fashion is itself a factor of contamination and hybridization between masculine and feminine. But for all the multiple gender codes, as well as the plugging of 'gender fluidity' in fashion magazines, advertising and popular culture, the upshot has not been equality of choice. For example, though there are proliferating cultural manifestations of sexuality and femininity, and while women can nowadays choose from among a variety of styles and 'scripts' in putting over their own version of femininity, they still have to juggle with self-control on various fronts: having a good career, nice family and attractive appearance becomes an imperative rather than an option; and it calls for the ability to keep taking a new stance vis-à-vis a gender order that is constantly altering (McRobbie 2004). This seems to take place not by moving beyond gender distinctions as such, but by distilling difference in an ever-new, more sophisticated and subtle guise.

But the point that many authors, especially women, have stressed in recent decades (Brownmiller 1984; Chapkis 1986; Jeffreys 2015 [2005]) is the link between the search for beauty and feminine identity. If he neglects his appearance, a man is no less male for that: he is simply an unkempt man. But not so the woman. An undisciplined, unmanipulated, unkempt, unembellished woman's body is a non-feminine body, femininity being construed as attention to pretty looks and the art of seduction. Picking up Foucault's arguments about the *Panopticon*, Sandra Bartky (1990) analyses the daily cosmetic ritual as an introjection of a sense of inferiority instilled by outside cultural agencies: women absorb the idea that femininity is made concrete when it is visible, that their body needs constant control and embellishment because it is imperfect. Trained to discipline and monitor it incessantly, women feel watched and judged according to their outward look. In the end, they have introjected the stare from outside and assume 'a state of conscious and permanent visibility'. This, argues Bartky, means they only gain access to real intimacy of self via the outsider's stare; hence their sense of self is ousted by a sense of being appreciated by others. Woman's sexual alienation (that is, how she is alienated from her own sexuality the way a factory hand is from the fruit of their own work in a capitalist economy) rests on the fact that supervisor and supervised dwell within her: she ends up viewing herself as a body, not just for others but for herself too. So, while there is an element of coercion in making women aware of such reification, even by polite appreciation and compliments on her look, there is also a much-needed recognition. A whole series of beauty practices do make a woman who agrees to them feel fully 'feminine'. In which case femininity is being reduced to the reflection of a body practice, much more than masculinity.

The idea that a woman is permanently accompanied by her self-image because of gender socialization figured in many feminist-based studies between the 1970s and 1990s. On this argument, if women are attentive to their outward appearance, it is because the image is made to represent the body, and the self takes refuge in that image. But the result of such self-concentration is that the outer world gets lost from sight: a way of relating to others sets in that is based on the insatiable quest for reflected confirmation of self-worth (the French philosopher Simone de Beauvoir went deep into this subject). But as we saw in the second chapter, Bourdieu (2001 [1998]) argues that women's acceptance of being 'a body for others' simply reflects patriarchal domination. When women submit to a condition that is actually degrading and impoverishing, it is both something 'spontaneous' and an act of 'extortion', since in thinking, and even thinking of themselves, the dominated party can only make use of language and patterns of thought based on vocabulary and cognitive categories that are insidiously imbued with the trappings of domination. This is even more evident in regards of non-white and non-Western bodies. Having incorporated the colonial gaze over their own bodies, many women struggle to maintain self-worth in a world that associates non-whiteness as otherness, as bell hooks (1992) has so vividly pointed out.

By contrast, some scholars have stressed the effect of mass culture in teaching women to be desirable first and foremost (Brumberg 1997; Chapkis 1986) and to try and adapt their body to unattainable aesthetic standards, while beauty industries deliberately seeded women with body dysmorphic disorder to induce them to purchase products (Greer 1999). However, in the course of the 1990s, sociologists, especially inspired by culturalism, post-colonialism and post-structuralism, broke away from this view as being unduly deterministic and failing to do justice to those women who do not conform to aesthetic ideals. The main problem – as Kathy Davis (1995) comments in research based on interviews with Dutch women who had undergone cosmetic surgery – is that the traditional pressure-of-the-media approach paints women as 'cultural dopes', intoxicated by their culture, less capable than others of distancing themselves or critically assessing messages from the celebrity world. In short, feminism ultimately ends up demeaning the mental abilities of women. Patricia Gagné and Deanna McGaughey (2002) argue along similar lines: they too work from interviews with facelift patients and conclude that many women actively choose surgery so as to be sexually freer and increase their chances of meeting partners. In their accounts, cosmetic surgery simply lies on a continuum stretching from make-up to dieting, dyeing one's hair or using special bras. These women claimed that surgery had been more of a liberation than an imposition. In which case, the authors conclude, beauty really can be a tool of personal empowerment for the individual woman, though it does turn out to be a way of removing power from women as a group.

Indeed, from a Foucauldian angle we see how the body is the prime area for wielding power, but for that reason also a crucial battleground for resisting it. Thus, a whole series of practices embellishing the body may be recast more or less consciously by the subject, leading to novel and transgressive stances towards patriarchal power, including cross-dressing (Butler 2006 [1990]), anorexia (Bordo 2003 [1993]) and extreme body art (Pitts 2003). But stepping out from social pressures around normative standards of beauty can be less drastic than that. In an ethnographic study of a beauty salon, Frida Kerner Furman (1997) gives voice to older women, who, in a sexist and ageist society, are frequently invisible as such. The older, mostly Jewish clients of Julie's International Salon interviewed by Furman articulate their experiences of bodily self-presentation, femininity, ageing and caring. They demonstrate their capacity to compensate for the negative effects of ageing in terms of body appearance and functionality by taking advantage of a greater freedom from obligations, emotional growth and a sense of contentment with being alive.

Men's bodies in patriarchy

One further argument against interpreting beauty care as a power substitute in a patriarchal world is that it is nowadays not just a woman's domain. For a long time, of course, virility was based on scorn for vanity and low regard for bodily appearance, especially under the productivist ethos of Fordist societies and their ideology of the *male breadwinner*, father of the family, devoted to work and uninterested in his appearance (Connell 2005a; Kimmel 2018 [1996]). The market for body products was in fact very cautious in wooing the male public at the time. But with the post-industrial restructuring of production, with the expansion of the service economy, it became necessary for the corporate man to interact with customers and clients and develop interpersonal skills and looking good. The bounds of male heterosexuality have extended to the use of explicit beauty products and eroticizing of the body. Men are expected to be more responsible for their appearance (Bordo 1999), a change which has been set down to mass-media culture, consumerism, the gay rights movement and feminism. If middle-class *metrosexual* (Salzman, Matathia & O'Reilly 2005) man, liberated from former codes of conduct, can now indulge in open and eager purchase of products enhancing the body with no fear of eccentricity or overstepping the limits of heterosexual normality, it is because heterosexual masculinity has broadened its confines.

Tristan Bridges (2014) explores various sides to the masculine hybridization discourse, in which young white heterosexual men admit to adopting features that were once associated with marginalized individuals (non-white, gay, lower-class trappings of masculinity and sometimes even of femininity). But Bridges is quick to point out that this by no means represents a challenge to sexual inequalities since it brands certain features of gay culture as 'gay', carrying on the belief that sexuality is pre-social and symbolically confirming the boundaries between gay and straight. Secondly, while the men observed theoretically departed from specific patterns of dominant masculinity, they were not necessarily against reaping the privileges that go with it. Kristen Barber's (2008) ethnographic work in a small Southern California men's hair salon reaches very similar conclusions. The author illustrates how white, middle-class, heterosexual men engage in beauty work formerly coded 'feminine' by highlighting their heterosexuality (e.g., by preferring being massaged by female professionals, or by stating that they do not want to look stylish for themselves; rather, they need to look good to succeed professionally). At the same time, they also naturalize distinctions between themselves and working-class men (e.g., by positioning themselves as classy and enjoying the beauty salon as different from the barbershop where men talk about beer, women, sports and cars). This contributes to their reproduction of gender and class hierarchies despite being involved in activities which transgress boundaries.

Clearly a new image of masculinity is circulating: more prepared to look after children, do the shopping, express feelings and a series of things that were once codified as feminine. Some research reveals how displaying the fact that one has worked on the body may be a source of pleasure and not a threat to one's masculinity (Holliday & Cairnie 2007). That is not to say that male prerogatives in terms of power have been waived: the 'new man' can also be viewed as a form of masculinity better suited to retaining or reviving patriarchal control over women in the contemporary age, including aesthetic flaunting of his muscles (Connell & Messerschmidt 2005). A whole range of studies, often called 'inclusive masculinity theory' (Anderson 2009) and based largely on observation of peer-group dynamics, show that many types of heterosexual male are more prone to voicing their emotions, accepting body proximity and condemning homophobia. But not for that do they shake off the underlying fear of being stigmatized as gay, nor does this necessarily entail more tactility or emotional openness across all social classes (McCormack 2014; for a different account of the relationship between hybrid masculinity and hegemonic masculinity and whether hybrid masculinities are 'shifts in – rather than changes to – systems of power and inequality', see Bridges & Pascoe 2014, 256).

According to Kathy Davis (2003), the prevailing connotations of the male body still tether it to feigned irrelevance, meaning that its needs or vulnerabilities must be transcended by rationality; or to the sphere of action, meaning it is essentially a performing body, a body that 'does' and is 'ready to do', not one to which things 'are done'; something that holds even when performance and aesthetic body culture go hand in hand. Hence the act of going to a beautician, for example, still symbolizes transgression of the rules, so that men need greater justification when they openly confess to it. Studies in this field also show that the danger of sounding effeminate or vain is neutralized by deliberately playing up the social and psychological, but not physical, advantages of beauty practices (Adams 2010; Holliday & Cairnie 2007), or else by ironic detachment (Gill, Henwood & McLean 2005), which goes to confirm the idea that focusing on appearance is a woman's prerogative. In other words, men nowadays claim the right to bodily self-determination, but the upshot is still in line with the historical position: aesthetic body care is not expected to increase masculinity to the same extent as it will femininity, since beauty still bears a specific gender identity (Davis 2003; Dull & West 1991).

2. The medicalization of ugliness

'Get the body of your dreams with our world class services and state-of-the-art technologies'; 'Rhinoplasty can improve the appearance and proportion of your nose enhancing facial harmony'; 'Have you experienced the fullness of your breast and want the volume back?'; 'Correct your asymmetries'; 'This powerful surgical improvement is for facial rejuvenation to reposition underlying tissues and smooth over skin, effectively erasing years from your appearance'. Nowadays it is common to talk of unsightliness in medical or pathological terms, as these advertisements show. A wrinkled face is one that 'has lost congruence with the bone structure', a small breast needs an 'enhancement surgery' meant to 'improve its fullness, shape, and contours', or to fill up 'the excess, or droopy, skin'; blepharoplasty removes the 'excess skin' resulting from 'eyelids stretching with age', and 'the weakening of the muscles'. According to Peter Conrad (2007), we are facing a widespread medicalization of society where recourse to medical-style frameworks has expanded onto new planes of social life. Now even ugliness and outward signs of ageing have been sucked into this mill, so that more and more goods and services are designed to fit the body into (Caucasian) standards of beauty and youthfulness, legitimized by scientific language and new technologies. As Foucault argued, application of medical knowledge has historically been a privileged space for defining normality and deviance, and also for the fabrication of the self (Osborne 1994), since it teaches one to view the body as a terrain for intervention. The whole history of medicine is punctuated with new techniques and routine checks and practices that have rendered bodies legible and perfectible in numerous ways.

The link between beauty and medicine has roots deep in the past. In his historical reconstruction of Western techniques of beautification, Bruno Rémaury (2000) showed them to have been viewed in ancient times as a shameful women's affectation, but nonetheless a medical-hygienist vision of body care continued to coexist and came to the fore at the dawn of the modern age. From the late nineteenth century on, in particular, cosmetic techniques, especially targeting middle-class women in countries of the Global North, swept the manufacturing market, promoted and legitimized increasingly by the language of fitness. Broader and broader swaths of the population came to see unsightly features as incompatible with the demands of daily living, while tolerance of ugliness diminished in all social classes. The body needed constant embellishment but also inner and outer cleansing. If it were neglected, it would degenerate (white hair, wrinkles, flab) or be contaminated by atmospheric agents and pollution.

The history of cellulite is a case in point. It has been shown (Ghigi 2004) that in the second half of the nineteenth century, French doctors and masseurs began claiming the existence of inflamed subcutaneous nodules all over the body. The term was coined for what we now identify as localized infiltrations on the thighs and buttocks which a host of products and treatments are claimed to offset (creams, massage, special garments). In those times the points where this 'wholly feminine' pathology was located differed from nowadays: in the 1920s, when cellulite became a proper 'maladie à la mode', many French women wrote to magazines complaining that they could see and feel it on the back of the neck and the ankles, while doctors suggested exercises and products to eliminate it. As more female flesh and body contours went on display to the public gaze according to the changing rules of fashion and decency, women were induced by magazines, masseurs, cosmetic sellers and beauty doctors to feel the need to treat this medicalized 'problem' of cellulite. And cellulite got 'relocated' by medical gaze, now affecting the thighs, the calves and the buttocks. Likewise, the doctors appearing in the magazines kept changing their tune about its composition: from 'lymphatic congestion' to 'absorption of toxins via the intestinal mucosa', or 'degenerate flesh, a mixture of water and matter closer to urine than to blood' (ibid., 67).

The so-called 'enemy even of skinny women' crossed the frontiers of other European countries during the 1940s and washed up in the United States at the end of the 1960s in the magazine *Vogue*. The cellulite epidemic thus went through its historical phases, spreading a fatphobic message: war on fat, blaming the overweight for lack of will-power (Fischler 1990; Stearns 1997). This example, like the story of acne (Brumberg 1997) and a host of other stories, is a clear indication of how the branding of bodily unsightliness as pathological altered its targets. What is interesting to note is the constant refrain: cellulite is a woman's thing and a spontaneous degeneration of her body.[1] Just like around 1890 technology and dentists' talk historically 'invented' the mouth as a discrete entity, an organ to manage and monitor constantly, separate from the rest of the body (Nettleton 1994), so products and services available on the market turned adult female flesh into something separate and sick.

The history of cellulite is part of a more general fat phobia culture, which spread over the last two centuries especially in Western societies and was haunted by moral judgements. The social stigmatization of obesity began in the closing decades of nineteenth-century Europe and the United States when stylists, physicians and nutritionists started painting it as something negative invading the body without forming part of it, while the media joined in with praise for dieting and weight control (Fischler 1990; Monaghan 2008; Stearns 1997). As we have seen (see chapter 3), the sociologist Sabrina Strings, through a historiographical exploration, illustrates the racialized roots of the thinness ideal. In the United States, fatness became stigmatized as both black and sinful. And by the early twentieth century, slenderness was increasingly promoted in the popular media as the correct embodiment for white Anglo-Saxon Protestant women.

In fact, Strings shows, fat phobia did not originate with medical findings, as one might think, but with the Enlightenment-era belief that fatness was a sign of 'savagery' and racial inferiority. 'Savage' blackness was juxtaposed to the disciplined whiteness and the discourse of fatness as 'immoral' and 'black' worked to denigrate Black women. During the eighteenth and nineteenth centuries, body size became a sign of race, morality and national identity. Today, in relation to the alleged 'obesity epidemic' in the United States, poor

Black women are particularly stigmatized as 'diseased' and a burden on the public healthcare system. And so are mothers, as Natalie Boero (2009) pointed out. A long-lasting discourse of mother blame in popular and professional understandings has historically created 'bad mothers' to explain phenomena as wide ranging as homosexuality, crime, autism, depression, poverty and birth defects. Today, mother blame is expressed in (especially working) mothers' moral reproachment about the size of their children, as being too permissive and passing on bad eating habits. Adopting a 'bad mothers' discourse, Boero notes, obscures very real discriminations and inequalities based on race, class, gender and fat phobia.

Cosmetic surgery

Standing as it does midway between medicine and the market, cosmetic surgery is the most striking phenomenon in the whole process of medicalization of ugliness. It began in the late nineteenth century as an independent branch of plastic surgery,[2] and in the course of the twentieth swept the world, finding its way into the daily discourse of men and especially women of every social class, age, race and nationality. As Deborah Sullivan (2001) showed, this stemmed from a determined publicity drive by surgeons in the media, especially in periodicals, but it was also helped by the coincidence of various favourable circumstances, such as the honing of techniques, greater affluence, a widespread consumer turn, changes in healthcare systems and the development of a profit-oriented health culture (Gimlin 2012). More generally speaking, it was the culmination of long-maturing cultural dynamics: the democratization of beauty as a right/duty, and the quest for happiness via changing one's body and shaking off inferiority complexes (Gilman 1999; Haiken 1997). Small wonder, then, that cosmetic surgery has been studied by many sociologists, especially since the 1990s.

Given the strong gender association (even today almost nine out of ten patients are women[3]), cosmetic surgery has mostly been studied by feminist sociologists, combining critiques of the cultural background with attention to patients' individual testimony and views on the phenomenon (Heyes & Jones 2009). Many studies based on media messages and interviews have focused on the cultural violence which forces women to embody an ageless youth, the outcome of patriarchal domination and conditioning by the media and the cosmetics industry (Blum 2003; Sullivan 2001). The more radical versions describe such surgery as based on a fundamental 'deception': that one can take one's life in hand by working on one's body (Jeffreys 2015 [2005]; Morgan 1991).

Other social analysts have gone deeper into their interviews using techniques of ethnographic observation, often reaching a softer judgement. Julien Mirivel (2007) analysed the language and gestures of (female) patient–surgeon meetings at a small US clinic, captured on video recordings. The study emphasized the surgeon's need to talk of cosmetic surgery as medically relevant though without appearing like a salesman, balancing the roles of gatekeeping (of the patient's expectations) and marketing (of the service). However, the patient does have an active role, co-constructing her body as a medical issue, hence a candidate for surgery, though she needs to reassure the surgeon that her expectations are realistic. Likewise, Davis (1995), in her already mentioned research on Dutch patients, shows that the interviewees are well aware of being under pressure to make their body conform to a norm, but they do display a certain agency, as being protagonists seeking a change in their own right.

What emerges altogether is a tension between ideals and practice of which the patients are often conscious: they skilfully dose declarations of appropriation with a defensive attitude, making light of the operation, but also talking of the sense of liberation and the advantages it brought (Adams 2010; Atkinson 2008; Gill, Henwood & McLean 2005; Gimlin 2002; Holliday & Cairnie 2007). In a similar vein, Samantha Kwan and Jennifer Graves (2020) shed light on the paradox of the 'natural fake', the desire of a natural-looking but surgically altered body. Based on interviews with women from diverse backgrounds in California around their motivation to have cosmetic surgery (such as breast augmentation, tummy tuck, liposuction, facelifts, etc.), the authors show how women handle and negotiate surgery meanings, complications and disappointments. For example, they assert that they do not aim to totally transform their appearance, but, rather, to enhance their natural look and 'restore' the 'authentic' appearance they enjoyed when younger. No matter their race or class, they engage in sometimes contradictory boundary work to distance themselves from 'surgical others' who had 'bad' (i.e., fake-looking) procedures, or misinterpretations of what surgical procedures should be. The result was generally felt as empowering but, on the other side, many women's satisfaction with the results had changed over time and they had to keep on managing their postoperative body.

The most subtle analyses draw the appropriate distinction between the individual's expressed viewpoint and the social factors that lie behind it. In one study on Asian-American women in San Francisco the ethnographer Eugenia Kaw (1993) quotes patients' accounts of how they changed their facial features closer to a Western model. 'They all stated that an eyelid without a crease and a nose that does not project indicate a certain "sleepiness", "dullness", and "passivity" in a person's character' (ibid., 79). It is intriguing to note how, in blending a modern image with a sense of activeness and the Western social model, these women had introjected a racial ideology whereby natural Asian features equal passivity and lack of emotion. It is precisely 'the medicalization of racial features, which reinforces and normalizes Asian American women's feelings of inadequacy, as well as their decision to undergo cosmetic surgery', Kaw comments (1993, 86; for a critique of this analysis, see Heyes 2009).

All in all, though, the picture that emerges from such studies is one of individual choice within powerful structural pressures, both a gratifying and an oppressive position. Cosmetic surgery is a means of controlling women via their bodies, but also a way women can exercise control over some dimensions of their lives. As Davis (1991, 33) puts it, 'Feminist theory on beauty needs to be grounded; that is, it must take the ambiguous, contradictory, everyday social practices of women as its starting point.'

3. Body management: from fitness to body art

Among the most popular body-transforming practices in the Global North is now a growing attention to fitness, involving commercial gyms and wellness centres. For many people these have taken the place of sport as a leisure activity. But unlike doing sport (Bourdieu 1978; Heikkala 1993), fitness does not aim to provide any specific skills (such as tapping a ball over a net in coordination with five other players as in volleyball, or swimming a set distance as fast as possible in a set style, competing against other athletes) but to work on the body to make it more responsive and alluring in daily life, keeping it youthful, trim, with toned muscles, etc. All in all, the fit body has been branded as an icon of the neoliberal order, demonstrating the subject's capacity to work on itself and to achieve ever more demanding goals (Martschukat 2021 [2019]).

Possibly because of its growing popularity across genders, the fitness craze has met with conflicting diagnoses (Sassatelli 2010a). It has been hailed as democratization of sport open to segments of the population, like women, that used to be excluded from sport as a recreation, or it has been decried as the triumph of consumer narcissism and a signal that postmodern hedonism is gaining ground.

The success of Jane Fonda's aerobic videos in the 1980s, for example, was interpreted by feminist thinkers as evidence that women are still victims of a patriarchal regime that forces them to pay undue attention to their outward appearance (Dinnerstein & Weitz 1998). Various other points have been raised by feminist studies: that the aerobic fixation with fat is akin to the obsessions of women with eating disorders; that constant monitoring of self during exercise does not liberate women's lives but makes them less inclined to accept their bodies; or that the aerobic turn is tightening up the norms of femininity and once again segregating women's sports (Lloyd 1996; Maguire & Mansfield 1998).[4] As the range of fitness activities expanded and fitness culture developed, a number of studies have highlighted the ambivalent potential of keep-fit exercise for women: femininity is increasingly associated with a strong body which challenges the classical skinny portrayal of women while continuing to mirror the hegemonic archetype of attractive and heteronormative femininity (Boepple, Ata, Rum & Thompson 2016; Washington & Economides 2016).

Such works have highlighted important issues; but in order to grasp the mechanisms by which keeping fit takes on significance for those who devote themselves to it, one has to delve beyond a simplistic equation between body workout or modification and superficiality or manipulation. Again, taking Davis's suggestion of observing women's everyday social practices, we need to go right into the world of the gym and look at how the layout and exercises are planned and how an institution can respond to a host of complex and sometimes contradictory demands (Sassatelli 2010a).

Going to the gym is definitely a voluntary act. Yet once inside, customers must reckon with an environment that compels them to work out: a world with rules of its own, designed to aid and maintain focus on performing set physical activities. Gym goers typically appreciate the environment for driving them to work, and keep working, on their bodies even when they least feel like it. They derive the intrinsic gratification of being able to stand the pace, something which partly acts as a filter for the body ideals on which fitness is based. Nonetheless, keep-fit activities promote the ideal of fitness and that is what inspires those who practise them. Ever-developing though fitness activities always are, there are certain physical characteristics that appear to play a hegemonic role (Dworkin & Wachs 2009; Labre 2005; Markula 1995; Sassatelli 2016). The notion of being in good physical shape, for instance, hinges on the idea of energy and other factors like toned muscles, strength, resilience, agility, suppleness, vascular capacity, breathing and so on. Fitness embraces a set of body-related aspirations as assets to use in everyday life. It is reflected in a toned, supple body emphasizing its strength, energy and efficiency. A fit body, in short, is a sign of health, youth, potential, performance and attractiveness. The fitness fan is asked to recognize that you don't achieve the right bodily appearance without being fit or in good form and that a fit body is the best symptom of good health.[5]

The dual connotations of fitness – work on the body as in a gym, and the body this produces – thus become a primary and hegemonic value, so to speak. This joins together aesthetics and function: the aesthetics of function underpinning fitness seek not a large, but a strong, responsive, agile body, a youth-centred androgynous ideal that values toned, supple and well-defined muscles rather than the bulging kind. Partly thanks to the fitness craze, there has been a fashion for sports and physical recreation that blurs certain features of the male/female opposition, where one can find a strong mediation by business interests, but also the downplaying of competition and an emphasis on fun (Sassatelli 2010a). Yet even in unisex sports cultures, women can not only bolster qualities traditionally thought of as masculine, such as strength and courage, but at the same time, as though in compensation or defiance, they are inclined to exhibit traits of traditional femininity, for instance in their dress code, nail art and body allure. Thus, when doing a sport apparently devoid of gender distinction, like windsurfing, researchers have suggested that women seem to make up for the masculine overtones of sport by sticking to aspects of traditional femininity, with the erotic and the emotional to the fore (Wheaton & Tomlinson 1998). Still, as a study of female climbers observed (Dilley 2012), the display of traditional feminine traits in clothing may act as a subversive move which qualifies the femininity centred on bodily prowess and bravery they are embracing.

Although women's boxing entered the Olympics in 2012, prompting a spate of research on women who pursue boxing and other contact sports (Nash 2015; Paradis 2012), sport is still one of the crucial arenas of reproduction of a combative masculinity. Through contact sports, males are socialized into appreciating danger, toughness and physical strength. It is hardly surprising that research into masculine identity in sport often focused on violence (McKay, Messner & Sabo 2000). Boxing is unlike fitness and wellness activities, which teach practitioners to find pleasure in routine, order and discipline, as far as possible risk-free. As Loïc Wacquant (2004) writes in his well-known ethnographic research, boxing leads to the acquisition of resistance to the excitement of violence, to take risks without letting it get the upper hand, to face violence in a tough, natural manner. In men's case, the practice of contact sports geared to aggression generally not only seems correlated with a natural recourse to violence outside the sporting setting, but also reinforces the impression that men are more violent, thus naturalizing one of the standard gender stereotypes about masculinity.

Body art

Physical exercise is not the only way people voluntarily remodel their body, however. Forms of mutilation, decoration or application of surface accessories are common practices, attributing social and cultural messages to the human body that we may find in all societies. Some of them today, such as make-up, hair dyeing and ear piercing, are performed across the population on a fairly routine basis. In his research into the way people relate their experience with body alteration, Nick Crossley (2005) found it was rare to hear practices such as these described as a 'project' calling for at least some minimal act of reflection by the individual. However, more radical, permanent and invasive manipulations of one's own appearance fitted Giddens's notion of a 'body project' more closely (see chapter 2) and elicited greater justification in people's account of their own life story.

'Body art' is one such. By this term we normally mean a range of techniques including tattooing, body piercing, scarification, branding and permanent make-up – all of which were long thought of as deviant behaviour in Western society. Tattoo and piercing are the commonest forms of body art in the Global North. As Margo DeMello (2000) points out, the practice of permanently colouring the skin made its European debut in the late eighteenth century, chiefly among sailors, artisans, criminals and slaves. Since then, it has had a fluctuating reception, ranging from exotic fascination to outspoken hostility for being a barbaric tradition. Little by little, prisoners began to decorate their bodies with tattoos, assuming an identity that was once fraught with stigma. With the advent of capitalist consumerism, techniques and apparatus had reached a high pitch; permanent decoration of the skin came in among certain kinds of Americans and Europeans who wished to proclaim their worldly sophistication and artistic leanings. At the end of the nineteenth century, most tattooists' customers were from the military, especially the navy, who got tattooed with sailor, soldier and military symbols. But any women also were, and soon became attractions in travelling showbusiness in the United States. As DeMello describes it (2000, 57–8):

In the 1880s, however, tattooed women arrived on the scene and upstaged men completely. This was because they had to show their bodies (legs and thighs) to display their tattoos and during the Victorian period it was considered quite racy to see a woman's thighs. Another aspect of their appeal was that tattooed women were seen as docile and chaste, which was an exciting contrast to the idea of tattoos, which had only been seen on men. While men were tattooed on their hands and neck, tattooed women left their neck, hands, and heads free of tattoos to appear modest when wearing clothes – and so that they could have an alternate career when they retired from show business.

Over time, tattooing took on a new connotation, being typical of especially working-class men. During the first half of the twentieth century until the 1970s, women were largely absent from the tattoo scene: 'nice' (middle-class, attractive, heterosexual) girls and ladies did not get tattoos. Especially in the 1940s and 1950s, the tattoo culture in the United States was a masculine world. Only from the 1950s on did tattooing catch on among dissident youth subcultures in Europe and the United States: bikers, hippies (DeMello 2000) and above all punks (Hebdige 2003 [1979]). The practice of transgressive bodily *bricolage* grew: ordinary objects would be turned into gadgets for piercing and decorating the body, which conferred group identity. DeMello continues (2000, 77):

> With the peace, gay, and women's liberation movements came new designs that were both more feminine and also appealed to middle-class tastes more than the classic working-class designs. Peace symbols; the yin/yang image; astrological signs; and animals like dolphins, butterflies, rabbits, and kittens (considered more feminine), began showing up on women's shoulders, breasts, and ankles, and also on young middle-class men's bodies.

As Clinton Sanders (2008 [1989]) remarks, body art at that time was labelled by critics and practitioners alike as a sign of disaffection with society. Gradually other subcultures took up tattoo and piercing as marks of belonging: heavy metal fans, skinheads and many rock stars. Erotic and neotribal forms of body piercing, not to mention scarification and branding, gained a certain popularity among gay and lesbian sadomasochist (SM) communities as the 1980s turned into the 1990s. As Victoria Pitts (2003) points out, many contemporary subcultures of protest, like the Modern Primitives, the Queer movement and BDSM, took over radical forms of body art to express their rejection of contemporary Western values, especially individualism, destruction of the ecosystem, and capitalism, and overtly challenge the normative boundaries of gender, sexuality and ethnicity. As a whole, such cultures of protest share the idea that the body is political in being the prime place of social control and regimentation, though it is also an arena upon which to enact powerful alternative identities (Wojcik 1995; see chapter 3).

Many sociologists now agree that the transgressive potential of body art became enfeebled by commercialization as styles typical of consumer culture came onto the market. From the late 1980s on, many forms of body art were included in mainstream culture and became mass phenomena with a turnover of billions. The rise of body art is still more pronounced among the younger generations in need to assert control over their own changing bodies through permanent embellishment bearing the hallmarks of authenticity (or so they hope; see also chapter 5). As Fred Davis (1992) points out, the antifashion spirit of such rebel subcultures has more in common with middle-class taste than with ethnic minorities and marginal groups: their styles display 'more subversion from inside than opposition from outside the system'. But the widespread popularity of body art across the lines of gender, ethnicity, age and social class also stems from overt promotion by the music industry and media culture, as well as a marketing boom (Atkinson 2004) that has stressed the popular roots of tattoo to make it more attractive to new segments of the population.

However, even in its commercial forms, according to some (Randall & Polhemus 1996), body art expresses a wish for continuity, community and commitment to stemming fragmentation and anonymity. While wholeness, health and handsomeness of the body are praised in consumer culture, the violation of the organism by cutting, scarifying or branding would anyhow mark a challenge to the dominant ideology. Michael Atkinson (2003), with an ethnographic work on tattoo enthusiasts, shows that for those indulging in it, body art stands distinct from more ephemeral alterations to the body surface: its being so hard to reverse sounds like a rejection of capitalist consumer ideology with its praise for social mobility and endless modification. Another line altogether is taken by Bryan Turner (2000) who argues that the meaning and motivation behind tattooing are signs of individualistic self-expression, not statements of belonging to some community. In such interpretation, body art is 'optional, decorative, impermanent and narcissistic' (ibid., 42), and marking the body surface is just a playful attempt to cope with alienation.

Whatever its meaning in relation to consumer culture, body art is also an embodied practice and can be studied as such. Analysing how the painful side to body art is borne, Paul Sweetman (1999) and David Le Breton (2005) both claim that bleeding, pain and healing spring from the need to focus on self and make the subject reflect more deeply on what her or his body is going through. This is far from neutral with regard to gender and the construction of subjectivity, though. Traditional conceptions of 'hegemonic masculinity' associate it with strength, risk-taking and the ability to withstand pain and injury. So having one's own body tattooed or pierced could be experienced as a subversion of gender norms for heterosexual women not just in relation to the history of body art, which has long been masculine, but also in relation to the experience of having the body inked or tattooed as such. This is one of the issues raised by Michael Atkinson (2003) studying tattoo enthusiasts in Canada. By exploring the interpretation attributed to their tattoos, interviews revealed a composite variety of meanings and experiences ascribed to their body art, expressing culturally established, but also resistant, and negotiated images of femininity. Indeed, many women took their tattoo as signifier of 'hegemonic masculine' constructions of femininity, for example as a means to enhance their body aesthetically or to sexualize it. But for others, marking the skin can be a privately negotiated act of dissent or even, especially for those heavily tattooed, a flagrant crusade into a historically masculine body practice. Ethnographic research by Beverly Yuen Thompson (2015; 2019) similarly shows that heavily tattooed women feel they challenge the dominant beauty culture. For some of them, this entails fiercely showing off their body art; for others, hiding their tattoos from their family members.

In this chapter we have seen how power, gender and body appearance are strictly related to each other. We have seen that for centuries beauty has been considered a sort of 'poisoned' gift: it confers power, but vicarious or ephemeral, distinct from the advantages of authority. The value placed on body care and outward appearance has changed accordingly. Over time – and especially with the advent of modern capitalism and the consumer society – beauty has ceased to be a gift: it became a result. It is the result of self-disciplines imposed on the body, presented as free self-expression and gratifying, and related to meritocratic visions of body works. Feminism has interpreted the pressure to be beautiful differently, considering it both as a tool of patriarchy, as well as a value to invest in, and a practice to be explored from the subjective point of view of those who engage in it. From this perspective, male beauty care challenges many of the classic feminist positions, even if empirical research shows how it ends up confirming the asymmetries of power between men and women and the construction of female subjectivity. We then saw how in contemporary society body modification, sometimes legitimized by the scientific language of medicine, can be experienced as oppressive and gratifying at the same time. We now turn to another aspect of the visualization of gendered bodies, moving from social interactions and everyday practices to media contents.

7

Visualizing Gendered Bodies

In 2017 Adidas launched a new campaign. At first sight, the model, the Swedish artist Arvida Byström, appears as a conventional petite blonde. Her dress is a soft pink with laces and ribbons. She sports white Adidas shoes with pink socks. As the camera pans in, we see that her legs are unshaved. The hair on her legs is apparently the only non-conforming detail in a body which Byström herself pointed out on Instagram is otherwise 'abled, white, cis'. Indeed, her posture, sitting sideways on the floor with her legs crossed, as well as her glances and gestures, underlined a conventional femininity using the codes that advertising conventionally deploys to do gender in visual images.

The advert received quite heated and very mixed reactions. Byström in particular reported harsh criticism and even violent threats for her choice of being unshaved. The advert tapped into a taboo. Women removing their body hair has become increasingly widespread in contemporary society, at least since the first decades of the twentieth century (Hope 1982; Synnott 2002 [1993]). Indeed, it is used to stress femininity in a binary gender order whereby male and female bodies are constructed as different and opposed. The ad campaign addresses what is a mundane reproduction of normative femininity as women overwhelmingly construct body hair removal as a taken-for-granted practice that produces an 'acceptable' femininity (Toerien, Wilkinson & Choi 2005).

Women who don't conform to hair removal norms are perceived as dirty, gross and repulsive (Lesnik-Oberstein 2006), their very femininity being put into question. This is especially true for Black women and working-class women: being too hairy in the wrong places makes them excessive and adds to the other aspects of their marginalization (Fahs & Delgado 2011). But there is more to the advert. In it Byström claims: 'I think femininity is usually created from our culture, I think everybody can do feminine things, can be feminine. And I think in today's society we are very scared of that!'. We may indeed consider the advert as suggesting that femininity is produced through specific bodily practices and ensuing representations whose normativity obscures their constructive role. We may consider that it is in fact enlarging the way femininity may be portrayed and experienced. And yet, to do femininity, as suggested, a number of conventional codes were deployed: it is precisely because of the success of these codes that Byström could be seen as a woman, and that the detail of the unshaven legs was able to stand out and become the object of criticism.

Advertising reveals often in extreme, typified form many aspects of our bodily culture and it is a fundamental source of body ideals. More often than not, it plays on gender binaries and what is commonly accepted as femininity and masculinity. In our daily lives we are confronted by colourful advertising: maybe a young woman seductively simpering in a swimsuit, another with a cheerful smile presents the latest in dental cleaning to the sleepy companion, another all agog at her gleaming floor so magically cleaned of her thoughtless little boy's footprints. Or again, it may be a man smugly driving his car through a wood, or hugging a silent ecstatic girl, or sipping his coffee in a double-breasted suit, or nonchalantly displaying his muscular chest as he clutches a favourite aftershave.

Such poses reinforce the facile, and yet insidious, gender stereotypes, as usual taking blithely for granted not just the difference but the inequality between men and women. If once again we mentally invert the genders as displayed, the lack of symmetry will be evident: in some, status is being pumped up, in others demeaned. Any deviance from the norms regulating the acceptable visibility of gender and of other intersecting axes of identification would receive strong reaction, and sometimes advertising plays precisely on this. As Byström herself commented on social networks, 'I can't even begin to imagine what it's like to not possess all these privileges [being able, white and cis] and try to exist in the world'.

As distilled forms of culture and cultural differences, advertising images have been the target of much criticism, from feminist scholars in particular. Hardly surprising, therefore, advertising may wink at feminism and play on reversals and traditionally devalued bodily aspects. It was some decades ago that the cosmetic sector began campaigns – such as the 2004 Dove campaign for 'real beauty', carving the brand out as a site for female activism about the dominant ideology of beauty (Murray 2013), or the classic 1997 The Body Shop anti-Barbie doll Ruby with her rounder silhouette offering an example of 'commercial reflexivity' (Sassatelli 2010b) – which selectively embraced elements of feminist criticism claiming to place emphasis on 'self-esteem'.

As we shall see in this chapter, images of the gendered body are a battlefield. How bodies are portrayed by advertising and the media plays a crucial role in gender politics, and we must consider them closely to appreciate not only their surface claims but also the way bodies are engaged through taken-for-granted mannerisms. Images make powerful statements about gender and the body; we may not think about them, they are a sort of wallpaper in our daily lives, but their immediacy strikes home. Or they may be controversial and paradoxical, teasing us into discussing them for the issues they raise about male, female, freedom of expression, entrenched differences, inequality and the reproduction of inequalities. The following pages will deal with the visual representation of gendered bodies in the media, inspecting the ways these interact with age-old stereotypes and new forms of representation. While for a long time women's bodies have been displayed through ritualized forms of submission, in recent times advertising is proposing more active and 'empowered' images of femininity. Indeed, what we may find in the media is the persistence of inequality together with the development of new images of men's and women's bodies which contribute to complicate the image of the gendered body and of gender itself.

1. The male gaze

The images of the body proposed by a range of cultural products – from Hollywood cinema to TV talk shows, from video games and comics to ads in the press, from plays at the theatre to Instagram memes – tend to be coded by gender. Laura Mulvey's work, especially, has been a decisive influence on the way cinema and gender have been studied, paving the way for reading what we see on screen as holding a latent meaning that reflects the most entrenched classifications and hierarchies of the society and culture from which it derives. In her classic essay on cinema and visual pleasure, she develops the idea of the 'male gaze' (Mulvey 1989 [1975]; see King 2021). Mulvey argued that Hollywood classics reflected a patriarchal idiom steeped in the dominant gender differences, depicting women as objects not subjects, a materialization of the male unconscious, with no voice in their own right. The classic Hollywood film portrays a 'woman-object' via a masculine gaze that projects its fantasy onto the female figure in two ways – 'voyeuristic' (seeing the rebelling woman as a temptress and prostitute) or 'fetishist' (the docile redeeming woman portrayed as a virginal or maternal figure).[1]

Looking is structurally unbalanced, just as the social world itself is, says Mulvey (1989 [1975], 19): '(i)n a world ordered by sexual imbalance, pleasure in looking has been split between active/male and passive/female. The determining male gaze projects its fantasy onto the female figure which is styled accordingly'. Sexual difference is thus affirmed *relationally*: the view of the female depends on that of the male, and vice versa.

As Mulvey maintains, the viewer is invited to take pleasure from a particular arrangement of the viewpoints whereby the male hero acts while the women are observed and exhibited, their appearance 'coded to make a strong visual and erotic impact'. Women indeed somehow impersonate the essence of being gazed at: they are characterized by their *'to-be-looked-at-ness'*. From that relation there emerges a 'scopic regime' (Jay 1993) that fixes the gender identities in an irremediably hierarchical structure. The male gaze – which does not mean the gaze of individual males, but the way a certain culture defines its own way of looking as a representation system – basically circumscribes the woman as a body, and her body as an object of pleasure. The only form of identification left to the woman would thus be a kind of super-identification with herself as an image, an object of desire and pleasure, pain and suffering (Doane 1991). All she is offered is constant confirmation of a precise gender identity.

Though Mulvey's arguments have come under heavy fire – for embracing the heterosexual matrix, for example, and not giving due credit to the many possible different interpretations of men and women viewers (Creed 1993; Mirzoeff 2023 [1999]) – her work remains fundamental (Oliver 2017). Mulvey shows us the relational nature of gender identity and the important role played by the passivity/activity dynamic between the genders. To Mulvey, the fact of visual representation is crucial in the forming of gender identity, but the dominant or determining male gaze tends to make the effects of such representation weigh especially heavily on women. To appreciate the power of the gender order in coding artistic images, one need only play the gender-reversing game. Art critic Linda Nochlin (1989) did just that with minor artists of the late nineteenth century. In her work on power, women and art, she showed how art's gender conventions become manifest in pornographic picture postcards. If you invert the picture of a naked woman offering fruit (and actually offering herself to the male gaze and desires), and in its place put a male equivalent (a naked man wearing no more than shoes and socks and exhibiting fruit and himself), the lack of symmetry becomes apparent. The depiction of the woman strikes us as 'normal'; the man looks like a joke inviting a guffaw. So only women look right to us for exhibiting as sex objects, and representation of the contrary gaze may be shocking or disturbing (which ties up with our remarks on pornography in chapter 3).

Similar points emerged from the work of John Berger and his well-known *Ways of Seeing* (2008 [1972]) based on a popular series of BBC documentaries where he sifted the history of Western art to show how 'men *act* and women *appear*. Men look at women. Women watch themselves being looked at' (ibid., 47). Berger makes the apt point that we never just look at something, but inevitably imagine a relation between us and what we are beholding. In other words, the gaze is never innocent because it is positional, and the image succeeds in making the standpoint more obvious to us when it constructs us as a subject of the gaze.

Depiction of women in Western art from the Renaissance on contrives to place the viewer in a specific visual standpoint which in turn constructs masculinity as dominant and femininity as objectified (Leppert 2007). With the female nude, for example, a genre that gradually gained strength over time, woman is depicted as an object of male desire, passive and open to the onlooker's stare, which turns her into a spectacle of vanity (mirrors being a frequent feature), as often as not de-subjectified (she will tend to be looking at us through a mirror, putting the viewer into the position of a voyeur). The woman surveyed transforms herself into a spectacle, an object to be looked at. So, the female nude in art sets the relationship between men and women, and also that of women with themselves. To understand oil canvases from the European mainstream therefore means focusing not just on the kind of womanhood being conveyed, but also the type of masculinity targeted and legitimated, from which emerge the cultural coordinates on which the gender order is constructed. As Berger reminds us, images are not just important for what they show, but for what they don't show, for what they skate over or take for granted.

An intersectional lens

Like Mulvey, Berger himself rather takes heterosexuality for granted (the gaze they refer to is also heterosexual rather than simply male, it has been suggested), and does not contemplate the possibility of divergent forms of sexuality. The male gaze is also often racialized, as race is another of the aspects latent in images such as the classic female nude. We may thereby also speak of a 'white gaze' as suggested by George Yancy (2017) in his *Black Bodies, White Gazes: The Continuing Significance of Race in America.* Taking up Fanon's suggestions and deconstructing the white gaze, he demonstrates how it functions in everyday life being implicated in an ongoing oppression of Blacks. On the racist content latent in images, we may recall a celebrated essay by Paul Gilroy (1987) which considered a strategy of assimilation that is very much the order of the day, especially for subjects of colonial diasporas living in the Global North. Gilroy studied British electoral posters of the early 1980s at the height of the Thatcher era. One of them shows a young man of Afro-Caribbean origin smartly dressed in a dark suit, collar and tie, short hair, arms folded, legs slightly akimbo. The caption reads: 'Labour says he's black, Tories say he's British'. The would-be inclusive poster gives Black people a very precise collocation: they are 'in' if they forgo the assumed signs of ethnic belonging that the picture does not show (dreadlocks, casual attire, a less stiff posture, ethnic accoutrements). Inclusion by assimilation, therefore, cancelling out the Afro-Caribbean identity of Black subjects as they do not fit in with the dominant white middle-class idea of masculinity. Here the male gaze turns out to be not just tarred with gender hierarchy but also, intersectionally, with hierarchical ranking supported by ethnic and class classifications (see chapter 5).

The Black body is not only suppressed and tamed in the media, but also ceaselessly represented as 'other'. As bell hooks (2004) has shown in her *We Real Cool: Black Men and Masculinity*, the Black body is simultaneously feared and desired, especially in relation to masculinity and sexuality: '"hypermasculine Black male sexuality" is feminized and tamed by a process of commodification that denies agency and makes it serve the desires of others, especially white sexual lust' (ibid., 74). There has been a considerable increase in Black bodies appearing in advertisements and the media, but the differences, albeit increasingly subtle, have by no means disappeared (Downing & Husband 2005; Titley 2019). Advertising offers up plenty of symbolic resources that often rely upon dichotomies whereby visions of the feminine, the Black and the poor stand in opposition to the masculine, the white and the privileged. A Black body is sometimes put in publicity to give 'a note of colour' to an image of would-be pluralism, sometimes to convey a reassuring vision of assimilation of ethnic identities, and sometimes to contrast a specific ethnic and cultural look with that of the dominant white body. In their study of skin representation in advertising, Janet Borgerson and Jonathan Schroeder (2018) found that while racial categories are slippery and arbitrary, racial as well as gender categorizations are still very much in the picture. The softness of the skin is still associated with femininity and youthfulness and skin colour is used to portray the surface pluralism of 'racial mixing', where models' skin colour functions to reduce their identity to skin colour alone, masking deeper processes of racialization with the effect that categories are created based solely on the surface of the body itself turned into a supposedly reliable system of signs.

Images actively confer a position and a form on the individuals they depict (Pollock 1988). Clearly, the nature of the subject created by the gaze that is triggered by visual images – in art, advertising and elsewhere – is always evolving. Thus, as we shall elaborate further later, as the gender order has gradually changed, so has representation of the gendered body. To be sure, there has been a great increase in sexualized, objectified male images suggesting that the erotic and aesthetic body look is being included in the hegemonic male profile (see chapter 6). According to Susan Bordo (1999) in her *The Male Body*, this process is due to the coming out of gay and Afro-American culture, though it has not been matched by any greater relaxation about displaying the male body or inverting the traditional male-gaze subject into a male *object* of observation, especially if the new gaze is likewise male. But objectification and stigmatization are still heavier on Black women. Black feminist Moya Bailey (2021) coined the term 'misogynoir' to stress that misogyny weighs particularly on Black women, who are still portrayed in the media as more ugly, hypersexual and unhealthy than their non-Black counterparts; and has likewise documented the wealth of actions and discourses that Black women have developed especially on social media to confront anti-Black misogyny.[2]

We thereby need to observe the old and new male and female looks which are cropping up in media and advertising, critically considering how they relate to each other, and how they reproduce or modify dominant ways of seeing the body. Indeed, innovative images of the gendered body may conceal coded or tacit references to old-style hierarchies or harbour new contradictions and ambivalences which propose complex ways of visualizing gender.

2. Gendered bodies in advertising

Advertising is a fundamental source of body and gender representation in contemporary society. In advertising, representation of gender differences as related to bodily manners and appearances takes a special form: attitudes and styles are concentrated, overstated in the extreme. This may be called 'hyper-ritualization' (Goffman 1979). Hyper-ritualization proves to be based on open exaggeration, sometimes ironic, at times dreadfully earnest, of the ceremonial forms of gender difference that we all recognize from our everyday experience. For this reason, advertising is a rich source for our understanding of embodiment: it visualizes in a subtle and yet overstressed manner those differences which, in everyday life, often go unnoticed and at the same time works on our taken-for-granted feelings and categories.

Displaying gender differences and hierarchies

On these premises, in his influential book *Gender Advertisements*, Erving Goffman (1979) looks at the way gender is presented in advertising images. Goffman analysed a large corpus of print adverts from the 1970s considering the spatial and expressive micro-configurations of the images, such as the way bodies are positioned, movements are shown, gazes are organized, facial expressions are made, and so on. And he illustrates how they thus construct differences between the genders which then appear as 'natural'. For Goffman, advertising images distil the 'gender displays' which occur in everyday life. In everyday life, people create their own masculinity and femininity via a 'canvas of appropriate expressions' or 'gender displays'. Gender displays are customarily viewed as expressing an underlying pre-social reality ('sex'). Gender may hence be conceived of as a dramatization of ideal cultural views of male and female nature (see chapter 2). Yet what is natural, in both men and women, is their ability to learn to produce and interpret displays of masculinity and femininity and their desire to join in a precise scheme to create displays of the kind – 'this capacity they have by virtue of being persons, not females or males' (ibid., 8). Any scene, indeed, 'can be defined as an occasion for the depiction of gender difference, and in any scene a resource can be found for effecting this display' (ibid., 9). Shared cultural resources allow for such displays to be clear and often taken for granted by the doers and the onlooker.

In advertising, expressions of gender are realized through signals and symbols that are directly anchored in our body. That is precisely the language that visual representation in photographs captures (and exploits), especially in the hyper-ritualized form of commercial messages. They are snapshots not so much of real life as of a ritual idiom: a body idiom that usually places women in a subordinate position. Many of the images that Goffman analysed organized around what he called the 'child–parent complex'. This is a frame that holds together male–female relations and parent–child relations, whereby both children and females are placed under a 'paternalistic' custody. For example, one body ritual from everyday life as well as in advertisements is a woman leaning against a man who holds his arm around her. The result, Goffman comments, is that women obtain protection and care in exchange for a violation of their own sphere of privacy, autonomy and even their right to be treated as full individuals, as happens to children. Gender displays thus assert a basic structure of society in keeping women 'in their place'. These ritual displays make asymmetrical use of communication strategies like treatment as a non-person or benevolent control, extending from children to women: 'ritually speaking females are equivalent to subordinate males and both are equivalent to children' (ibid., 5).

Through what he calls 'pictorial pattern analysis', Goffman elaborated a number of categories which summarize the 'genderisms', that is the gendered codes of non-verbal behaviour, through which femininity and masculinity were displayed and portrayed. In their interlockings, men's bodies – action, posture, manner, gaze, movement, facial expression – tended to carry out ritualistic forms of domination and women's bodies tended to carry out ritualistic forms of submission. Once again, in Goffman's study, images tended to cast men as active and women as passive. When portrayed as engaged in an activity together, in particular, he observed the workings of 'function ranking' (ibid., 36ff.) among the genders: in ritual displays, the men were inclined to carry out the main active role, and the women the passive, decorative, subsidiary role. This was often coupled with 'relative size', whereby women are predominantly depicted as smaller and in lower positions than men. These are in turn reflected in the portrayal of 'the family': 'in the mocked-up families of advertisements one finds that the allocation of at least one girl and at least one boy ensures that a symbolization of the full set of intrafamily relations can be affected. For example, devices are employed to exhibit the presumed special bond between the girl and the mother and the boy and the father' (ibid., 37), underlining the binary construction of gender. Women's bodies were also shown to be cast more often as object, visually dissected in specific body parts, especially the hands, something that goes under the category of 'the feminine touch', or the fact that women more than men were shown stroking or hugging an object or gently touching themselves in a decorative way. We furthermore find the 'ritualization of subordination' with women being placed in lower positions, lying down or canting their head, knees and bodies and 'licensed withdrawal' with women, more than men, appearing to retreat from the situation at hand, withdrawing their gaze from the camera or closing their eyes, or being carried away by emotions.[3]

One of the powerful features of Goffman's analysis is his stress on the relationality of gender displays, so that he often considers how men and women reciprocally construct the genderisms at hand. The pictorial details may appear innocent, but the visible is often an invisible upholding of power differences and relations (Schwalbe 2022). Thus, for example, Anthony Cortese (2008) takes up his observations by documenting examples of women being portrayed in advertising as the object of what Goffman had called the 'mock assault' one plays with children, where the boundary between play and violence is subtle and compelling enough to make the image more powerful in an ever more crowded mediascape.

Over the years, Goffman's genderisms have been widely drawn upon, integrated and expanded in visual and media studies to consider advertising, social media and virtual communities (Belknap & Leonard 1991; Bell & Milic 2002; Cougar Hall, West & McIntyre 2012; Jha, Raj & Gangwar 2017; Kang 1997; Mager & Helgeson 2011; Milburn, Carney & Ramires 2001; Tsichla & Zotos 2016). Classic genderisms such as feminine touch, withdrawing gaze and laying posture as well as new social media-related categories (e.g., kissing pout and muscle presentation) dominate self-presentation on Instagram (Döring, Reif & Poeschl 2016). Even in music videos, female performers' displays of touching hair and delicate self-touch appear as consistent with Goffman's study of gender display in print advertisements (Wallis 2011). Overall, some of his proposed genderisms, such as relative size and function ranking, have diminished in advertising portrayals of women while male depictions are moving from mere traditional masculine portrayals to a greater variety of roles, including decorative ones. Still, old ways of displaying gender have not disappeared. But they coexist with novel images of femininity and masculinity, which re-elaborate or overturn, at least in part, the active/passive dichotomy that lies at the core of Goffman's corpus.[4]

Towards a new femininity

In contemporary advertisements we may find significant new trends that accommodate both the permanence of gender inequality and the emergence of new male and female subjectivities. In particular, from the 1970s onwards advertising has ridden the wave of protest or progressive movements, such as feminism (Goldman 1992). Rosalind Gill (2007a), for example, illustrates how the male and female image has changed in the media. The hybrid feminine image has arrived, such that it is fairly common to mix features of feminist awareness as to body choices with others depicting the more traditional woman – both of them locked into the consumer culture. One will find post-feminist femininity hinting at women's power as due to their active, provocative sexuality, or their consumer choice to improve their body according to cultural standards of youthfulness and beauty, or their bodily awareness and constant working upon their body.

In a recent study of advertising for middle- and upper-middle-class women in glossy magazines, Kirsten Kohrs and Rosalind Gill (2021) identify 'confident appearing' as a new tendency in the configuration of visual tropes for representing women which taps into (middle- and upper-middle-class) women's raising consciousness. In such adverts women are depicted (ibid., 358)

> head held high, face turned forward, eyes meeting the gaze of the viewer and looking directly back at her or him. Smiling is rare, and sometimes the gaze has an almost defiant aspect ... Other tropes in the visual construction of 'confident appearing' involve control or movement, for example with the figure of the woman striding confidently forward through an urban landscape. In such representations the stride is typically exaggerated – much longer than is actually typical of walking – to highlight a sense of a forward-moving woman.

This configuration, reinforced by suitable text which stresses power and choice, is clearly aimed to suggest self-belief, empowerment and confidence, and corresponds to a shift towards tropes of 'empowerment' which has been recognized as having four themes.

Besides empowerment we find 'an emphasis upon the body, a shift from objectification to sexual subjectification, a pronounced discourse of choice and autonomy' (Gill 2008, 41).

Such media images partly subvert the gender stereotypes and partly re-propose them in far subtler form (Gill 2007a; 2007b; 2008; Lazar 2014; 2017; McRobbie 2004). According to Michelle Lazar (2014), advertising often seeks to articulate feminist ideas and more traditional versions of femininity, incorporating bodily signals of emancipation and empowerment as well as circulating the assumptions that feminist struggles have come to fruition and can be ended so that women today can 'have it all'. Such contradictions can be traced in a variety of visual media. Advertising campaigns devoted to female empowerment and backed by major firms – promptly dubbed 'femvertising' – are a clear example. They claim to improve women's lot by fostering individual growth in awareness (as by women taking responsibility for their lack of self-confidence) but without mentioning the structural and collective conditions behind gender inequality – or of course that they are promoting brands and reducing social issues to consumer choices (Lazar 2014).

On this account, aesthetic labour is recontextualized as fun and play in cosmetics advertising (Lazar 2017), re-framing the traditional emphasis on beautification in terms of self-realization: while postfeminist culture has intensified the aesthetic regime of women, by increasing the scope and scale of perfecting the female body, the empowered, pleasurable, feminine subjectivities on offer in cosmetics advertising are set against a phantomatic vision of feminist critiques of power which are rejected as 'old school', 'censorious' and 'uptight'. In all this, the postfeminist woman, far from being a helpless victim, is situated as a willing participant, whose pursuit of beauty is a form of entrepreneurial, relentless and self-generated discipline in the name of personal desires (see chapter 6). The body becomes even more central to female subjectivity. In this view, she is sexualized not as an object, but as a subject choosing to pose as an apparent object since that suits her own free, active, strong, self-confident interest. So instead of being the object of a male gaze, such bodies become objects of a female gaze that has internalized the commercial pressure to take oneself in hand in the expansive, narcissistic way that suits consumerism and the dominant heterosexuality. As we shall see in the following pages, these trends in the representation of women and their bodies are thereby deeply ambivalent. In many respects, what is going on is simply a visual equivalent of that abduction of major feminist conquests regarding the body and sexuality which Nancy Fraser (2013) has so poignantly criticized.

3. Visions of gender in everyday images

Critical analysis of how men and women are depicted in the media and in other forms of visual communication has grown more widespread and sophisticated. Nowadays there are many forums for contesting gender stereotypes in the cultural products we consume, from the academe to the web. But though it is relatively easy to highlight and criticize classic stereotypes like woman as 'nothing but an obedient housewife' or 'just an eroticized body', or man as 'simply dominant' or 'just a fighter', it is harder to spot genderisms and ritualized displays of masculinity and femininity. Yet it is essential we understand how gender codes work in terms of bodies and communication, if we are to dig at all deeply into what we take for granted about our visual language.

To see how bodies are socially constructed in the media and in everyday images by the lens of gender one thus needs to read between the lines of visual discourse, which correlates more or less with written texts in a composite intertextual form (Kress & Van Leeuwen 1996). A broad output of essays and documentaries penetrate as far as the (albeit important) awareness of how the media hypersexualize bodies asymmetrically; they more rarely capture the genderisms in less overtly sexist images.[5] Gender-analytic glasses with thicker lenses nonetheless enable us to grasp how body politics are also at work in less evidently stereotyped ways of depicting masculinity and femininity.

Subtle stereotypes

For many decades, a wealth of research has demonstrated that media communications are imbued with traditional gender stereotypes, be it adverts, magazines or TV talk shows. Even today, few films would pass the Bechdel test. This famous test stemmed from a 1985 comic strip by Alison Bechdel, *Dykes to Watch Out For*, and set three simple criteria for rating a film as non-sexist: does it have at least two named women characters; do those two women talk to one another at any point; and, if they do, do they talk about a subject other than a man? But gender stereotyping cannot be reduced to a simple matter of role assignment: it is created by multiple semiotic elements interacting with one another.

Stereotyping is a multifaceted process. In toys advertising – a strikingly gendered media content – the traditional meanings of femininity and masculinity are reinforced not just by the fact that little girls are chosen for dolls or toy kitchens, while little boys are chosen for toy cars or monsters that squirt sticky green gunge. The gender attribution process is based on everything depicted, bodies and products, and it is produced in all the intertextual and compositional features of the advertising video or image. Beyond the content, commercials differ in terms of sound and technical picture specifications. Thus, while 'jingles' accompany all targets, they are likely classical or melodic in adverts for girls, but modern rock, pop or house music for boys. The rate at which the picture changes is faster in ads for boys, while fade-out is commoner in those for girls. Colours are brighter and more varied for boys, softer and mellower for girls. Such features mark the difference in the activity being proposed (for girls, care activities or fashion; in the case of boys, competition or manipulation, geared more to amusement and physical strength). To the former is reserved the domain of the magic, based on the instantaneity of an innate or acquired gift from the outside; to the latter the domain of technique, based on the sedimentation of knowledge. Girls are reassured in the ease of the task, protected in the hope of domesticity, in the care of others or of their own physical appearance; they are more likely to be portrayed while gossiping, courting, staring at the mirror or taking care of others; they are told to be a body at the disposal of the environment and not to cross borders. Boys, on the other hand, are more likely to be represented in outdoor settings, and encouraged to compete, to build, in some way to venture beyond the boundaries of the known. Overall, girls are assigned to the domain of relations, boys to that of performance. And so on. In other words, it is a whole universe of meanings that are mobilized in defining femininity and masculinity, much more than the simple differences between the objects advertised, and this universe is resistant to change, despite changes in social institutions and interactions (see Browne 1998; Kahlenberg & Hein 2010; McArthur & Eisen 1976; Smith 1994).

Indeed, advertisements also reflect the material culture which surrounds us. The world of objects is indeed a domain where gendered bodies can be visualized and engaged. From razors to shampoos, from mineral water to yoghurts, male and female versions of products are spreading out, always covering (and creating) new rentable niches of market. Packaging and textures, colours and even prices of the same product change according to the gender of the target (Petersson McIntyre 2018). We could just take a quick look at the toiletries in a supermarket to see to what extent products are gendered and what meanings for each gender are suggested. In the case of male versions of products provided in double format, be they shower gels or deodorants, we typically find packaging full of buzzwords and fully capitalized texts, numbers and expressions like 'active', 'extra fresh' or 'power'; dominant colours are black, green or blue; containers are made to be held; fragrances are woody and pungent, evoking the sense of action and wildness. In female versions of the same products, we find words evoking beauty, care and relaxation, like 'restoring', 'natural', 'soft'; dominant colours are pastel, light, especially pink or purple; we see fruits and flowers, curved lines instead of straight ones; containers remind of the female silhouette, are elongated and with no edges, textures are smoother, fragrances are floral and fruity, evoking nurturance and relaxation. These associations seem straightforward and natural: we even see pink as an inherently 'feminine' colour. Historical and anthropological studies proved that it is not. Well-known research by Jo Paoletti (2012) on the gendering of clothing for children showed that in the early twentieth century there was little agreement among manufacturers, retailers and consumers on which colour was feminine or masculine, and whether they could signal gender markers at all. Today, we grow up immersed in such a sea of visual codes of gender, consistently replicated from objects to the advertisements of objects; the gendering of bodies is still evoked by such codes (see also chapter 6). Despite some retailers, such as the UK store John Lewis, having removed 'boys' and 'girls' labels from their children's clothing, and the spread of gender-neutral children's fashion, especially addressed to upper-class families, the market has remained extremely reluctant to change in the face of this and still favours gender stereotypes, as they create and satisfy specific segments. Anyway, it's difficult to see where nature ends, and nurture begins.

Toys, clothes and consumer goods are not the only repertoires where we can find cultural footholds communicating how much our bodies are expected to be gendered right from childhood. Male and female representations in children's literature and textbooks have been researched extensively for more than fifty years. This is no surprise, since they are deemed fundamental sources for communicating what is expected of women and men and their place in the social structure for people during their first socialization to the world and the identity formation process. As early as 1971, in a study of illustrations of women in children's books, Alleen Pace Nilsen noticed that most of them showed women's bodies as wearing aprons – which made her conclude that there was a 'cult of the apron' which sounded anachronistic already at that time – standing in doorways or at the window looking out at the action. In the same year, Mary Key summarized gender roles in children's books as 'boys do: girls are' (Key 1971, as quoted in Kortenhaus & Demarest 1993).

Even when 'girls' are meant to 'do', and high-performing female adult bodies are considered, as in the case of athletes, gender becomes focal in their representations. Since the 1980s, a great amount of research has been devoted to the portrayal of female and male athletes in popular sports magazines, newspapers and television (Cooky, Messner & Musto 2015; Duncan 1990; Messner 1988). It has been largely documented that while male athletes are depicted by the popular media in terms of their sporting performance and muscularity, female athletes are feminized, if not sexualized, and often their sporting achievements are trivialized. By examining hundreds of cover photographs in the National Collegiate Athletic Association media guides in the 1990s, for example, Jo Ann Buysse and Melissa Sheridan Embser-Herbert (2004) investigated whether athletes were portrayed on or off the court, whether they were pictured in or out of uniform, whether in active or passive pose or position, and what the theme of the photo was. The findings showed, for example, that male athletes were more likely to be portrayed in uniform, on the court, in action, than women, and that female athletes were more likely to be portrayed as 'feminine' and sometimes in sexually suggestive poses. They also showed the tendency to portray women and men in traditionally gender-appropriate sports. Nevertheless, some changes were registered over time in the way female athletes were depicted.

Body positivity and representation

From social media campaigns to the glossy press, the bodies usually displayed are toned, slim and youthful, toeing the line of current standards of beauty and health. But such discipline is heavily gendered, both quantitatively and qualitatively. In quantitative terms, the frequency with which men and women have access to media space whenever their bodies depart from the norm in being flabby, fat, wrinkled or disabled is grossly disproportionate. Older men's bodies are allowed to appear, perhaps because of the social roles they more frequently play, whereas older women are almost invisible, either thanks to the scalpel, or because they are just not there.

Famous research such as that by Claire Wiseman and colleagues (1992) on the bodies of candidates for Miss America and models for *Playboy* has shown a widening gap over time between the models' weight and the mean weight of the female population in the same age bracket. Besides, from a qualitative viewpoint one notes that the meaning itself of body discipline changes according to gender. As Susan Bordo (2003 [1993]) pointed out, a female body deviating from the norm in being fat (for example) is shown as an alien transgressor in media culture. It is not just a question of weight: a woman's body needs keeping under control in its drives, whether hunger-based or sexual, while only toned and slim – not merely thin – denotes those managerial qualities that the middle classes have always hailed as upwardly mobile on a typically masculine social scale (see chapter 6). Moreover, such disciplined bodies make it invisible how much time-consuming, expensive and sometimes painful labour they require to be made so (Gill 2008). Overall, the spread of beautiful (and often altered) bodies in the social media also means, for some, feeling pressure to conform to idealized body standards, experiencing cyberbullying or engaging in harmful behaviours like excessive dieting or over-exercising, since the social media offer ample opportunities for appearance-based comparisons and considerable exposure to thin ideal content. Zoe Brown and Marika Tiggemann (2016) found that exposure to Instagram images that depict attractive and thin celebrities and peers was associated with higher body dissatisfaction levels, mediated by social comparison.

Note that the recent fashion for the curvy look is only an apparent exception to the rule. No sooner do we look admiringly at a softer, rounder form of body than we find it is being countered by make-up, clothes and postures explicitly designed to slim it. Again, we see the same sociocultural expectations of gendered bodies even as they are supposedly being challenged. As it has been suggested, many images of so-called 'curvy beauties' reinforce, rather than criticize, society's preoccupation with appearance over other attributes; and they often portray conventionally attractive white women, excluding other marginalized bodies. As Susan Sontag (1977 [1972]) pointed out in her classic essay 'The double standard of aging' (seen in chapter 5), to women in contemporary Western society, femininity equates with beauty and beauty with youth: the female body is not allowed to grow flaccid or wrinkled like a male one, since in growing old it gets less feminine.

Nevertheless, in recent years, the body positivity movement has emerged, especially on social media. New generations are one of the most important targets of this movement, as well as one of its main protagonists. Nowadays teenagers use their bodies on social media in various ways, often as a means of self-expression, to seek validation or to engage with others. They frequently take selfies, or self-portraits, and share them on social media platforms such as Instagram, Snapchat and TikTok to showcase their appearance, fashion choices and make-up skills, as well as express their emotions and moods.

Platforms like TikTok and Instagram Reels have popularized short-form videos where users, largely teens, dance or lip-sync to trending songs. They often participate in viral dance challenges, showcasing their skills and creativity. Moreover, those who are passionate about fitness, sports or physical activities often share photos or videos of their workouts, competitions or achievements on social media. This can include weightlifting, yoga, running or team sports. But such platforms also provide an opportunity for teenagers to share their fashion and style choices. They may post photos of their outfits, accessories or hairstyles, and seek feedback or validation from their followers. This means promoting body positivity and self-acceptance, when teenagers share photos that showcase their bodies in a positive light, discussing body image issues, or joining communities that support one another in embracing body diversity. But it is not exempt from ambiguities, since, firstly, it creates a new pressure on girls to 'love' their bodies (and therefore may make them feel worse about themselves if they do not); secondly, despite the positive messaging around bodies, such content still focuses on appearance thus making it relevant; thirdly, it keeps on objectifying specific body parts (Cohen, Newton-John & Slater 2021).

Other researchers explored engagement in self-presentation and peer comparison on social media through interviews with teenage girls, who were found to negotiate their self-presentation efforts to achieve the standards of beauty projected by their peers, and used likes and followers to measure approval of physical beauty and gain validation (Young, Smith & Batten 2022). Laura Ramsey and Amber Horam (2018), for example, argue that young women often post sexualized photos of themselves on social media because they desire attention, which is also associated with self-objectification and feelings of sexual empowerment.

Ambivalences

Body positivity messages are not confined to social media. Periodicals, TV and advertisements are increasingly proposing images, roles and behaviours that (apparently) subvert the traditional gender order, with counter-stereotypes of the male and especially the female. As Sarah Banet-Wiser (2018) suggests in her book *Empowered: Popular Feminism and Popular Misogyny*, feminism may be defined as 'popular' for three reasons: it is manifest in discourses that are broadly accessible as they circulate in popular and commercial media; it is admired by like-minded people and groups; and it is a terrain of struggle. Indeed, Banet-Wiser suggests that feminism is as popular as misogyny and examines the deeply interwoven relationship between the two as it plays out in advertising, online and multimedia platforms and non-profit and commercial campaigns, so that discourses that emphasize self-confidence, body positivity and individual achievement stand alongside violent misogynist phenomena such as revenge porn and toxic geek masculinity, as they are co-constituted in the media.[6] The 'two movements are conjunctural even as they are asymmetrical, intersecting in their various patterns of actions and expressions, echoing each other in complex and contradictory ways' (ibid., 40). To counter the popularity of misogyny, we have to interrogate the politics of 'visibility' of which popular feminism is itself part and be alert to its ambivalence.

In their study of *Genderblend*, a visual trend aimed at portraying gender identities and relations in ways that are more inclusive and diverse in the supplier of stock images and editorial photography 'Getty Images', Giorgia Aiello and Anna Woodhouse (2016), for example, show how rising above gender clichés in these images translated into an unequal representation of both gender non-conforming and transgender persons. The visual analysis they adopt goes across the *typing* (using objects as attributes which define the portrayed subjects), the *juxtaposition* (making comparisons to highlight deviations from the norm) and the *texturization* (conferring texture to emphasize material and physical specificity). In the case of persons portrayed as engaged in activities traditionally associated with the other gender, we see a reversing of roles which in fact sharpens the boundaries. In the case of transgender persons, images focus on a marginal aspect of gender limits that abstracts individuals from the social context, thus making their 'difference' more visible.

For example, by examining the texturization of two series of studio portraits entitled 'transvestite Asian senior man' and 'woman breaking the rules of gender' we see (ibid., 364):

[the first as portrayed] against a black theatrical backdrop as he poses and dances wearing a red corset, a black split front skirt, fishnet stockings, high-heeled red shoes, red lipstick, and a choker around his neck. His long white hair, beard, wrinkles and thin, wiry body stand in sharp contrast with these accessories and are foregrounded through subtle chiaroscuro lighting. [The second] is pictured in 'men's clothes' (i.e. a black tie, a sleeveless white shirt, and white trousers), and both the textures of her full sleeve tattoo and of a mask that looks like a web of black lace around her eyes stand out against the flat dark background and the neutral colours of her clothes. ... In sum, in the world of Genderblend queer identities are foregrounded in relation to individuals' physical attributes, but are dissociated from the everyday contexts in which they may live, work, or relate to others. ... (T)hese images design difference as embodied, but also as disembedded from broader society.

As the authors note, such communication about gender non-conforming identities is almost entirely limited to their visibility, and their visual treatment is limited to their inherent ambiguity discursively taken out of everyday life contexts, particularly realms like work and the family. As such, a globally powerful corporation like Getty Images 'strategically deploys substantial challenges to major inequalities to define its own brand and remit. It is in this sense that corporate capitalism moves into the realm of actual social critique and, in doing so, also begins to colonize difference' (ibid., 355), the authors comment.

Ambivalence is even more evident in many visual campaigns aimed at denouncing gender violence and femicide. Despite the intention to raise awareness of violence and empower women, most images of male and female bodies in such campaigns often contradict their purpose. It is enough to enter a string such as 'gender violence' in internal search engines of stock photo repositories to immediately get an idea. The typical visual representation of violence against women takes first of all the point of view of the public or of the abusive man: almost never the point of view of the abused woman. The man is almost never represented, and if he is, he is more frequently seen from behind, or is metonymically represented by his closed fist. The woman is often on the ground, and we see her from a high angle (which is meaningful, since, as in Gunther Kress and Theo Van Leeuwen's classic work (1996), the viewer is implicitly evoked as more powerful than the subject of the image). She is often squatting and closed in on herself, her face covered by her hands. Alternatively, she holds one or both her hands out, showing us her palms as an invitation to stop or as a sign of defence. In any case, we are invited to assume her aggressor's point of view, so we are invited to identify with him rather than with her. Moreover, she is typically white, young, slim, often beautiful, with some bruises on her face or faded make-up but in a way that reinforces her charm, in an aestheticization of violence.

Whatever the intentions of those who create such images, they end up confirming that gender violence is a women's problem and not men's, and that women are more victims than potential survivors able to react and find support. Women are portrayed as completely lacking in agency. The men who mistreat them, on the other hand, are almost never represented; neither are men who symbolically could stop other men from engaging in violence. In such images, women are nothing more than helpless 'victims' and gender violence still remains a women's issue.[7]

While women are portrayed as victims when it comes to gender violence, the other way around is also true in visual media: victims are often portrayed as women. Heather Johnson (2011) studied photo archives of the United Nations High Commissioner for Refugees (UNHCR) and other institutional sources, with the idea that visual framing of refugees reflects and contributes to changing policies and practices of international refugee regimes. Johnson found that visual representation of international refugees has undergone three shifts across sixty years, especially since refugees from the Global South have captured the attention of northern policymakers: racialization, victimization and feminization. From the heroic, powerful political individuals, to the nowadays nameless flood of poverty-stricken women and children, these shifts marked a depoliticization trend, which symbolically denied any political agency to subjects.

In other words, their representations increasingly established a visual condition of political voicelessness. The refugees began to be depicted as abstracted away from a political and historical context, sometimes covering their face, in unrecognizable backgrounds, to represent the universal condition of the human being as a mute victim. Interestingly, this depoliticization, despite being strategic to mobilize public support for humanitarian causes, has been established through the feminization of the subject, deemed to embody vulnerability and dependence upon others at the highest levels. As Johnson comments, 'To construct a representation is an act of power; representations are fundamentally political. ... How we imagine particular categories of people deter-mines how we engage with them, who we accept as legitimate political actors, and who is able to participate in our world' (ibid., 1017).[8]

Indeed, there is a wide awareness of the fact that body politics can be performed through images and that the way we gender bodies through images is inherently political. The public is more sensitive than in the past to visual representation politics and calls for more equitable representation of genders, races, generations and abilities, albeit, as we shall see, often in postfeminist terms.

Postfeminist turns and continued exclusions

The market is increasingly responding to such claims and so, again, advertisements are instructive. As suggested, we see an increasing presence of an empowerment discourse in advertising depicting women. As Rosalind Gill's (2008) analysis showed, young women are now frequently depicted as active, independent and sexually powerful, rather than simply passive sexual objects. However, these still tend to exclude older women, disabled women, fat women or women that do not visually fit female beauty standards. At the same time, the agency of these (typically) white heterosexual women is depicted as confined to the aestheticization of physical appearances and consumerism. In fact, powerful women in 'battle of the sexes' roles appear to be more emotionally tied to objects (be they cars, watches or new perfumes) than to their male partners. They are depicted as playing men at their own game, 'a game, it should be noted, whose rules she had no part in determining and which, in a sexist culture, have the odds stacked against women, particularly as they grow older', Gill (2008, 49) comments.

Since the mid-1980s, a hyper-visibility of men as gendered subjects also occurred in the mainstream media, and men's images have been changing accordingly. Again, Gill (2003) discusses the changes in the way masculinities have been portrayed (both in verbal and visual languages) in fashion and lifestyle magazines and advertising: from the 1980s' images of masculinity which encompass many of the traits previously thought of as feminine (like being emotional, nurturing and caring) to the 1990s' revival of classical patriarchal features of masculinity (constructed around knowingly misogynist and predatory attitudes to women as part of a cultural backlash against feminism, even if more prone to consumerism and sexual freedom than bread-winner responsibilities).

In the meantime, other changes occurred in the way gender is visualized in mainstream communication. An appropriation and commodification of homoerotic images by media elided masculinity from activity, and showed men not only as active sexual subjects, but also as objects of desire. According to Suzanne Moore (1988), already in the 1980s the eroticization of men's bodies in the hetero-sexual scopic regime suggested a new kind of gaze among women, now implicitly constructed as subjects of desire. This doesn't entail necessarily that the meaning of sexualization is the same for female and male bodies: as Bordo (1999) notes, in the case of women it can suggest victimization, while for men it can suggest confidence. Moreover, as shown by a content analysis of images of women and men inspired by Goffman's work on more than four decades of *Rolling Stone* magazine covers, being just naked or sexualized is different from being 'hypersexualized' and 'nothing more than' a sexual object, which still remains peculiar to female subjects

(Hatton & Trautner 2011). At the same time, representations of explicitly sexualized men have become widespread in the media. This turn holds the potential of radically challenging the dependence of successful masculine identification on the repudiation of objectification, in a more general diversification of masculinities in the media (see also Moss 2011).

The analysis of visual media content is today increasingly engaged with an intersectional perspective (see chapter 5). It is not just a matter of how and how much gendered and racial features are depicted, but of how they mutually constitute each other, in both the gendering of race and in the racializing of gender in visual codes of representation (Weber 2001). This may imply, for example, documenting the patterns of racialization operating in the 'sexualized' visual economy of advertisements through the lenses of gender, age and social class (Gill 2009). It may also imply considering how age, gender and race intersect and impinge on how users construct and manage their profile photographs on the internet as Sanja Kapidzic and Susan Herring (2015) have done in their study of a chat site designed for and used by teens.

But it may also extend to the appreciation of the ambiguities of the exploitation of intersectionality itself as a theme in marketing and advertising. For example, Francesca Sobande (2019) analyses a number of campaigns which adjust to new egalitarian sensibilities in matters of gender, race and sexuality and brands them as 'woke-washing': using 'woke' (the investment in issues of social justice) and drawing on commercialized notions of feminism, equality and Black social justice activism, they primarily endorse the neoliberal idea that success and social change just requires individual ambition and consumption. A telling example is also the study of the Diesel advertising campaign 'Nature: Love it while it lasts' by Anthony Barnum and Anna Zajicek (2008). In the advertisement a variety of genders and races are represented: the colourful mix of bodies, each half dressed with an item from the brand collection and portrayed as taken by desire and enjoyment of an element of nature (a flower, a tree, a shell, and so on) in a forest that evokes a fantastic world of environmental purity, are decontextualized, their cultural specificity erased, gender and race reduced to aesthetic detail. By looking at the effects of gender within a race category and at the differences of race within a gender category, the authors unveil multiple matrices of domination. Their analysis shows that the equality among race, ethnicity, gender and sexuality displayed by the campaign is achieved at the expense of imposing a 'culturelessness of whiteness' upon all groups and identities represented: 'in reproducing the Other (race, ethnicity, gender, and sexuality) as the spice for white mainstream culture, whiteness is being imposed upon the Other. Importantly, this whiteness is not just whiteness but also heterosexuality, maleness, and Westerness' (ibid., 124).

Content analysis studies of mass media images have long discussed gender and race issues in visual imagery. Several studies on Western commercials, for example, have shown the persistence of both sexist and racist stereotypes: whites outnumber African American and Asiatic people (Latinx were virtually non-existent) and are more likely depicted in authoritative roles; African Americans are portrayed as aggressive and menacing, African American women in particular as instinctual, hypersexualized and exotic (often animal-like, wearing predatory animal-print clothing and striking animal-like poses; see Plous & Neptune 1997). Jeffrey Brown (1999) discusses the contradictory representations of Black male bodies as physical threats but powerless in social hierarchies. On the one hand, 'not all Others have been constructed as equal by the dominant masculinist ideology. While the gay man, the Jewish man, the Asian man (and many other "Others") have been burdened by the projection of castrated softness, the black man has been subjected to the burden of racial stereotypes that place him in the symbolic space of being too hard, too physical, too bodily' (ibid., 28). On the other hand, those features which are attributed to hegemonic masculinities, like power, control and authority, have been denied to Black masculinities. The analysis of African American male superheroes in comic books of a black-owned publishing company, Milestone, allows Brown to shed light on the possibility of developing alternative images of Black superheroes through the infusion of gentler and more cerebral qualities in the visual codes of muscularity and hypermasculinity.

Gender-neutral displays

However, despite gender remaining an 'easy' criterion for market segmentation, today we are witnessing a trend towards gender-neutral advertising, which is sometimes very direct and vocal. This reflects a growing trend for the diffusion of gender-neutral and gender-fluid people in the population both in the United States and in Europe, but also of new sensibilities around these topics, especially among new generations. Several brands have turned to gender-neutral advertising, such as Calvin Klein and Benetton, and the cosmetics industry is proposing gender-neutral make-up such as in the case of unisex cosmetics brands JECCA or Milk Make Up with its famous campaign

'Blur the lines'. If we consider Benetton, a brand that has always been at the forefront of controversial advertising with a social slant, we may appreciate some of the particulars.

Benetton arrived at a gender-neutral campaign after a symbolic incident which happened in 2017 when it launched a campaign which received criticism for 'sexist' and 'outdated' communication, with consumers calling for a boycott of the brand. The campaign featured three male kids with different skin tones with their arms linked, all wearing colourful clothes from the brand's collection. The caption accompanying the image read 'Sorry ladies. Girls not allowed!'. Not surprisingly, the Italian fashion brand then switched to a different strategy and launched the campaign 'Colours don't have gender' in 2018. The lead image of this campaign features an assorted collection of girls from all over the world surrounding a boy, all dressed in colourful tulle skirts, flowers and with jumpers that sport the claim of the campaign, a new logo which combines the male and female symbols and the words 'gender free zone'. They are all smiling. One of the girls is jumping, therefore nullifying Goffman's 'relative size'. A gender-neutral image on many accounts, and yet we still spot some details which contradict the claim. Shoes are still heavily gendered: the girls wear ballerina slippers, the boy conventional black male shoes. What is more, there is only one boy, and he stands in the middle, holding the hand of the only kid in the picture. Even in an image like this, the realization of gender-neutrality is tricky. And this is because, in everyday life, most of the population still lives their bodies in gendered ways: advertising only captures the rituals we deploy in everyday life to construct identity. Therefore, advertising often uses models who incarnate, with their embodied subjectivity, the meanings they want to convey.

Indeed, we draw on media images as repertoires of meanings to shape our own social identities and represent ourselves to others. An increasing amount of research is now documenting how people (especially youngsters) represent themselves on social media and networking technologies (from Twitter to Whatsapp, from vlogs to Facebook) through self-portraits and selfies. One recurrent finding is the sexualized self-presentation online of young girls and practices of 'self-commodifying' as a sexual object in stereotypical ways (Paasonen 2011; Kapidzic & Herring 2011).

At the same time, social media and the internet are also a space for self-invention and self-display.[9] Research now focuses on the interaction of gender with other identity characteristics and features, like (self-reported) sexual orientation, age and ethnicity, showing that findings in terms of displays of subordination or objectification may vary significantly (Cougar Hall, West & McIntyre 2012). For example, a study of hundreds of teens' profile photographs on a popular chat site (Kapidzic & Herring 2015) found significant differences in gaze, posture, dress and distance from the camera according to gender and race, and that racial differences were stronger for boys than for girls. Female users' postures and distance invited greater intimacy with their viewers, while male users maintained a greater distance. Again, girls posted profile pictures in which they displayed seductive behaviour significantly more frequently than boys did. Boys posted more variable images, from images in which they were not looking directly at the viewer, to images in which they seemed to be inviting friendship by looking directly at the viewer, and images in which they were looking down at the viewer significantly more often than girls did. White boys displayed seductive behaviour significantly more often than black boys, whereas white and black girls patterned together, overwhelmingly preferring seductive poses. Overall, to a surprising extent, the profiles reflected not only mainstream media images, but also previous findings of gender and race differences in face-to-face interaction. 'The teens manipulate, through image choice, their posture and gaze, dress, and distance from the viewer – all signals available in offline physical interaction; in the process, they unconsciously reproduce offline ideologies of gender and race', suggest the authors of the study, Sanja Kapidzic and Susan Herring (2015, 960). Indeed, we draw into media images and codes to shape our practice and gender scripts, but the other way round is also true.

Gendered norms of face-to-face interaction are internalized when we take a photo of ourselves, the same way as advertisements overstress ceremonial forms of gender difference that we perform in our everyday experience, as Goffman taught us. Visualizing the body, and making visible the gendered methods of its representation, is a meaningful way to understand how gender functions but also to dismantle it, since the more its pressure is powerful, the more it is invisible.

In this chapter we have considered the way bodies and gender are represented in the media. We started by discussing the male gaze and its continuous relevance for visualizing bodies: women's bodies are still very often objectified in the media, especially in advertising. The way the body is portrayed in advertising scenes through a variety of spatial and expressive micro-configurations helps construct images of masculinity and femininity. In traditional stereotypes men preferentially carry out ritualistic forms of domination and women, specularly, of submission. Old gender stereotypes coexist with new ways of representing the gendered body, which assign women a more active stance. Feminist consciousness has come to influence how women are portrayed and gender is displayed in advertising, with the development of messages that contain assertive images of femininity which are transmitted through posture, gaze and demeanour. Today, the body has become even more central to the representation of femininity, women becoming represented as the active agents of their own sexualization. All in all, the representation of the body is still very much organized along gender lines, but gender intersects with other dimensions of subjectivity such as class, race and age, contributing to an ever-growing complexity in the construction of social inequalities in the media.

Representation is a fertile terrain through which to understand how our bodies have been drawn inside contemporary capitalism in the West and how ambivalent is the liberation of the body which is promoted by commercial culture and neoliberalism. We have seen how much the gendering of bodies has been the vehicle of power and hierarchy. De-gendering bodies in consumer cultures and capitalism is far from problematic, though, as it is often predicated on an individual achievement. But abstract individualization erases the bodies' social and cultural contexts, their histories and their specificity as well as the structural constraints which impinge on them.

Conclusion

Throughout this book we have looked at the way society constructs the body and gender and conversely how gendered bodies are played out in interaction, culture and institutions. The body locates the individual in society, and it is shaped by society. The recent pandemic has certainly heightened our perception of the relevance of the body in society and of society for the body (Purnell 2021). But we can individuate other, more structural factors which have contributed to an increased awareness of the way bodies and society are intertwined. Chris Shilling (2016) has emphasized six phenomena that have heightened the relevance of embodiment, both in people's lives and in the academic debate. These are, in brief:

- The increasing critique of the way capitalism has enacted economic progress, with issues such as environmental sustainability bringing attention to the limits of human existence on this planet.
- The process of population ageing which has highlighted the inequalities that unfold through age and their different relevance to different populations, especially in relation to the stigmatization of old age and the myriad social practices through which individuals try to keep their bodies young.

190

- The fact that the body has become, in the Global North, an important object around which processes of consumption are articulated, and that it is valued by countless practices that seek to modify it, beautify it, satisfy and guide its needs.
- The intensification of control over the body by political institutions, following the increasing pressure of migration, especially after the 9/11 terrorist attacks on the United States.
- Scientific and technological developments that have facilitated unprecedented control over aspects of our corporeality that previously seemed unavailable.
- But the first phenomenon that gave relevance to embodiment, according to Shilling, is feminism, for having made political many personal bodily issues.

Since the 1960s, feminist thinking at first (and gender approaches in academia that followed) has put its finger on the inequalities that are realized through male and female bodies, and the objectification of the female body. The interest in inequalities that pass through the body then extended to other social identities that are related to other aspects of embodiment such as race, age and class, as have been touched on in this book.

We have taken up this important legacy and tried to connect it with classical authors of sociology. We have concentrated on gender and the body since this is a fundamental aspect of embodiment, of how it is managed in interaction and invested by power. Gendered bodies are interlocked in a series of complex relationships which define both femininity and masculinity and the possibilities of going beyond binarism. We have explored the way normative femininities and hegemonic masculinities are patrolled through interaction, institutions and culture, and how, simultaneously, the gender order is changing to accommodate new visions of the body, gender and sexuality. The gendered body is therefore a contested terrain where competing visions are often set against each other. Still, some bodies are privileged over others, with culturally prized bodily characteristics providing some people with advantages while disadvantaging others.

Despite the presence of female bodies in the public sphere being revolutionized in many ways thanks to women's hard-fought conquests during the twentieth century, the subordination of women through their bodies is far from being a thing of the past. In her ethnography on super-rich club parties, where fashion models and beautiful women are invited to join wealthy businessmen and tycoons' tables in exchange for their mere presence, the sociologist

Ashley Mears (2020) revives Veblen's original critique of women's role in conspicuous consumption (see chapter 6). As Mears points out, despite the difference between the nineteenth-century leisure class and contemporary nouveau riche, in both scenarios we find men conspicuously displaying their status through the symbolic ownership of women. Such dynamics often return again and again throughout history. This is just one example of how the legacy of the classics can also come in handy in contemporary analysis of social phenomena inspired by feminist thought, and it is the approach we have advocated throughout the book.

As we have argued, gender is fundamental to embodiment. Gendered embodiment is fraught with differences that 'make all the difference' when it comes to accessing institutional roles, being able to take action, or having opportunities for personal growth. And gendered embodiment is, above all, naturalized. The very idea of human nature, dating back over centuries of Western thought, has exercised a tacit symbolic power that has rendered the feminine invisible except as 'otherness' (see chapter 1). And from the assumption of a natural – i.e., so obvious that it does not have to be justified – place in the field of sexual classifications of bodies, a particular, unequal and hierarchical sexual division of labour, emotions, expectations, ideals and so on, derives.

However, in contemporary Western society the boundaries of the natural are continuously constructed and challenged. And this has contributed to foreground issues of power and inequality as they unfold and materialize through gendered bodies. Power and bodies are deeply intertwined, and such intertwining is often referred to as body politics (see chapter 3). Both the processes through which societies regulate the human body or use (part of) it to regulate themselves, and the struggles over the degree of individual and social control of the body, its parts and processes are considered under this label. Power and resistance are indeed always coupled in the constitution of embodied subjectivities and gender. So where is it possible to find a space for agency and resistance outside the patriarchal power? Can the body be such a space?

Since patriarchal power has historically manifested itself over the body and through it, at the expense of women's conditions, it was precisely from the body that feminist movements decided to start, both to understand women's material experience and to create new subjectivities and to find a space of opposition against the workings of power. Subversive bodily actions have always been one of the most important elements of feminist praxis: from imprisoned English suffragettes' hunger strikes asking for the right to vote in the first decade of the twentieth century, to feminists throwing their bras at Miss America beauty pageants and other performative struggles in the 1970s, to Iranian women today unveiling themselves, asking for freedom and cutting their hair on social media and on the streets. The history of feminist praxis is made of a constant dialogue between theory and experience, through both specific bodily actions in the political space (like strikes and protests) and bodily practices in everyday life (such as subversive body art, cross-dressing, refusal of female beauty standards like shaving legs and so on).

But using the body as a site of resistance to the productive (and not only repressive) side of power is far from simple, though. In *Gender Trouble*, as we have previously seen, Judith Butler argues that gender is performative, and precisely because gender is nothing other than bodily performances, it can be re-signified through bodily performances, such as drag. However, Butler felt that the (quite wishful) interpretations of gender subversive bodily performances that the book stimulated had to be delimited to come to terms with practices. In *Bodies that Matter*, Butler (1993) suggests that we have to take the materiality of bodies into account and cannot think of performances as depending on the free will of a self-contained subject. By arguing that genders are performative, Butler did not mean that

> one woke in the morning, perused the closet or some more open space for the gender of choice, donned that gender for the day, and then restored the garment to its place at night. Such a willful and instrumental subject, one who decides on its gender, is clearly not its gender from the start and fails to realize that its existence is already decided by gender. Certainly, such a theory would restore a figure of a choosing subject – humanist – at the center of a project whose emphasis on construction seems to be quite opposed to such a notion. (ibid., x)

According to Butler, social identities are always both unstable and incomplete, and they precede the individual. Performativity's repetitive actions are given power through persistence and instability. Therefore, there is no singular and deliberate bodily act which can be subversive as such. Identity (naming oneself as a woman or a man, or referring to 'women' or 'men' in the plural form) is a necessary error: 'necessary' to mobilize politically, but an 'error' because it will never fully describe those it is meant to represent. That's why the use of 'queer' as an autonomous self-naming project is, according to this perspective, preferable, as it is more inclusive, anti-essentialist, fluid and self-critical.

In fact, in the post-structuralist view, the identity claims and body politics of minorities arose from discourses of domination (patriarchy, racism, heterosexism, etc.). In Foucauldian terms, those identities were but the outcomes of a productive power to name, distinguish and marginalize people through labels. So, it was suggested, the objective of those movements should be to empty such categories (man/woman, black/white, lesbian/gay/heterosexual, etc.) of any social meaning. The problem is that those categories did function in social practices and did have shared meaning with material consequences in the lives of individuals. As the meaningful and provocative title of an essay by the historian Laura Lee Downs (1993) puts it, 'If "woman" is just an empty category, then why am I afraid to walk alone at night?'.

Such dilemma kept new studies anchored to individuals' material reality, made up of ties and restrictions, but also recognition and gratification. It was not a matter of ducking the biological facts, but of involving materiality in social processes: 'Bodies have a reality that cannot be reduced; they are drawn into history without ceasing to be bodies. They do not turn into signs or positions in discourse, their materiality continues to matter' (Connell 2021, 47–8). Body politics and resistance should start from the awareness that the biological and the social construct one another.

Indeed, contemporary societies work on our bodies intensely and we have become more reflexively aware of our bodies (see chapter 2). Body care practices are viewed as a pleasant way of asserting one's own uniqueness at a time when anchoring oneself to socially defined groups and institutions is problematic and social vulnerability is on the increase. This growing phenomenon would appear to stem from a mentality based on economic exchange and commodification, which lead people to seek individual answers to collective problems (Bauman 1999; Giddens 1991; see also Sassatelli 2012). In late modern societies, as Christopher Lasch puts it in his classic work *The Culture of Narcissism* (1991 [1979]), we are unable to project ourselves into future generations and we have fragile relationships with others. Bodily appearance becomes essential to a sense of self (ibid., 92):

[a]ll of us, actors and spectators alike, live surrounded by mirrors. In them, we seek reassurance of our capacity to captivate or impress others, anxiously searching out blemishes that might detract from the appearance we intend to project. The advertising industry deliberately encourages this preoccupation with appearances.

In the new millennium, a new generation of women has become informed about feminism both informally and globally via the media and the internet. Besides working together towards a common goal of ending violence against women or of supporting women in non-liberal countries worldwide, they were focused on (white, Western) women's individual empowerment and self-esteem. At the same time, a new discourse directed at women slowly reached mainstream media, based on messages of 'leaning in' and 'having it all' in current patriarchal economies without questioning their basis nor what or who was excluded by these messages (Rottenberg 2017). Embraced by high-powered women and celebrities, this approach abandoned key terms, such as equal rights, wealth distribution and liberation, advocating, instead, for a life of balance and happiness.

What we are currently witnessing, Catherine Rottenberg (2018) argues, is the rise of a 'neoliberal feminism' that helps to ensure that all responsibility for reproduction and care work falls on the shoulders of individual women. Social problems are deemed to be individual again. And, again, white, upper-class native-born women ask for power, regardless (and often at the expense) of 'unworthy' disposable female 'others' (largely non-white, low-class, migrant) who perform, for instance, the domestic and care work for them. It is a time when, according to the philosopher Nancy Fraser, the traditional feminist quest for recognition gains ascendancy at the expense of another important principle of feminism: the quest for redistribution and solidarity (Fraser 2013).

In this overall new sensibility enmeshed with neoliberalism, 'postfeminism' (Gill 2016), the body becomes a site of individual performance in a world made of choices, agency and individualism, more than resistance to structural and cultural inequalities. In such context, the patriarchal power is 're-territorialized' in women's bodies and the beauty-industrial complex intensifies and extends their surveillance, monitoring and disciplining. In neoliberal times, the enterprise form is extended to all dimensions of life and to subjectivity itself; ambition and calculation are part of the new entrepreneurial self, defined by its capacity to consume and being self-reflexive and responsible for one's own look (Elias, Gill & Scharff 2017), but also in all aspects of body care. Again, to put it in Foucauldian terms, in their body women are called to find 'the truth of their being'.

Mass media and social media play a crucial role in such dynamics (see chapter 7). They shape public perceptions of gender, and these perceptions can influence societal norms and expectations for a number of reasons. Representation matters: the way that men and women are portrayed in the mass media can have a significant impact on how they are perceived in society. Stereotypical portrayals of gender roles can perpetuate harmful norms and expectations, while more diverse and accurate representations can help to challenge and break down these stereotypes. Despite progress in recent years, mass media still often perpetuate traditional gender stereotypes: women are often portrayed as emotional, submissive and focused on their appearance, while men are depicted as rational, dominant and unconcerned with their looks. These representations can reinforce dominant expectations and limit the opportunities available to individuals based on their gender. They also objectify women, focusing on their appearance and sexual appeal rather than their skills, intelligence or accomplishments. This can lead to women and girls internalizing these messages, resulting in body dissatisfaction, eating disorders and other mental health issues. But this can also shape people's career choices and aspirations by reinforcing stereotypes about which careers are suitable for men and women. Social media platforms certainly provide new opportunities for individuals to challenge traditional gender norms and expectations; however, they can also perpetuate harmful stereotypes and contribute to issues such as online harassment and the spread of misinformation.

But stereotypes are also about men. Nowadays feminist themes may need to be complemented by research into the social pressures bearing upon the male body too, pressures that are ever more common and contradictory as the gender order changes. The ways in which men experience their bodies is also conditioned by patriarchy as a power structure imposing the model of heterosexual masculinity, binding on everybody including men. The post-structuralist conceptual turn has brought awareness that masculinity too may be studied as a social, symbolic, ritual construct, whose many practices and meanings as related to the body are no less to be contested.

It has been observed that the way a factory worker embodies masculinity is not the same as the way an intellectual or a freelance professional embodies his masculinity. Talk of man in actual fact always means talk of men, as the classic study by Connell argues (2005a): there are multiple masculinities even in a patriarchal system. The way male bodies are envisaged and constructed in discourse and practice especially reflects the social order. In this case too there is no shortage of research demonstrating how the male body is likewise sanctioned and disciplined by knowledge and power, from sport to body care to displays of masculinity in youth subcultures. At the same time, studies on the traditional symbols of virility such as muscles, or on less overtly masculine areas such as fashion, or emotion management and caring for others, show how the old image of masculinity is being negotiated, with ambivalent results, in the face of the changing balance of power between men and women (Gough 2018; Messerschmidt 2018; Wacquant 1995).

Of course, gender is just one possible factor of hierarchization of bodies, albeit one of the most important. Intersectional analysis is a framework that helps us understand how various social categories, such as race, gender, class, sexual orientation and disability, intersect and influence individual experiences and outcomes (chapter 5). This means we need to take into account our position in the interlocking system of privilege and oppression. Our view of the world depends on such partiality. When applying this framework to bodies, we consider how these intersecting factors shape our understanding of bodily experiences, body image and bodily autonomy. Western ideals of health and ability are unattainable or exclusive for many people and impact how individuals perceive their own bodies and the bodies of others. Intersectionality helps us recognize that these ideals are not universal, but rather, are shaped by factors such as race, gender and class which contributed to the very creation of such ideals. In other words, they have been set against the 'othernesses' of non-white, non-heterosexual, non-abled bodies. And, of course, non-male.

The 'view from nowhere' attributed for centuries to male, heterosexual, white bodies in modern Western societies has been challenged by the awareness of the importance of our standpoint. Postcolonial thought has been crucial in this acknowledgement (see Bhabha 1994; Bhambra 2007; Chakrabarty 2000), as it has greatly contributed to unveiling the racialized and gendered premises of Western modernity. The very discourse of civilization and modernity may overstate cultural difference and historical discontinuity and position Western (and in particular European) civilization as an ideal point of arrival for all humanity. In her seminal essay 'Can the subaltern speak?', Gayatri Chakravorty Spivak (2010 [1988]) argues that subalterns are those who, belonging to colonized countries, cannot make their voices heard as colonial rule has reinforced divisions by gender, class, caste, religion and region which keep them divided and impede them forming a unified narrative to counter the Eurocentric view of Western modernization and rationalization. Gender itself may be seen as a colonial imposition, as Maria Lugones (2010) has suggested in her work on decolonial feminism. Drawing on historical examples of pre-colonial Native American tribes, Lugones situates gender, and its binary, as a colonial classification system that divides and subjugates indigenous people, opening the way to racialization.

At the same time, our perceptions and attitudes towards our own bodies can also be influenced by intersecting factors. For example, someone's body image may be impacted by their race, as certain racial and ethnic groups may experience unique beauty standards and expectations. Intersectional analysis can help us understand how different groups may experience varying levels of control over their own bodies, or even experience varying levels of health and access to health care. Black, transgender individuals and people with disabilities may face unique health challenges due to discrimination, stigma and lack of access to culturally competent health care, but they also may face unique challenges in asserting their bodily autonomy.

Bodily autonomy is a far from simple notion, though. How can we turn inside out the labels that a patriarchal culture has attached to our bodies and identities and use them as battlegrounds and sites of resistance? To many authors, the answer was that subjectivation (and resistance to it) were to be sought (also) outside the conscious battles waged by activists with their bodies: they had to be found in new sites of everyday life, previously conceived as unrelated to power and patriarchy in society. In recent years, the body has become an increasingly prominent site for the critique of heteronormativity and of the male/female binary. Gender-fluid, non-binary and queer identities have gained visibility in the public sphere, especially among younger generations from the 1990s onwards (see chapter 4). But this, too, brings us to a paradox of the postmodern turn. On the one hand, we aim to dismantle gender categories by deconstructing and subverting them. On the other, unequal life chances remind us continuously of how much these categories are material in their consequences. As Judith Lorber puts it (2021, ix): '(t)oday's new gender paradox is a rhetoric of gender multiplicity undermined by a continuing bi-gendered social structure that supports continued gender inequality. Underneath the seeming erasure of a rigid gender binary and its discriminatory norms lurks the persistence of men's power and patriarchal privilege.'

Broadly speaking, what contemporary perspectives add to classical theory is the awareness that male and female construct one another: the one can only stand in relation to the other, following conflictual and relational patterns that change with time. We need to spotlight the two genders' mutually determining experience, avoiding a view that crystallizes differences without leaving room for individual freedom from the expected sexual roles. As we have seen, that does not mean espousing a disembodied view of identity as freely and individually formed at will. Our embodiment construes experience for ourselves while we work on such experience, both for ourselves and the others. This is a laborious work which brings society right into our bodies, while we bring our bodies into society. Social practices and representation contribute to define human embodiment in a reflexive circularity which helps us go beyond the nature/culture divide.

Amid the constant flow of everyday life, the human being imitates the gestures, movements, postures and emotions it encounters. In so doing, it dons a body and with its own body takes its place in society. It is a typical non-reflexive body know-how, independent of intellectual or cognitive processes – John Dewey would say 'anoetic' – hence pre-conscious, which makes us feel at home with certain ways of being in the body, feeling, moving, seeing, touching and so forth (Garrison 2015; Shilling 2008). Thus, embodiment allows us to consider, so to speak, not only what society does to bodies, but also what bodies do to society.

Notes

Chapter 1: The Social Body

1   In many ways people 'do' pain, they become persons-in-pain through a process of 'naming': this very process influences bodily responses, thereby breaking down the dichotomies between culture and nature, body and mind (Bourke 2014). So, for example, in Western culture the metaphors used to describe the body and pain shifted and the way the body 'feels' pain has shifted accordingly: from a view that regarded pain as a demon and the result of an imbalance circulating in the whole body in the eighteenth century, to military metaphors which invoke the use of selective and parcelled out painkillers today. Such metaphors are deeply interwoven with our capacity to construct and account for ourselves in interaction and are likewise fundamental for a variety of institutions in their encounter with the body – from medical institutions to the market.

2   The Black body may, however, become a cultural weapon and an asset. As noticed by Mpho Mathebula (2022) through a study of naked protest in Africa, African women's naked bodies in protest may work as a link to generational power that creates a rupture and undermines coloniality. Naked protest may transform a woman's bodily vulnerability into a site of militancy, defiance and solidarity.

3   Friedrich Engels was attentive to women's sexual exploitation, though.

In *The Origin of the Family, Private Property and the State* (2010 [1884]), he states that in the nineteenth century's capitalist mode of production women lost the rights and honourable place they had in primitive communist societies. With the arrival of private property and systems of inheritance, fathers now demanded that paternity be established beyond doubt in order to pass their property on to their biological offspring. This was translated into strict limitations on female autonomy and sexuality. Capitalism ushered into 'the world the historical defeat of the female sex. The man took command in the home also, the woman was degraded and reduced to servitude; she became the slave of his lust and a mere instrument for the production of children' (ibid., 99).

4 According to Cas Wouters (2007, 167), we are witnessing a process of 'informalization' pointing to a reversal in the trend that Elias portrayed as a fundamental trait of the genesis of Western modernity, namely a move 'from detailed and stricter regimes of manners and emotions to other less formal and rigid regimes of manners and emotions'. Even more, in late modernity, we may be witnessing a process of 'carnivalization' (Langman 2008), whereby the boundaries which once kept the transgressive space of the carnival separated from everyday life have imploded: fuelled by media and consumer culture, there emerges a ludic and transgressive spirit which involves embodied forms of pleasure, rule-breaking and enjoyment of stigmatized desires.

5 In a well-known work on the affinities between romantic ethics and modern consumerism, Colin Campbell (1987) reminds us that it was mainly middle-class women who consumed the 'romantic' novels that disseminated a special new form of hedonism linked to the pleasures of the imagination. Campbell argues that a romantic lesson lies behind the hedonistic ethics, prompting people to fulfil themselves as individuals opposed to society, going in search of meaningful, different experiences. Captured as it is by the 'pleasures of the imagination', romantic hedonism thus proves related to the ability to process emotions, for example by vicariously enjoying thrilling situations of risk as when reading a novel. It was the bourgeois woman who could, and indeed had to, become the consumer *par excellence*; she it was who needed to 'daydream'. Women's capacity for consumption was to be fostered but also reined in by careful refinement of taste enabling them to appear 'naturally' and virtuously sophisticated (Jones 1998).

6 Even today, consumption is gendered in many domains, i.e., from shopping to fashion, from domestic consumption to leisure activities (Campbell 1987; Casey & Martens 2006; De Grazia & Furlough 1996; Scanlon 2000). Consumer goods can also be gendered: even apparently unisex items such as jeans can be sexualized, by branding and consumers alike, and this often happens in a binary fashion (Sassatelli 2011).

7 Understood as a social structure of relations, gender has been seen as structured at various levels or dimensions of social organization: interactional, individual and institutional (according to Barbara Risman

2004) or on the dimension of power, economic, emotional and symbolic relations according to Juliet Mitchell (1971, taken up by Connell 2021).

8   If we also consider ethnic and class differences at a point where physical traits intersect (see chapter 5), we shall see that in the last twenty years of the twentieth century in the United States, when obesity was a huge social issue, it was chiefly poorly educated, low-income, Black adult women whose body mass index went right up, whereas that of middle-aged, highly educated, very high-income white men grew at a lower rate (Ailshire & House 2011).

Chapter 2: Gendered Bodies and Subjectivity

1   Civil inattention is fundamental in a situation of unfocused co-presence, i.e., when sharing a space but not a focus of attention (Goffman 1990 [1963]). For everyone knows they are being seen, witnessed by onlookers, and will orient part of their behaviour according to the identity being perceived and the initial response of the audience.

2   Goffman took his distance from the Cartesian dualism which prevailed in sociology. Given that the body as the vehicle of the self needs to be monitored in everyday interaction, and that partial failure to do so, as is inevitable, leads to embarrassment, stigmatizing or ostracism, the self is clearly a constant process of unfoldment: practical, embodied and not fully strategic (Crossley 1995; Williams & Bendelow 1999). The emphasis is on the ambivalences, possibilities and predicaments of body management, something that is particularly evident in his work on stigmatization (Goffman 1990 [1963]). If someone is stigmatized, their body tends to become an intense focus of attention, attempting to manage the impairment to identity by techniques to cope with the stigma, hiding it, making up for it, reclassifying it and turning the tables on it.

3   To Goffman, gender is not one attribute among many, even if it is often carried out when actors are involved in doing something else. Thus, for example, he is well aware of the pervasive burden of gender for women. No one is ever free of it, even within the walls of the home: '(w)hereas other disadvantaged groups can turn from the world to a domestic scene where self-determination and relief from inequality appears possible, the disadvantage that persons who are female suffer precludes this; the places identified in our society as ones that can be arranged to suit oneself are nonetheless for women thoroughly organized along disadvantageous lines' (Goffman 1979, 9).

4   There has been prolific research on the construction of lovers' and couples' feeling in everyday life, for example, the books by Eva Illouz (2013) and Ann Swidler (2001). These works have to be set against the background of a growing therapeutic culture which offers individualizing scripts for the management of emotions (Illouz 2008). Emotions and

health have also been construed differently as Gillian Bendelow (2009) suggests, with the development of more sophisticated notions of stress that address the intertwining of emotion, embodiment and social factors and the idea of emotional health.

5   Marjorie DeVault (1991) highlighted the amount of preparatory work that women as wives and mothers have to go through so that what has been purchased for family consumption actually gets consumed, and the negotiating and conflict management skills they need to satisfy all the members' needs. Recent studies show, for example, how even today, especially when the family has young children, women still feel the greatest responsibility for feeding the family. In a work on food and femininity among Canadians, Kate Cairns and Josée Johnston (2016) show how, although gender relations are becoming more even and men more involved in the business of meals, women are the managers of family feeding. The business of getting food ready is still closely connected to the female role in looking after the family's bodies and health, while it is women who decide for the family through daily planning.

6   Gender shapes family life and everyday practices in multiple ways. First, it moulds intergenerational relations, as it provides the blueprint for the new generations' practices of socialization. Parental care and education have long been considered as the first domains to provide children with gender role models and cultural expectations. The strongest influence on gender role development seems to occur within the family settings as parents pass on, more or less explicitly and certainly through their bodily demeanour and emotion work, their beliefs about gender (Witt 1997). The family may remain a terrain for the reproduction of traditional gender dichotomies: a recent study focused on Germany, for example, showed that despite some elements of modernization of gender roles in female-breadwinner families, traditional gender concepts and practices prevailed (Jurczyk, Jentsch, Sailer & Schier 2019).

7   More generally, commodification of intimate life means that more and more often emotional and practical caregiving in families is being paid for. This has enabled women to enter the labour market but has failed to change gender models enough. Women still work a 'second shift' to take care of the family (Hochschild 1989). Hochschild (2003) seems to leave us hope that a different care model may gradually come in – alternative to the 'postmodern cold' in which caring has been held in little regard and everyone has had to get by as best they could, buying from a wide range of services on the market. She calls it the 'warm modern' model in which care is recognized as important work. In this model, institutions (the market, and also the State) do their part, while men and women share the part the institutions don't do.

8   Such an approach implies a critical stance, as we cannot simply choose any body (and any self) we want. Choice is here a continuous burden to be taken with a smile: we have 'no choice, but to choose' (Giddens 1991, 81; see also Beck 1992). Together with choice comes self-responsibility,

and risk-perception changes accordingly: now risks are in the region of anomie, linked to the incapacity to perform convincingly a body that fits. Thus, late modernity confronts the individual with a complex diversity of choices which is 'non-foundational', produces anxiety and offers 'little help as to which options should be selected' (Giddens 1991, 60). Circularly, the solution to such risk and anxiety found in contemporary society is, for Bauman (1992), merely 'technical': consumer culture solves the problem of the durable and coherent self-presentation by treating all problems as solvable through specific commodities. Each of them may be highly functional to a precise task, but they still have to be arranged in a coherent, credible whole, meaningful and revealing of the self.

9   As it is conceived as a creative, but structured, mechanism generating behaviour that is both relatively unpredictable and limited in its diversity (McNay 1999), the notion of 'habitus' seeks to keep together embodiment and intentionality, social determinacy and personal strategy. There is now a rich and ever-growing literature that explores social reality through the lenses of habitus across disciplines and fields; see, for example, Hillier and Rooks (2005) and Costa and Murphy (2015).

Chapter 3: Body Politics

1   The focus on the implication of medical truths in the power relations network was developed by Foucault in *Birth of the Clinic* (2012 [1963]). By analysing several medical treatises, Foucault investigated the sea-change that institutionalized pathological anatomy: disease became a 'collection of symptoms' necessarily expressed in the human body, instead of an abstract pathological 'essence'. All this went with medical observation 'dominating' the body, turning its hidden depths into a visible object. This is mostly true in the history of medical gaze on women's bodies, as testified by the work of Barbara Ehrenreich and Deirdre English's (2005 [1978]), a historical study on how previous religious justifications for patriarchy were transformed into scientific ones. The authors analyse 150 years of medical and professional knowledge on every aspect of women's lives – be it health care, childcare, motherhood, diet, housework or sex. In so doing, prescriptions and advice contributed to 'create' women as frail, prone to disease, vulnerable and inept due to their very nature.

2   Foucault has been blamed for his 'androcentric' omissions and the silence on the fact that the genealogy of knowledge, disciplines and power to tell a person's inner truth from their sexuality was different if it concerned men or women. For important readers of feminist interpretations of Foucault and feminist works taking on his legacy, see Diamond and Quinby (1988), Hekman (1996) and McNay (1992).

3   While the movement developing between the late nineteenth and early decades of the twentieth century concentrated on attainment of formal rights (civil and political, especially suffrage), feminist movements in the second half of the twentieth century, especially the 1960s and 1970s, were more interested in patriarchal mechanisms manifesting in men and women's daily lives. They thus focused on parity between spouses within the family, emancipation of women in the public sphere and labour market, as well as topics hitherto deemed private and personal in being more strictly bound up with the body, such as freedom from sexual violence, free sexuality, contraception and abortion. In other words, they acknowledged that the female body was a 'battlefield', to quote the title of a famous 1989 work by the feminist artist Barbara Kruger.

4   The term 'gender' was extended beyond linguistic grammar long before Rubin actually, denoting the sexual difference of bodies and sexuality. While American sexology commonly spoke of 'gender roles' back in the 1960s, in fact, already Johnson's 1785 *A Dictionary of the English Language* gives the meaning of *Sex* under the heading 'Gender' (Glover & Kaplan 2009).

5   Some authors prefer the term 'modifications' to contest evil intentions by the individual performers and feel they are not accurate to account for the broad range of possible practices and meanings they are surrounded by.

6   The term 'prostitution' indicates the practice of engaging in sexual activity for payment. It is generally used by those who see it as a form of sexual exploitation and is generally understood in terms of deviant or illegal or immoral activity. The term 'sex work', in its larger meaning, refers to various forms of economic exchange for sexual services, including prostitution, pornography, erotic dance, erotic massages and other performances. But the term 'sex worker' is also used instead of prostitute, considered demeaning and stigmatizing, to recognize that sex work is work. Here we use the term according to the approaches that are being presented.

Chapter 4: Gender, Sex and Sexuality

1   But post-structuralist theories of gender went down a road that Garfinkel would not pursue. Ethno-methodological indifference – seeking to study the actors' accounts 'wherever and by whomever they are done, while abstaining from all judgements of their adequacy, value, importance, necessity, practicality, success, or consequentiality' (Garfinkel & Sacks 1970, 345) – does not easily marry with the kind of politics of body, gender and sexuality which, with many nuances, is the hallmark of feminist thought, above all in its post-structural and queer versions.

2   The idea that sex, like gender, is constructed is backed by scholars of language, gender and sexuality, who have explored the ways bodies and

body parts are invested with gendered meaning (Motschenbacher 2009; Zimman, Davis & Raclaw 2014).

3   In 2018, fifty years after Garfinkel's interviews with Agnes, sociologists and filmmakers Chase Joynt and Kristen Schilt produced the short documentary 'Framing Agnes', which has subsequently expanded into a full documentary on transgender history and experience and presented at the Sundance Film Festival in 2022 (https://www.framingagnes. com/). The documentary reconstructs some of the scenes between Agnes and Garfinkel and uses archival material on Agnes' case, which was found in 2017, together with material on eight other cases of gender non-conforming people who never made it into the research. Several pre-eminent transgender personalities feature in the documentary as the people who were interviewed by Garfinkel. The documentary unfolds by juxtaposing their personal experiences and the precise re-enactment of the original interviews as retrieved from never-before-seen case files in Garfinkel's archive. In particular, American trans woman, multimedia artist and LGBTQ activist, Zackary Drucker stars as Agnes. Interrogated about how she feels listening to the recordings of the interviews between Agnes and Garfinkel, Drucker suggests that Agnes was in a 'strait-jacket', which amounted to the culture around sex and gender at the time. As pointed out by Joynt and Schilt, the documentary illustrates the importance of having 'a language' that helps conceive and recognize transgender identities beyond the cultural constraints of binary thinking, and suggests that the medical profession was thinking that the surgery was the trauma whereas the people who were seeking it considered the stigma that accompanied their situation as the most traumatic experience.

4   Anne Fausto-Sterling suggests that the prevalence of intersex people might be as high as 1.7% and this has attracted wide attention in the scholarly press and the popular media. There have been discussions as to how to classify intersex and thus percentages may vary according to principles of classification (Sax 2002).

5   While many surgeons performing genital reconstruction – in trans and intersex persons – concentrate on fashioning 'vaginas that seem real', the often-disappointed hope of many who undergo surgery is to have a vagina that makes them 'feel real', i.e., one that truly 'feels' (Kessler 1998). This contradiction gives a new depth to the basically pessimistic image Garfinkel provided of sexual passing and in so doing begins to throw clearer light on certain possible tactics of resistance and subversion. These probably entail giving priority to sexual pleasure as a fundamental human experience, over and above differences of gender/sex (Butler 1999).

6   The sex/gender binary is upheld in the sphere of sport, especially competitive sport where levels of testosterone are measured for athletes competing as females, that are trans or intersex or may not look squarely to gender bodily standards. Considering the case of the Indian female

sprinter Dutee Chand, Madeleine Pape (2019) explores how sexed bodies have been defined and illustrates how the two-category model of biological difference has ultimately been reasserted.

7   That does not mean we should place race, sexuality or gender in relation as though separate spheres of power. In *Bodies that Matter*, Butler (1993) suggests that theoretical pluralist separation of categories is based on exclusionary operations that attribute a false uniformity to them and serve the regulatory purposes of the State: power delimits what counts as a viable sex and what not. What we need to find is a possibility of action laying bare the arbitrariness of gender and sex distinctions, which seem natural in being discursively reproduced in time via the materiality of the bodies they refer to. But that materiality fails to capture the full extent of the discourse and representation: the body is somehow always unruly, which is why it 'counts'; it matters in its matter. Via body performance one can achieve the political feat of breaking the chain of repeated action. That act of liberation (rupture) challenges the claim to originality of gender and the heterosexual norm. In this light, 'drag' is an example of the performativity of subjectivity. In recent years these concepts have taken on a special importance for those who see gender as fluid – genderqueer, genderRebel, nogender – as well as for non-medicalized transgender persons, complicated though it may be by the interaction with the body's materiality and social conditioning.

8   The research by Laumann and colleagues clearly builds on Alfred Kinsey's famous research in the 1940s. Kinsey and his colleagues conducted a series of surveys of the sexual behaviour of middle-class Americans, associating such activities as pre-marital sex, masturbation, homosexuality with age, class and gender variables. The huge amount of data collected revealed the variety of sexual practices within the United States, shedding new light on the gap between social norms and actual behaviours. Kinsey discovered that homosexual activity, especially among men, was more widespread than expected. Homosexuality and heterosexuality were not two discrete and dichotomic categories, but two poles on a continuum – the so-called 'Kinsey Scale', a ranking scale ranging from those who solely have desires for or sexual experiences with the opposite sex, to those who have exclusively same-sex desires or experiences. In the middle there were people who have mixed levels of desire or experiences with both sexes, including 'incidentally' or 'occasionally'.

Chapter 5: Intersectional Experiences and Identities

1   Sofie Lau, Nanna Kristensen and Bjarke Oxlund (2020, 210), in their provoking ethnography of a death case in Denmark during the pandemic crisis, refer to the questioning of contemporary medical technology: 'Overall, the fact that hospitals have been overwhelmed by Covid-19 cases, combined with an absence of a successful cure or vaccine, has

disrupted the modern regime of life sustaining efforts'. The pandemic has revealed the relevance of social factors in the treatment of illness and the communal dimension of medical practices and arrangements (Purnell 2021).

2 Indeed, intersectionality can also be deployed to study superordination in the intersection of gender, class and race, concentrating on masculinity, whiteness and elite social groups (Leek & Kimmel 2015).

3 Du Bois was well aware that stigmatization often takes place on corporeality; in particular it works on the 'colour line' as he would put it in his classic *The Souls of Black Folk* (Du Bois 2015 [1903]).

4 Sexual development is a topic that can be addressed even before puberty. As Breanne Fahs and Eric Swank (2015) point out, children's sexualities are often constructed as immature entities. Children's bodies are seen either as expressions of playfulness or as victims of abuse, but not as desiring subjects in their own right. There are debates about where to draw the line between what is sexual and what is not among children, but indeed children recognize their own genitals as pleasant and private, and there are studies on childhood masturbation, to the extent that some studies identify the age of ten as the actual onset of sexual feelings. However, there is still limited research on incorporating children as sexual subjects.

5 As Sandra Bartky (1990) pointed out, women internalize a judgemental gaze towards their bodies and the idea that if they let themselves go, they will become undesirable. This contributes to their self-perception, wherein even though they may recognize beauty care and body maintenance practices (such as hair removal, toning, make-up, exfoliating, etc.) as societal impositions, they won't easily give them up unless they question their own sense of self. The problem, according to Bartky, is that in this process, an idea of the female body's inferiority to the male body is also internalized, which poses the risk of becoming alienated from their own bodies.

Chapter 6: The Power of Appearances

1 The different meanings attaching to the phenomenon over time are now given two distinct names in English: *cellulite* and *cellulitis*. The first is a deposit of subcutaneous fat; the second a circumscribed inflammation of interstitial and perivisceral adipose tissue.

2 By 'plastic surgery' one means those surgical techniques, known from ancient times, designed to reconstruct bodies and faces ravaged by disease, deformation, organ removal or accident. Cosmetic or aesthetic surgery, by contrast, includes techniques for remodelling healthy bodies and faces in line with the prevailing standards of beauty.

3 Methodologically reliable data are difficult to collect in such domain since cosmetic surgery (differently from the reconstructive one) is

performed in professional private settings and statistics are based on questionnaires that members of national professional societies are invited to complete. According to the 2020 Plastic Surgery Statistics Report, produced by the American Society of Plastic Surgeons, 92% of all cosmetic surgical procedures were performed on women; and according to the Global Survey, produced by the International Society of Aesthetic and Plastic Surgeons in 2022, around 86.5% of non-surgical procedures were performed on women.

4   For example, bodybuilding as a competitive physical activity has been ascribed to the creation of subcultures where both a complex and partly subversive kind of femininity and a more traditional but often ambiguous masculinity are reproduced. Alan Klein's work on Californian male bodybuilders showed two tendencies: building up muscle is a typically male attempt to compensate for physical, cultural or economic deficiencies; at the same time, it points to the bodybuilders' economic, sexual and personal contradictions and the unachieved search for masculinity (Klein 1993; see also Marshall, Chamberlain & Hodgetts 2020 for recent tendencies and tensions). Women gradually entered the subculture of bodybuilding. Tanya Bunsell's ethnographic study provides a perspective on the world of women bodybuilders, exploring the ways in which they resist, negotiate and accommodate pressures to engage in conventional feminine activities and appearances: while deliberately building up muscle mass these women seemingly defy distinctions of gender; when it comes to competitions, they find they need to display their femininity by ornaments and hyper-feminine posturing (Bunsell 2013; see also Boyle 2005; Lowe 1998). For bodybuilding there is the important issue of steroid consumption and how it relates to masculinity and masculinization of the body (Kotzé & Antonopoulos 2021) as well as femininity and a muscular look (Andreasson & Johansson 2021).

5   The fit and healthy body is increasingly promoted through apps and wearable devices which invite users to monitor their own body very closely: as Deborah Lupton (2020) has suggested in a study of Australian women, there are numerous tensions between the different demands that women face trying to conform to the idealized and normative femininities proposed and their everyday lives and bodies.

Chapter 7: Visualizing Gendered Bodies

1   Mulvey mentioned a way round this when exploring alternative strategies of film representation, primed, inter alia, by avant-garde cinema and feminist thinking: together with Peter Wollen she created documentaries on certain strong, active, creative women like Amy Johnson the aviator (*Amy*, 1980), photographer Tina Modotti and painter Frida Kahlo (*Frida Kahlo and Tina Modotti*, 1982) (see Sassatelli and Mulvey 2011).

2 More broadly, in her study of coming out *Come Out, Come Out, Whoever You Are*, Abigail Saguy (2020) examines how coming out has become an important social ritual and has moved beyond gay and lesbian rights groups to be deployed also by, for example, immigrants and fat acceptance activists to resist stigma and enact social change, shifting in meanings and power in the process.

3 In a close-up on the genderisms of femininity that appeared in French translation, Goffman (1977b) elaborated on the latter including: the 'hidden woman' (sheltering behind an object or hanging back on the fringe of the action); the 'distant woman' (where, by some secondary involvement like speaking on the phone, she is shown abandoning a scene where she ought to be, and actually is, involved, which diminishes her agency); the 'submissive woman' (stretched out on a bed or floor, lower than the other figures portrayed, indicating ritual submission, or slightly bending at the knee as a token of accepting subordination); 'hand game' or 'womanly happiness' (where the woman is again dissociated from what she is doing and losing agency: for example, putting her hand over her mouth to hold back a bursting emotion, thus emphasizing her own emotional nature or a childlike gush of joy at tasting a product); the 'docile woman' (where she is under supervision from a man who holds her hand, encircles her waist, guides her gesture in kinaesthetic learning mode); the 'childlike woman' (where women strike an infantile pose); the 'toy woman' and 'playful woman' (where the woman is the object of a game like chase-and-capture and grab-and-squeeze that one plays with children, or where she herself with all her body puts on a comic display like a marionette or clown).

4 Goffman indeed also collected advertising images where dominant genderisms were turned upside down – though these 'reversals' were a relatively small part of his sample (Chadwick 1988). Gender displays may ironically reflect basic traits of the social structure, but may also go against such traits, reversing or offsetting them. As they distil everyday displays in typified forms, adverts are ambivalent: they may not just put across a vision of identity, family, gender, race, etc., serving to reproduce social hierarchies and differences, but also stage minority or even subversive visions, especially where new consumer identities are becoming important and vocal.

5 Of course, there is also the issue of how media images of the body are received and consumed, thereby influencing audiences' perceptions of their own bodies. In their book *The Media and Body Image: If Looks Could Kill*, Maggie Wykes and Barrie Gunter (2005) discuss both some important aspects of body representation and idealization in the media and the theories and empirical studies that have been developed around matters of reception and influence.

6 As detailed by Wendy Anderson (2021) in *Rebirthing a Nation: White Women, Identity Politics, and the Internet*, neoliberal culture also marries white nationalism to produce an ostensibly pro-women racist

rhetoric: in the United States, conservative women placed in positions of political and communicative power, including Sarah Palin, Kellyanne Conway and Ivanka Trump, have validated racial fears through a form of racism which is articulated through white identity politics and classification of womanhood based on motherhood and 'maternal feminism'.

7   In much media content, early images of battered women as pure victims are now set aside more recent images of battered women as 'survivors'. This is a reversed ideal type showing the subject as making choices and being self-sufficient, at the opposite pole of an agency continuum. The resulting discursive dichotomy contributes to the stigmatization of battered women who stay in violent relationships and do not actively struggle for their survival, and reduces the issue to a matter of individual choice, whatever the social, economic, cultural reasons for experiencing a long-lasting violent intimate relationship (for an example of content analysis of the abusive relationship 'victims vs. survivors' dichotomy in literature, see Dunn 2005; for an example of analysis of visual representations of rape myths and portrayals of victimhood in news photographs, see Schwark 2017).

8   This recalls what Imogen Tyler (2006) also noted about the figure of asylum-seekers in media representations, created by the mountain of images of beings with qualities that invoke fear, anger and disgust amongst 'native' communities. While xenophobic discourses depict the asylum-seeker as a dehumanized, undifferentiated mass, humanitarian discourses invite the public to recognize 'the human face' of specific asylum-seekers, asking us through photographic close-ups to recognize that they are 'just like us' and to identify with 'the victims' of repressive asylum laws. But in so doing, humanitarian 'subjects' place themselves in the position of agents for asylum-seekers. As a consequence, they visually obliterate asylum-seekers' agency, and depend on the same categories of inclusion/exclusion, authentic/inauthentic, us/them, as xenophobic discourse, thus reinforcing abjection (Ahmed 2014).

9   In a book drawing on ethnographic studies of trans video blogging, Tobias Raun (2016) explores the ways in which the video blog (or 'vlog') enables trans people to construct their stories in multimodal messages offering new ways to construct and archive bodily changes, and to revise the story endlessly. The author suggests that video blogs have a transformative and therapeutic potential and can be used as a site for community building and resistance.

Bibliography

Abelson, M.J. (2019) *Men in Place: Trans Masculinity, Race, and Sexuality in America*. Minneapolis, MN: University of Minnesota Press.

Adams, J. (2010) 'Motivational narratives and assessments of the body after cosmetic surgery', *Qualitative Health Research*, 20, 6: 755–67.

Adelman, M. & Ruggi, L. (2016) 'The sociology of the body', *Current Sociology*, 64, 6: 907–30.

Ahmed, L. (1992) *Women and Gender in Islam*. New Haven, CT: Yale University Press.

Ahmed, S. (2014) *Cultural Politics of Emotion*, 2nd edn. Edinburgh: Edinburgh University Press.

Aiello, G. & Woodhouse, A. (2016) 'When corporations come to define the visual politics of gender: The case of Getty Images', *Journal of Language and Politics*, 15, 3: 352–68.

Ailshire, J.A. & House, J.S. (2011) 'The unequal burden of weight gain. An intersectional approach to understanding social disparities in BMI trajectories from 1986 to 2001/2002', *Social Forces*, 90, 2: 397–423.

Alaluf, Y.B. (2018) '"It's all included – without stress". Exploring the production of relaxation in Club Med seaside resorts', in: Illouz, E. (ed.) *Emotions as Commodities: Capitalism, Consumption and Authenticity*. London: Routledge.

Almaguer, T. (1991) 'Chicano men: A cartography of homosexual identity and behavior differences', *Differences: A Journal of Feminist Cultural Studies*, 3, 2: 75–100.

Almeling, R. (2015) 'Reproduction', *Annual Review of Sociology*, 41, 1: 423–42.

Amadieu, J.-F. (2002) *Le Poids des apparences: Beauté, amour et gloire*. Paris: Odile Jacob.

Anderson, E. (2009) *Inclusive Masculinity: The Changing Nature of Masculinities*. London: Routledge.

Anderson, W.K.Z. (2021) *Rebirthing a Nation: White Women, Identity Politics, and the Internet*. Jackson, MS: University Press of Mississippi.

Andreasson, J. & Johansson, T. (2021) 'Negotiating female fitness doping: Gender, identity and transgressions', *Sport & Society*, 24, 3: 323–39.

Annandale, E. (2021) 'Health and gender', in: Cockerham, W.C. (ed.) *The Wiley Blackwell Companion to Medical Sociology*. Hoboken, NJ: Wiley-Blackwell.

Anzaldúa, G. (1987) *Borderlands/La Frontera: The New Mestiza*. San Francisco, CA: Spinsters.

Ariès, P. (1962 [1960]) *Centuries of Childhood: A Social History of Family Life*. New York: Alfred A. Knopf.

Ariès, P. (2008 [1977]) *The Hour of our Death: The Classic History of Western Attitudes Toward Death Over the Last One Thousand Years*. New York: Vintage Books.

Atkinson, M. (2003) *Tattooed: The Sociogenesis of a Body Art*. Toronto: University of Toronto Press.

Atkinson, M. (2004) 'Tattooing and civilizing processes: Body modification as self-control', *Canadian Review of Sociology*, 41, 2: 125–46.

Atkinson, M. (2008) 'Exploring male femininity in the "crisis": Men and cosmetic surgery', *Body & Society*, 14, 1: 67–87.

Bailey, M. (2021) *Misogynoir Transformed: Black Women's Digital Resistance*. New York: New York University Press.

Banet-Wiser, S. (2018) *Empowered: Popular Feminism and Popular Misogyny*. Durham, NC: Duke University Press.

Barber, K. (2008) 'The well-coiffed man: Class, race, and heterosexual masculinity in the hair salon', *Gender & Society*, 22, 4: 455–76.

Barnes, M. (2015) 'Fetal sex determination and gendered prenatal consumption', *Journal of Consumer Culture*, 15, 3: 371–90.

Barnum, A.J. & Zajicek, A.M. (2008) 'An intersectional analysis of visual media: A case of Diesel advertisements', *Social Thought & Research*, 29: 105–28.

Bartky, S.L. (1990) *Femininity and Domination: Studies in the Phenomenology of Oppression*. London: Routledge.

Baudrillard, J. (1998 [1970]) *The Consumer Society: Myths and Structures*. London: Sage.

Bauman, Z. (1992) *Intimations of Postmodernity*. London: Routledge.

Beauvoir, S. de (1989 [1949]) *The Second Sex*. New York: Vintage Books.

Beccia, A.L., Baek, J., Austin, S.B., Jesdale, W.M. & Lapane, K.L. (2021)

'Eating-related pathology at the intersection of gender identity and expression, sexual orientation, and weight status: An intersectional multi-level analysis of individual heterogeneity and discriminatory accuracy of the Growing Up Today Study cohorts', *Social Science & Medicine*, 281: 1–11.

Beck, U. (1992) *Risk Society: Towards a New Modernity*. London: Sage.

Becker, H. (1953) 'Becoming a marihuana user', *American Journal of Sociology*, 59, 3: 235–42.

Beemyn, G. & Eliason, M. (1996) *Queer Studies: A Lesbian, Gay, Bisexual, and Transgender Anthology*. New York: New York University Press.

Beemyn, G. & Rankin, S. (2011) *The Lives of Transgender People*. New York: Columbia University Press.

Belknap, P. & Leonard, W.M. (1991) 'A conceptual replication and extension of Erving Goffman's study of gender advertisements', *Sex Roles*, 25, 3–4: 103–18.

Bell, P. & Milic, M. (2002) 'Goffman's Gender Advertisements revisited. Combining content analysis with semiotic analysis', *Visual Communication*, 1, 2: 203–22.

Bell, R.M. (1987) *Holy Anorexia*. Chicago, IL: The University of Chicago Press.

Bendelow, G. (2009) *Health, Emotion and the Body*. Cambridge: Polity Press.

Benhabib, S. (2002) *The Claims of Culture: Equality and Diversity in the Global Era*. Princeton, NJ: Princeton University Press.

Berger, J. (2008 [1972]) *Ways of Seeing*. London: Penguin.

Bericat, E. (2016) 'The sociology of emotions: Four decades of progress', *Current Sociology*, 64, I3: 491–513.

Bernstein, E. (2007) *Temporarily Yours: Intimacy, Authenticity, and the Commerce of Sex*. Chicago, IL: University of Chicago Press.

Berry, B. (2016 [2008]) *The Power of Looks: Social Stratification of Physical Appearance*. London: Routledge.

Bhabha, H. (1994) *The Location of Culture*. London: Routledge.

Bhambra, G. (2007) *Rethinking Modernity: Postcolonialism and the Sociological Imagination*. Basingstoke: Palgrave.

Billings, D. & Urban, T. (1982) 'The socio-medical construction of transsexualism: An interpretation and critique', *Social Problems*, 29, 3: 266–82.

Bird, C.E. & Rieker, P.P. (2012) *Gender and Health. The Effects of Constrained Choices and Social Policies*. Cambridge: Cambridge University Press.

Bishop, K. (2016) 'Body modification and trans men: The lived realities of gender transition and partner intimacy', *Body & Society*, 22, 1: 62–91.

Blackman, L. (2016) 'New biologies: Epigenetics, the microbiome and immunities', *Body and Society*, 22, 4: 3–18.

Blackman, L. (2021) *The Body*. London: Routledge.

Blum, V. (2003) *Flesh Wounds: The Culture of Cosmetic Surgery*. Berkeley, CA: University of California Press.

Boepple, L., Ata, R.N., Rum, R. & Thompson, K. (2016) '"Strong is the new skinny". A content analysis of fitspiration websites', *Body Image*, 17: 132–5.

Boero, N. (2009) 'Fat kids, working moms, and the "epidemic of obesity". Race, class, and mother blame', in: Rothblum, E. & Solovay, S. (eds) *The Fat Studies Reader*. New York: New York University Press.

Boero, N. & Manson, K. (2020) *The Oxford Handbook of the Sociology of the Body*. Oxford: Oxford University Press.

Bolin, A. (1994) 'Transcending and transgendering: Male-to-female transsexuals, dichotomy and diversity', in: Herdt, G. (ed.) *Third Sex, Third Gender*. New York: Zone.

Bolivar, A. (2021) '"Nothing feels better than getting paid": Sex working trans Latinas' meanings and uses of money', *Feminist Anthropology*, 2, 2: 298–311.

Boltanski, L. (1971) 'Les usages sociaux du corps', *Annales. Économies, Sociétés, Civilisations*, 26, 1: 205–33.

Bordo, S. (1999) *The Male Body: A New Look at Men in Public and in Private*. New York: Farrar, Straus and Giroux.

Bordo, S. (2003 [1993]) *Unbearable Weight: Feminism, Western Culture, and the Body*. Berkeley, CA: University of California Press.

Borgerson, J.L. & Schroeder, J.E. (2018) 'Making skin visible: How consumer culture imagery commodifies identity', *Body & Society*, 24, 1–2: 103–36.

Bornstein, K. (1994) *Gender Outlaw: On Men, Women and the Rest of Us*. New York: Routledge.

Bourdieu, P. (1977) 'Remarques provisoires sur la perception sociale du corps', *Actes de la Recherche en Sciences Sociales*, 14: 51–4.

Bourdieu, P. (1978) 'Sport and social class', *Social Science Information*, 17: 819–40.

Bourdieu, P. (1984 [1979]) *Distinction: A Social Critique of the Judgement of Taste*. Cambridge, MA: Harvard University Press.

Bourdieu, P. (1990 [1980]) *The Logic of Practice*. Stanford, CA: Stanford University Press.

Bourdieu, P. (2001 [1998]) *Masculine Domination*. Stanford, CA: Stanford University Press.

Bourke, J. (2014) *The Story of Pain: From Prayer to Painkillers*. Oxford: Oxford University Press.

Boyle, L. (2005) 'Flexing the tensions of female muscularity: How female bodybuilders negotiate normative femininity in competitive bodybuilding', *Women's Studies Quarterly*, 33: 134–49.

Brickell, C. (2022) 'Goffman and gender studies', in: Jacobsen, M.H. & Smith, G. (eds) *The Routledge International Handbook of Goffman Studies*. London: Routledge.

Bridges, T. (2014) 'A very "gay" straight? Hybrid masculinities, sexual aesthetics, and the changing relationship between masculinity and homophobia', *Gender & Society*, 28, 1: 58–82.

Bridges, T. & Pascoe, C.J. (2014) 'Hybrid masculinities: New directions in the sociology of men and masculinities', *Sociology Compass*, 8, 3: 246–58.

Brody, L.R. (1999) *Gender, Emotion and the Family*. Cambridge, MA: Harvard University Press.

Brody, L.R. (2000) 'The socialization of gender differences in emotional expression: Display rules, infant temperament, and differentiation', in: Fischer, A.H. (ed.) *Gender and Emotion: Social Psychological Perspectives*. Cambridge: Cambridge University Press.

Brown, A. (2021) 'Qualitative description and Black males: On race, the body, and researching the unimaginable', *Qualitative Inquiry*, 27, 10: 1159–68.

Brown, J.A. (1999) 'Comic book masculinity and the New Black Superhero', *African American Review*, 33, 1: 25–42.

Brown, Z. & Tiggemann, M. (2016) 'Attractive celebrity and peer images on Instagram: Effect on women's mood and body image', *Body Image*, 19: 37–43.

Browne, B.A. (1998) 'Gender stereotypes in advertising on children's television in the 1990s: A cross-national analysis', *Journal of Advertising*, 27, 1: 83–96.

Browne, I. & Misra, J. (2003) 'The intersection of gender and race in the labor market', *Annual Review of Sociology*, 29: 487–513.

Brownmiller, S. (1984) *Femininity*. New York: Simon & Schuster.

Brownmiller, S. (1986 [1975]) *Against Our Will: Men, Women and Rape*. New York: Simon and Schuster.

Brumberg, J. (1997) *The Body Project: An Intimate History of American Girls*. New York: Random House.

Bullough, V.L. & Bullough, B. (1993) *Cross-Dressing, Sex and Gender*. Philadelphia, PA: University of Pennsylvania Press.

Bunsell, T. (2013) *Strong and Hard Women: An Ethnography of Female Bodybuilding*. London: Routledge.

Burkitt, I. (1999) *Bodies of Thought: Embodiment, Identity and Modernity*. London: Sage.

Butler, J. (1993) *Bodies that Matter: On the Discursive Limits of 'Sex'*. New York: Routledge.

Butler, J. (1999) 'Revisiting bodies and pleasure', *Theory, Culture & Society*, 16, 2: 11–20.

Butler, J. (2006 [1990]) *Gender Trouble: Feminism and the Subversion of Identity*. New York: Routledge.

Buysse, J.A.M. & Embser-Herbert, M.S. (2004) 'Constructions of gender in sport: An analysis of intercollegiate media guide cover photographs', *Gender & Society*, 18, 1: 66–81.

Byrne, B. (2006) *White Lives: The Interplay of 'Race', Class and Gender in Everyday Life*. London: Routledge.

Cairns, K. & Johnston, J. (2016) *Food and Femininity*. London: Bloomsbury.

Campbell, C. (1987) *The Romantic Ethic and the Spirit of Modern Consumerism*. Oxford: Blackwell.

Cárcamo, C., Moreno, A. & del Barrio, C. (2021) 'Girls do not sweat: The development of gender stereotypes in physical education in primary school', *Human Arenas*, 4: 196–217.

Carpenter, L.M. (2015) 'Studying sexualities from a life course perspective', in: DeLamater, J. & Plante, R.F. (eds) *Handbook of the Sociology of Sexualities*. Cham: Springer International Publishing.

Carrillo, H. & Fontdevila, J. (2014) 'Border crossings and shifting sexualities among Mexican gay immigrant men: Beyond monolithic conceptions', *Sexualities*, 17, 8: 919–38.

Casey, E. & Martens, L. (eds) (2006) *Gender and Consumption: Domestic Cultures and the Commercialization of Everyday Life*. London: Routledge.

Cavanagh, S.L. (2010) *Queering Bathrooms: Gender, Sexuality and the Hygienic Imagination*. Toronto: University of Toronto Press.

Chadwick, M. (1988) *Gender and Symbol in Advertising Imagery: A Comparison of Goffman and Williamson*. Salford: University of Salford.

Chakrabarty, D. (2000) *Provincializing Europe: Postcolonial Thought and Historical Difference*. Princeton, NJ: Princeton University Press.

Chapkis, W. (1986) *Beauty Secrets: Women and the Politics of Appearance*. Boston, MA: South End Press.

Charrad, M. (2011) 'Gender in the Middle East: Islam, state, agency', *Annual Review of Sociology*, 37, 1: 417–37.

Cheng, R.P. (2009) 'Sociological theories of disability, gender, and sexuality: A review of the literature', *Journal of Human Behavior in the Social Environment*, 19, 1: 112–22.

Chu, A.L. & Drager, E.H. (2019) 'After trans studies', *Transgender Studies Quarterly*, 6, 1: 103–16.

Cixous, H. & Clement, C. (1986 [1975]) *The Newly Born Woman*. London: Tauris.

Clayson, H. (2003) *Painted Love: Prostitution in French Art of the Impressionist Era*. Los Angeles, CA: Getty Publications.

Cohen, R., Newton-John, T. & Slater, A. (2021) 'The case for body positivity on social media: Perspectives on current advances and future directions', *Journal of Health Psychology*, 26, 13: 2365–73.

Collins, P.H. (1990) *Black Feminist Thought. Knowledge, Consciousness, and the Politics of Empowerment*. Boston, MA: Unwin Hyman.

Collins, P.H. (2015) 'Intersectionality's definitional dilemmas', *Annual Review of Sociology*, 41, 1: 1–20.

Connell, C. (2010) 'Doing, undoing, or redoing gender?: Learning from the workplace experiences of transpeople', *Gender & Society*, 24, 1: 31–55.

Connell, C. & Mears, A. (2018) 'Bourdieu and the body', in: Medvetz, T. & Sallaz, J.J. (eds) *The Oxford Handbook of Pierre Bourdieu*. Oxford: Oxford University Press.

Connell, R. (1987) *Gender and Power: Society, the Person and Sexual Politics*. Stanford, CA: Stanford University Press.

Connell, R. (2005a) *Masculinities*, 2nd edn. Cambridge: Polity.

Connell, R. (2005b) 'Globalization, imperialism and masculinities', in: Kimmel, M.S., Hearn, J. & Connell, R. (eds) *Handbook of Studies on Men and Masculinities*. London: Sage.

Connell, R. (2009) 'Accountable conduct: "Doing gender" in transsexual and political retrospect', *Gender & Society*, 23, 1: 104–11.

Connell, R. (2021) *Gender: In World Perspective*, 4th edn. Cambridge: Polity.

Connell, R. & Messerschmidt, J. (2005) 'Hegemonic masculinity: Rethinking the concept', *Gender & Society*, 19, 6: 829–59.

Conrad, P. (2007) *The Medicalization of Society*. Baltimore, MD: Johns Hopkins University Press.

Cooky, C., Messner, M.A. & Musto, M. (2015) '"It's dude time!": A quarter century of excluding women's sports in televised news and highlight shows', *Communication & Sport*, 3, 3: 261–87.

Corsaro, W.A. (2003) *We're Friends, Right? Inside Kids' Culture.* Washington, DC: Joseph Henry Press.

Corsaro, W.A. (2015) *The Sociology of Childhood.* Los Angeles, CA: Sage.

Cortese, A.J. (2008) *Provocateur: Images of Women and Minorities in Advertising.* New York: Rowman & Littlefield.

Costa, C. & Murphy, M. (2015) *Habitus and Social Research: The Art of Application.* Basingstoke: Palgrave.

Cougar Hall, P., West, J.H. & McIntyre, E. (2012) 'Female self-sexualization in MySpace.com personal profile photographs', *Sexuality & Culture*, 16: 1–16.

Crawford, R. (2006) 'Health as a meaningful social practice', *Health*, 10, 4: 401–20.

Creed, B. (1993) *The Monstrous-Feminine: Film, Feminism, Psychoanalysis.* London: Routledge.

Cregan, K. (2006) *The Sociology of the Body: Mapping the Abstraction of Embodiment.* London: Sage.

Crenshaw, K. (1989) 'Demarginalizing the intersection of race and sex: A black feminist critique of antidiscrimination doctrine, feminist theory and antiracist politics', *University of Chicago Legal Forum*, 1: 139–67.

Crenshaw, K. (1991) 'Mapping the margins: Identity politics, intersectionality, and violence against women', *Stanford Law Review*, 43, 6: 1241–99.

Crocetti, D., Arfini, E.A.G., Monro, S. & Yeadon-Lee, T. (2020) '"You're basically calling doctors torturers": Stakeholder framing issues around naming intersex rights claims as human rights abuses', *Sociology of Health & Illness*, 42, 4: 943–58.

Crossley, N. (1995) 'Body techniques, agency and inter-corporality: On Goffman's relations in public', *Sociology*, 129, 1: 133–49.

Crossley, N. (2001) *The Social Body: Habit, Identity and Desire.* London: Sage.

Crossley, N. (2005) 'Mapping reflexive body techniques: On body modification and maintenance', *Body & Society*, 11, 1: 1–35.

Crossley, N. (2022) 'Goffman and the sociology of the body', in: Jacobsen, M.H. & Smith, G. (eds) *The Routledge International Handbook of Goffman Studies.* London: Routledge.

Cuthbert, K. (2019) '"When we talk about gender we talk about sex":

(A)sexuality and (a)gendered subjectivities', *Gender & Society*, 33, 6: 841–64.

D'Anglure, B.S. (2018 [2006]) *Inuit Stories of Being and Rebirth: Gender, Shamanism, and the Third Sex.* Winnipeg: University of Manitoba Press.

Darwin, H. (2017) 'Doing gender beyond the binary: A virtual ethnography', *Symbolic Interaction*, 40, 2–3: 317–34.

Darwin, H. (2020) 'Challenging the cisgender/transgender binary: Nonbinary people and the transgender label', *Gender & Society*, 34, 3: 357–80.

Davis, A. (1981) *Women, Race and Class.* New York: Random House.

Davis, F. (1992) *Fashion, Culture, and Identity.* Chicago, IL: University of Chicago Press.

Davis, G. (2015) *Contesting Intersex: The Dubious Diagnosis.* New York: New York University Press.

Davis, G., Dewey, J.M. & Murphy, E.L. (2016) 'Giving sex: Deconstructing intersex and trans medicalization practices', *Gender & Society*, 30, 3: 490–514.

Davis, K. (1991) 'Remaking the she-devil: A critical look at feminist approaches to beauty', *Hypatia*, 6, 2: 21–43.

Davis, K. (1995) *Reshaping the Female Body: The Dilemma of Cosmetic Surgery.* New York: Routledge.

Davis, K. (2003) *Dubious Equalities and Embodied Differences: Cultural Studies on Cosmetic Surgery.* Lanham, MD: Rowman & Littlefield.

De Grazia, V. & Furlough, E. (eds) (1996) *The Sex of Things: Gender and Consumption in Historical Perspective.* Berkeley, CA: University of California Press.

Defert, D. (1991) '"Popular life" and insurance technology', in: Burchell, G. & Gordon, C. (eds) *The Foucault Effect: Studies in Governmentality.* Hemel Hempstead: Simon and Schuster.

DeLamater, J. (1987) 'Gender differences in sexual scenarios', in: Kelley, K. (ed.) *Females, Males, and Sexuality.* Albany, NY: SUNY Press.

DeMello, M. (2000) *Bodies of Inscription: A Cultural History of the Modern Tattoo Community.* Durham, NC: Duke University Press.

Demos, J. & Demos, V. (1969) 'Adolescence in historical perspective', *Journal of Marriage and Family*, 31, 4: 632–8.

Denny, E. (2018) *Pain.* Cambridge: Polity.

DeVault, M. (1991) *Feeding the Family.* Chicago, IL: University of Chicago Press.

Diamond, I. & Quinby, L. (1988) *Feminism and Foucault: Reflections on Resistance.* Boston, MA: Northeastern University Press.

Dilley, R. (2012) 'Embodying difference: Gender, identity and climbing', in: Hughson, J., Palmer, C. & Skillen, F. (eds) *The Role of Sports in the Formation of Personal Identities.* New York: Edwin Mellen Press.

Dinnerstein, M. & Weitz, R. (1998) 'Jane Fonda, Barbara Bush and other aging bodies: Femininity and the limits of resistance', in: Weitz, R. (ed.) *The Politics of Women's Bodies: Sexuality, Appearance, and Behavior.* Oxford: Oxford University Press.

Doan, P.L. & Johnston, L. (2022) *Rethinking Transgender Identities: Reflections from Around the Globe*. London: Routledge.

Doane, M.A. (1991) *Femmes Fatales: Feminism, Film Theory, Psychoanalysis*. London: Routledge.

Döring, N., Reif, A. & Poeschl, S. (2016) 'How gender-stereotypical are selfies? A content analysis and comparison with magazine adverts', *Computers in Human Behavior*, 55, Part B: 955–62.

Douglas, M. (1984 [1966]) *Purity and Danger: An Analysis of the Concepts of Pollution and Taboo*. London: Routledge.

Douglas, M. (2003 [1973]) *Natural Symbols: Explorations in Cosmology*. London: Routledge.

Downing, J. & Husband, C. (2005) *Representing 'Race': Racisms, Ethnicities and Media*. London: Sage.

Downs, L.L. (1993) 'If "woman" is just an empty category, then why am I afraid to walk alone at night? Identity politics meets the postmodern subject', *Comparative Studies in Society and History*, 35, 2: 414–37.

Dozier, R. (2005) 'Beards, breasts, and bodies: Doing sex in a gendered world', *Gender & Society*, 19, 3: 297–316.

Dreger, D.A. (1998) *Hermaphrodites and the Medical Invention of Sex*. Cambridge, MA: Harvard University Press.

Du Bois, W.E.B. (2015 [1903]) *The Souls of Black Folk*. New Haven, CT: Yale University Press.

Duden, B. (1993) *Disembodying Women: Perspectives on Pregnancy and the Unborn*. Cambridge, MA: Harvard University Press.

Dull, D. & West, C. (1991) 'Accounting for cosmetic surgery: The accomplishment of gender', *Social Problems*, 38, 1: 54–70.

Duncan, M. (1990) 'Sports photographs and sexual difference: Images of women and men in the 1984 and 1988 Olympic Games', *Sociology of Sport Journal*, 7: 22–43.

Dunn, J. (2005) '"Victims" and "survivors": Emerging vocabularies of motive for "battered women who stay"', *Sociological Inquiry*, 75, 1: 1–30.

Duschinsky, R., Schnall, S. & Weiss, D.H. (eds) (2016) *Purity and Danger Now: New Perspectives*. London: Routledge.

Dworkin, A. (1981) *Pornography: Men Possessing Women*. New York: Putnam.

Dworkin, S.L. & Wachs, F.L. (2009) *Body Panic: Gender, Health and the Selling of Fitness*. New York: New York University Press.

Dwyer, C. (1999) 'Veiled meanings: Young British Muslim women and the negotiation of differences', *Gender, Place and Culture: A Journal of Feminist Geography*, 6, 1: 5–26.

Dyer, R. (1985) 'Male gay porn: Coming to terms', *Jump Cut*, 30, 1: 27–9.

Ehrenreich, B. (1989) *Fear of Falling: The Inner Life of the Middle Class*. New York: Pantheon Books.

Ehrenreich, B. & English, D. (2005 [1978]) *For Her Own Good: Two Centuries of the Experts' Advice to Women*. New York: Anchor Books.

El Guindi, F. (1999) *Veil: Modesty, Privacy and Resistance*. Oxford: Berg.

Elias, A., Gill, R. & Scharff, C. (2017) *Aesthetic Labour: Beauty Politics in Neoliberalism*. London: Springer.

Elias, N. (1985) *The Loneliness of the Dying*. New York: Basil Blackwell.

Elias, N. (2021 [1939]) *The Civilizing Process: Sociogenetic and Psychogenetic Investigations*. Oxford: Blackwell.

Elias, N. & Dunning, E. (1986) *Quest for Excitement: Sport and Leisure in the Civilizing Process*. Oxford: Basil Blackwell.

Elliot, P. (2010) *Debates in Transgender, Queer, and Feminist Theory: Contested Sites*. Farnham: Ashgate.

Engels, F. (2010 [1884]) *The Origin of the Family, Private Property and the State*. London: Penguin.

Entwistle, J. (2023 [2000]) *The Fashioned Body: Fashion, Dress and Social Theory*. Cambridge: Polity Press.

Fahs, B. & Delgado, D.A. (2011) 'The specter of excess: Race, class, and gender in women's body hair narratives', in: Bobel, C. & Kwan, S. (eds) *Embodied Resistance: Challenging the Norms, Breaking the Rules*. Nashville, TN: Vanderbilt University Press.

Fahs, B. & Swank, E. (2015) 'Unpacking sexual embodiment and embodied resistance', in: DeLamater, J. & Plante, R.F. (eds) *Handbook of the Sociology of Sexualities*. Cham: Springer International Publishing, pp. 149–67.

Fanon, F. (2021 [1952]) *Black Skin, White Masks*. London: Penguin.

Fausto-Sterling, A. (2000) *Sexing the Body*. New York: Basic Books.

Featherstone, M. (1982) 'The body in consumer culture', *Theory, Culture & Society*, 1, 2: 18–33.

Featherstone, M. (1991) *Consumer Culture and Postmodernism*. London: Sage.

Featherstone, M. (2010) 'Body, image and affect in consumer culture', *Body & Society*, 16, 1: 193–221.

Featherstone, M. & Hepworth, M. (1991) 'The mask of ageing and the postmodern life course', in: Featherstone, M., Hepworth, M. & Turner, B. (eds) *The Body: Social Process and Cultural Theory*. London: Sage.

Featherstone, M., Hepworth, M. & Turner, B. (eds) (1991) *The Body: Social Process and Cultural Theory*. London: Sage.

Federici, S. (2014 [2004]) *Caliban and the Witch: Women, the Body and Primitive Accumulation*. New York: Autonomedia.

Feher, M., Nadaff, R. & Tazi, T. (eds) (1989) *Fragments for a History of the Human Body*, 3 vols. New York: Zone.

Feinberg, L. (1996) *Transgender Warriors*. Boston, MA: Beacon Press.

Ferguson, H. (2000) *Modernity and Subjectivity: Body, Soul, Spirit*. Charlottesville, VA: University Press of Virginia.

Ferrero Camoletto, R. & Bertone, C. (2012) 'Italians (should) do it better? Medicalisation and the disempowering of intimacy', *Modern Italy*, 17, 4: 433–48.

Fine, C. (2017) *Testosterone Rex: Myths of Sex, Science, and Society*. New York: W.W. Norton & Co.

Firestone, S. (2015 [1970]) *The Dialectics of Sex: The Case for Feminist Revolution*. London: Verso.

Fischler, C. (1990) *L'Homnivore: Le Goût, La Cuisine et Le Corps*. Paris: Odile Jacob.

Fontdevila, J. (2009) 'Framing dilemmas during sex: A micro-sociological approach to HIV risk', *Social Theory & Health*, 7, 3: 241–63.

Foucault, M. (1977 [1975]) *Discipline and Punish: The Birth of the Prison*. London: Penguin.

Foucault, M. (1978 [1976]) *The History of Sexuality, Vol. 1: The Will to Knowledge*. London: Penguin.

Foucault, M. (1980a [1975]) 'Body/Power', in: Gordon, C. (ed.) *Power/Knowledge. Michel Foucault: Selected Interviews and Other Writings 1972–1977*. New York: Pantheon Books.

Foucault, M. (1980b) *Herculine Barbin: Being the Recently Discovered Memoirs of a Nineteenth-century French Hermaphrodite*. New York: Pantheon Books.

Foucault, M. (1990 [1984]) *The Use of Pleasure, Vol. 2: The History of Sexuality*. New York: Vintage Books.

Foucault, M. (2012 [1963]) *The Birth of the Clinic*. London: Routledge.

Franklin, S., Lury, C. & Stacey, J. (2000) *Global Nature, Global Culture*. London: Sage.

Fraser, M. & Greco, M. (eds) (2004) *The Body: A Reader*. London: Routledge.

Fraser, N. (2013) *Fortunes of Feminism: From State-Managed Capitalism to Neoliberal Crisis*. London: Verso.

Frosh, S., Phoenix, A. & Pattman, R. (2002) *Young Masculinities: Understanding Boys in Contemporary Society*. Basingstoke: Palgrave Macmillan.

Frost, S. (2020) 'The attentive body: How the indexicality of epigenetic processes enriches our understanding of embodied subjectivity', *Body & Society*, 26, 4: 3–34.

Furlong, A. & Cartmel, F. (1997) *Young People and Social Change: Individualization and Risk in Late Modernity*. Buckingham: Open University Press.

Furman, F.K. (1997) *Facing the Mirror: Older Women and Beauty Shop Culture*. London: Routledge.

Gagné, P. & McGaughey, D. (2002) 'Designing women: Cultural hegemony and the exercise of power among women who have undergone elective mammoplasty', *Gender & Society*, 16, 6: 814–38.

Gagnon, J. & Simon, W. (1973) *Sexual Conduct: The Social Sources of Human Sexuality*. Chicago, IL: Aldine.

Garfinkel, H. (1999 [1967]) *Studies in Ethnomethodology*. Cambridge: Polity.

Garfinkel, H. & Sacks, H. (1970) 'On formal structures of practical actions', in: McKinney, J.C. & Tiryakioin, E.A. (eds) *Theoretical Sociology*. New York: Appleton-Century-Croft.

Garrison, J. (2015) 'Dewey's aesthetics of body-mind functioning', in: Scarinzi, A. (ed.) *Aesthetics and the Embodied Mind: Beyond Art Theory and the Cartesian Mind/Body Dichotomy*. Dordrecht: Springer.

Gay, R. (2017) *Hunger: A Memoir of (My) Body*. New York: Harper.

Gerschick, T.J. (2000) 'Toward a theory of disability and gender', *Signs: Journal of Women in Culture and Society*, 25, 4: 1263–8.

Ghigi, R. (2004) 'Le corps féminin entre science et culpabilisation. Autour d'une histoire de la cellulite', *Travail, genre et sociétés*, 12, 2: 55–75.

Ghigi, R. & Sassatelli, R. (2018) 'Body projects: fashion, aesthetic modifications and stylized selves', in: Krevets, O., Maclaran, P., Miles, S. & Venkatesh, A. (eds) *The SAGE Handbook of Consumer Culture*. London: Sage.

Giddens, A. (1991) *Modernity and Self-Identity: Self and Society in the Late Modern Age*. Stanford, CA: Stanford University Press.

Gill, R. (2003) 'Power and the production of subjects: A genealogy of the New Man and the New Lad', *The Sociological Review*, 51, Supplement 1: 34–56.

Gill, R. (2007a) *Gender and the Media*. Cambridge: Polity.

Gill, R. (2007b) 'Postfeminist media culture: Elements of a sensibility', *European Journal of Cultural Studies*, 10, 2: 147–66.

Gill, R. (2008) 'Empowerment/sexism: Figuring female sexual agency in contemporary advertising', *Feminism & Psychology*, 18, 1: 35–60.

Gill, R. (2009) 'Beyond the "sexualization of culture" thesis: An intersectional analysis of "sixpacks", "midriffs" and "hot lesbians" in advertising', *Sexualities*, 12, 2: 137–60.

Gill, R. (2016) 'Post-postfeminism? New feminist visibilities in postfeminist times', *Feminist Media Studies*, 16, 4: 610–30.

Gill, R. (2021) 'Neoliberal beauty', in: Craig, M.L. (ed.) *The Routledge Companion to Beauty Politics*. London: Routledge.

Gill, R., Henwood, K. & McLean, C. (2005) 'Body projects and the regulation of normative masculinity', *Body & Society*, 11, 1: 37–62.

Gilleard, C. & Higgs, P. (2013) *Ageing, Corporeality and Embodiment*. London: Anthem Press.

Gilman, S. (1999) *Making the Body Beautiful*. Princeton, NJ: Princeton University Press.

Gilroy, P. (1987) *There Ain't No Black in the Union Jack: The Cultural Politics of Race and Nation*. London: Hutchinson.

Gilroy, P. (1993) *The Black Atlantic: Modernity and Double Consciousness*. Cambridge, MA: Harvard University Press.

Gimlin, D. (2002) *Body Work: Beauty and Self-Image in American Culture*. Berkeley, CA: University of California Press.

Gimlin, D. (2012) *Cosmetic Surgery Narratives: A Cross-Cultural Analysis of Women's Accounts*. Basingstoke: Palgrave Macmillan.

Glennie, P. & Thrift, N. (1996) 'Consumption, shopping and gender', in: Wringley, E. & Lowe, M. (eds) *Retailing, Consumption and Capital*. London: Longman.

Glover, D. & Kaplan, C. (2009) *Genders*, 2nd edn. London: Routledge.

Go, J. (2013) 'For a post-colonial sociology', *Theory & Society*, 42, 1: 25–55.

Goffman, E. (1959) *The Presentation of Self in Everyday Life*. New York: Doubleday Anchor Books.

Goffman, E. (1963) *Behaviour in Public Places: Notes on the Social Organization of Gatherings*. New York: Free Press.

Goffman, E. (1977a) 'The arrangement between the sexes', *Theory & Society*, 4, 3: 301–31.

Goffman, E. (1977b) 'La ritualisation de la féminité', *Actes de la Recherche en Sciences Sociales*, 14: 34–50.

Goffman, E. (1979) *Gender Advertisements*. New York: Harper & Row.

Goffman, E. (1981) *Forms of Talk*. Philadelphia, PA: University of Pennsylvania Press.

Goffman, E. (1982 [1967]) *Interaction Rituals: Essays on Face-to-Face Behavior*. New York: Pantheon.

Goffman, E. (1986 [1974]) *Frame Analysis: An Essay on the Organization of Experience*. Boston, MA: Northeastern University Press.

Goffman, E. (1990 [1963]) *Stigma: Notes on the Management of a Spoiled Identity*. London: Penguin.

Goffman, E. (2010 [1971]) *Relations in Public: Microstudies of the Public Order*. London: Routledge.

Goldman, R. (1992) *Reading Ads Socially*. London: Routledge.

González-López, G. (2006) 'Heterosexual fronteras: Immigrant mexicanos, sexual vulnerabilities, and survival', *Sexuality Research & Social Policy*, 3, 3: 67–81.

Gough, B. (2018) *Contemporary Masculinities: Embodiment, Emotion and Wellbeing*. Basingstoke: Palgrave.

Gray, B. (2010) 'Emotional labour, gender and professional stereotypes of emotional and physical contact, and personal perspectives on the emotional labour of nursing', *Journal of Gender Studies*, 19, 4: 349–60.

Green, A.I. (2007) 'Queer theory and sociology: Locating the subject and the self in sexuality studies', *Sociological Theory*, 25, 1: 26–45.

Green, A.I. (2008) 'The social organization of desire: The sexual fields approach', *Sociological Theory*, 26, 1: 25–50.

Greer, G. (1992) *The Change: Women, Aging, and the Menopause*. New York: Knopf.

Greer, G. (1999) *The Whole Woman*. New York: Knopf.

Gribaldo, A. (2020) *Unexpected Subjects: Intimate Partner Violence, Testimony, and the Law*. Chicago, IL: HAU Books.

Grosz, E. (1994) *Volatile Bodies: Toward a Corporal Feminism*. Bloomington, IN: Indiana University Press.

Gruenbaum, E. (2001) *The Female Circumcision Controversy: An Anthropological Perspective*. Philadelphia, PA: University of Pennsylvania Press.

Guillaumin, C. (1993) 'The constructed body', in: Burroughs, C.B. &

Ehrenreich, J.D. (eds) *Reading the Social Body*. Iowa City, IA: University of Iowa Press.

Guillaumin, C. (1995) *Racism, Sexism, Power and Ideology*. London: Routledge.

Guillaumin, C. (2016 [1992]) *Sexe, Race et Pratique du Pouvoir*. Donnemarie-Dontilly: Éditions iXe.

Guldin, A. (2000) 'Self-claiming sexuality: Mobility impaired people and American culture', *Sexuality and Disability*, 18, 4: 233–8.

Haber, H.F. (1996) 'Foucault pumped: Body politics and the muscled woman', in: Hekman, S. (ed.) *Feminist Interpretations of Michel Foucault*. University Park, PA: Pennsylvania State University Press.

Haiken, E. (1997) *Venus Envy: A History of Cosmetic Surgery*. Baltimore, MD: Johns Hopkins University Press.

Hakim, C. (2010) 'Erotic capital', *European Sociological Review*, 26, 5: 499–518.

Hall, L., Callister, L., Berry, J.A. & Matsumura, G. (2007) 'Meanings of menopause: Cultural influences on perception and management of menopause', *Journal of Holistic Nursing*, 25, 2: 106–18.

Halperin, D. (1995) *Saint Foucault: Towards a Gay Hagiography*. Oxford: Oxford University Press.

Halperin, D. (2002) *How to Do the History of Homosexuality*. Chicago, IL: University of Chicago Press.

Hanna, J.L. (1988) *Dance, Sex and Gender*. Chicago, IL: University of Chicago Press.

Harris, A. & Bartlow, S. (2015) 'Intersectionality: Race, gender, sexuality, and class', in: DeLamater, J. & Plante, R.F. (eds) *Handbook of the Sociology of Sexualities*. Cham: Springer International Publishing, pp. 261–71.

Hassin, R.R., Aviezer, H. & Bentin, S. (2013) 'Inherently ambiguous: Facial expressions of emotions, in context', *Emotion Review*, 5: 60–5.

Hatton, E. & Trautner, M.N. (2011) 'Equal opportunity objectification? The sexualization of men and women on the cover of *Rolling Stone*', *Sexuality & Culture*, 15, 3: 256–78.

Hausman, B.L. (1995) *Transsexualism, Technology and the Idea of Gender*. Durham, NC: Duke University Press.

Hebdige, D. (2003 [1979]) *Subculture*. London: Routledge.

Heikkala, J. (1993) 'Discipline and Excel: Techniques of the self and body and the logic of competing', *Sociology of Sport Journal*, 10: 397–412.

Hekman, S. (ed.) (1996) *Feminist Interpretations of Michel Foucault*. University Park, PA: Pennsylvania State University Press.

Henslin, J.M. & Biggs, M.A. (1971) 'Behaviour in public places: The sociology of the vaginal examination', in: Henslin, J.M. (ed.) *Down to Earth Sociology*. New York: The Free Press.

Herdt, G.H. (1993) *Ritualized Homosexuality in Melanesia*. Berkeley, CA: University of California Press.

Heyes, C. (2009) 'All cosmetic surgery is "ethnic": Asian eyelids, feminist indignation, and the politics of whiteness', in: Heyes, C. & Jones, M. (eds) *Cosmetic Surgery: A Feminist Primer*. Farnham: Ashgate.

Heyes, C. & Jones, M. (eds) (2009) *Cosmetic Surgery: A Feminist Primer*. Farnham: Ashgate.

Hillier, J. & Rooks, E. (2005) *Habitus: A Sense of Place*. Farnham: Ashgate.

Hines, S. & Sanger, T. (2010) *Transgender Identities: Towards a Social Analysis of Gender Diversity*. London: Routledge.

Hird, M.J. (2000) 'Gender's nature: Intersexuality, transsexualism and the sex/gender binary', *Feminist Theory*, 1, 3: 347–64.

Hochschild, A.R. (1989) *The Second Shift: Working Families and the Revolution at Home*. New York: Viking.

Hochschild, A.R. (2003) *The Commercialization of Intimate Life: Notes from Home and Work*. Berkeley, CA: University of California Press.

Hochschild, A.R. (2012a [1983]) *The Managed Heart: Commercialization of Human Feeling*. Berkeley, CA: University of California Press.

Hochschild, A.R. (2012b) *The Outsourced Self: Intimate Life in Market Times*. New York: Metropolitan Books.

Hockey, J., Meah, A. & Robinson, V. (2007) *Mundane Heterosexualities*. Basingstoke: Palgrave Macmillan.

Holliday, R. & Cairnie, A. (2007) 'Man made plastic: Investigating men's consumption of aesthetic surgery', *Journal of Consumer Culture*, 7, 1: 57–78.

hooks, b. (1981) *Ain't I a Woman: Black Women and Feminism*. Boston, MA: South End Press.

hooks, b. (1992) *Black Looks: Race and Representation*. Boston, MA: South End Press.

hooks, b. (2004) *We Real Cool: Black Men and Masculinity*. London: Routledge.

Hope, C. (1982) 'Caucasian female body hair and American culture', *Journal of American Culture*, 5, 1: 93–9.

Howson, A. (2013) *The Body in Society: An Introduction*. Cambridge: Polity.

Illouz, E. (2007) *Cold Intimacies: The Making of Emotional Capitalism*. Cambridge: Polity.

Illouz, E. (2008) *Saving the Modern Soul: Therapy, Emotions and the Culture of Self-Help*. Berkeley, CA: University of California Press.

Illouz, E. (2013) *Why Love Hurts: A Sociological Explanation*. Cambridge: Polity.

Illouz, E. (ed.) (2018) *Emotions as Commodities: Capitalism, Consumption and Authenticity*. London: Routledge.

Im, E. & Meleis, A. (2000) 'Meanings of menopause to Korean immigrant women', *Western Journal of Nursing Research*, 22, 1: 84–102.

Irigaray, L. (1985) *Speculum of the Other Woman*. Ithaca, NY: Cornell University Press.

James, A., Jenks, C. & Prout, A. (1998) *Theorizing Childhood*. Cambridge: Polity Press.

Jay, M. (1993) *Downcast Eyes: The Denigration of Vision in Twentieth-Century French Thought*. Berkeley, CA: California University Press.

Jeffreys, S. (2015 [2005]) *Beauty and Misogyny: Harmful Cultural Practices in the West*. London: Routledge.

Jha, A.K., Raj, A. & Gangwar, R. (2017) 'A semiotic analysis of portraying gender in magazine advertisements', *Journal of Humanities & Social Science*, 22, 5: 1–8.

Johnson, H.L. (2011) 'Click to donate: Visual images, constructing victims and imagining the female refugee', *Third World Quarterly*, 32, 6: 1015–37.

Jones, A. (2020) *Camming: Money, Power, and Pleasure in the Sex Work Industry*. New York: New York University Press.

Jones, R.W. (1998) *Gender and the Formation of Taste in Eighteenth Century England: The Analysis of Beauty*. Cambridge: Cambridge University Press.

Judovitz, D. (2001) *The Culture of the Body: Genealogies of Modernity*. Ann Arbor, MI: University of Michigan Press.

Jurczyk, K., Jentsch, B., Sailer, B. & Schier, M. (2019) 'Female-breadwinner families in Germany: New gender roles?', *Journal of Family Issues*, 40, 13: 1731–54.

Juteau-Lee, D. (1995) '(Re)constructing the categories of "race" and "sex": The work of a precursor', in: Guillaumin, C., *Racism, Sexism, Power and Ideology*. London: Routledge.

Kahlenberg, S.G. & Hein, M.M. (2010) 'Progression on nickelodeon? Gender-role stereotypes in toy commercials', *Sex Roles: A Journal of Research*, 62, 11–12: 830–47.

Kane, E.W. (2000) 'Racial and ethnic variation in gender-related attitudes', *Annual Review of Sociology*, 26: 419–39.

Kang, M.-E. (1997) 'The portrayal of women's images in magazine advertisements: Goffman's gender analysis revisited', *Sex Roles*, 37, 11–12: 979–96.

Kantorowicz, E. (2016 [1957]) *The King's Two Bodies: A Study in Mediaeval Political Theology*. Princeton, NJ: Princeton University Press.

Kapidzic, S. & Herring, S.C. (2011) 'Gender, communication, and self-presentation in teen chatrooms revisited: Have patterns changed?', *Journal of Computer-Mediated Communication*, 17, 1: 39–59.

Kapidzic, S. & Herring, S.C. (2015) 'Race, gender, and self-presentation in teen profile photographs', *New Media & Society*, 17, 6: 958–76.

Kaufmann, J.-C. (2001 [1995]) *Corps de femmes, regards d'hommes: sociologie des seins nus*. Paris: Pocket.

Kaufmann, J.-C. (2008) *The Single Woman and the Fairytale Prince*. Cambridge: Polity.

Kaw, E. (1993) 'Medicalization of racial features: Asian American women and cosmetic surgery', *Medical Anthropology Quarterly*, 7, 1: 74–89.

Keister, L.A., Thébaud, S. & Yavorsky, J.E. (2022) 'Gender in the elite', *Annual Review of Sociology*, 48: 149–69.

Kessler, S.J. (1998) *Lessons from the Intersexed*. New Brunswick, NJ: Rutgers University Press.

Kessler, S.J. & McKenna, W. (1978) *Gender: An Ethnomethodological Approach*. New York: Wiley.

Kimmel, M. (2018 [1996]) *Manhood in America: A Cultural History*. New York: Oxford University Press.

Kimmel, M. & Plante, R. (eds) (2004) *Sexualities: Identities, Behaviors, and Society*. New York: Oxford University Press.

King, S.C. (2021) 'The male gaze in visual culture', in: Goins, M.N., McAlister, J.F. & Alexander, B.K. (eds) *The Routledge Handbook of Gender and Communication*. London: Routledge.

Kipnis, L. (1996) *Bound and Gagged: Pornography and the Politics of Fantasy in America*. New York: Grove Press.

Klein, A.M. (1993) *Little Big Men: Bodybuilding Subculture and Gender Construction*. New York: SUNY Press.

Kline, S. (2005) 'A becoming subject: Consumer socialization in the mediated marketplace', in: Trentmann, F. (ed.) *The Making of the Consumer: Knowledge, Power and Identity in the Modern World*. Oxford: Berg.

Kohrs, K. and Gill, R. (2021) 'Confident appearing: Revisiting gender advertisements in contemporary culture', in: Angouri, J. & Baxter, J. (eds) *The Routledge Handbook of Gender, Language and Sexuality*. London: Routledge.

Kortenhaus, C.M. & Demarest, J. (1993) 'Gender role stereotyping in children's literature: An update', *Sex Roles*, 28: 219–32.

Kotzé, J. & Antonopoulos, G.A. (2021) 'Boosting bodily capital: Maintaining masculinity, aesthetic pleasure and instrumental utility through the consumption of steroids', *Journal of Consumer Culture*, 21, 3: 683–700.

Kress, G. & Van Leeuwen, T. (1996) *Reading Images: The Grammar of Visual Design*. London: Routledge.

Kristeva, J. (1982) *Powers of Horror: An Essay on Abjection*. New York: Columbia University Press.

Kulick, D. (1998) *Travesti: Sex, Gender, and Culture among Brazilian Transgendered Prostitutes*. Chicago, IL: The University of Chicago Press.

Kulick, D. & Rydström, J. (2015) *Loneliness and Its Opposite: Sex, Disability, and the Ethics of Engagement*. Durham, NC: Duke University Press.

Kwan, S. & Graves, J. (2020) *Under the Knife: Cosmetic Surgery, Boundary Work and the Pursuit of the Natural Fake*. Philadelphia, PA: Temple University Press.

Labre, M.P. (2005) 'The male body ideal: Perspectives of readers and non-readers of fitness magazines', *Journal of Men's Health and Gender*, 2, 2: 223–9.

Lampe, N.M., Carter, S.K. & Sumerau, J.E. (2019) 'Continuity and change in gender frames: The case of transgender reproduction', *Gender & Society*, 33, 6: 865–87.

Langman, L. (2008) 'Punk, porn and resistance: Carnivalization and the body in popular culture', *Current Sociology*, 56, 4: 657–77.

Laqueur, T. (1992) *Making Sex: Body and Gender from the Greeks to Freud*. Cambridge, MA: Harvard University Press.

Lasch, C. (1991 [1979]) *The Culture of Narcissism: American Life in an Age of Diminishing Expectations*. New York: W.W. Norton & Company.

Lasker, J., Egolf, B. & Wolf, S. (1994) 'Community, social change and mortality', *Social Science & Medicine*, 39, 1: 53–62.

Latour, B. (1999) *Politics of Nature: How to Bring the Sciences into Democracy*. Cambridge, MA: Harvard University Press.

Lau, S.R., Kristensen, N.H. & Oxlund, B. (2020) 'Taming and timing death during COVID-19: The ordinary passing of an old man in an extraordinary time', *Anthropology & Aging*, 41, 2: 207–20.

Laumann, E.O., Gagnon, J.H., Michael, R.T. & Michaels, S. (1994) *The Social Organization of Sexuality: Sexual Practices in the United States*. Chicago, IL: University of Chicago Press.

Lazar, M.M. (2014) 'Recuperating feminism, reclaiming femininity: Hybrid postfeminist identity in consumer advertisements', *Gender & Language*, 8, 2: 205–24.

Lazar, M.M. (2017) '"Seriously girly fun!". Recontextualising aesthetic labour as fun and play in cosmetics advertising', in: Elias, A., Gill, R. & Scharff, C. (eds) *Aesthetic Labour: Dynamics of Virtual Work*. London: Palgrave Macmillan.

Le Breton, D. (2005) *Anthropology of the Body and Modernity*. Paris: PUF.

Leek, C. & Kimmel, M. (2015) 'Conceptualizing intersectionality in super-ordination: Masculinities, whitenesses, and dominant classes', in: Jackson, S.A. (ed.) *The Routledge International Handbook of Race, Class, and Gender*. London: Routledge.

Leppert, R. (2007) *The Nude: The Cultural Rhetoric of the Body in the Art of Western Modernity*. London: Routledge.

Lesnik-Oberstein, K. (2006) *The Last Taboo: Women and Body Hair*. Manchester: Manchester University Press.

Liebelt, C., Böllinger, S. & Vierke, U. (eds) (2019) *Beauty and the Norm: Debating Standardization in Bodily Appearance*. Basingstoke: Palgrave Macmillan.

Lloyd, M. (1996) 'Feminism, aerobics and the politics of the body', *Body & Society*, 2, 2: 79–98.

Locher, B. & Prügl, E. (2001) 'Feminism and constructivism: Worlds apart or sharing the middle ground?', *International Studies Quarterly*, 45, 1: 111–29.

Löfgren-Mårtenson, L. (2004) '"May I?" About sexuality and love in the new generation with intellectual disabilities', *Sexuality and Disability*, 22: 197–207.

Lokot, M. & Avakyan, Y. (2020) 'Intersectionality as a lens to the COVID-19 pandemic: Implications for sexual and reproductive health in development and humanitarian contexts', *Sexual and Reproductive Health Matters*, 28, 1: 40–3.

Lorber, J. (1994) *Paradoxes of Gender*. New Haven, CT: Yale University Press.

Lorber, J. (2021) *The New Gender Paradox*. Cambridge: Polity.

Lorde, A. (1984) *Sister Outsider: Essays and Speeches*. Trumansburg, NY: Crossing Press.

Lovejoy, M. (2001) 'Disturbances in the social body: Differences in body image and eating problems among African American and White women', *Gender and Society*, 15, 2: 239–61.

Lowe, M. (1998) *Women of Steel: Female Body Builders and the Struggle for Self*. New York: New York University Press.

Lugones, M. (2010) 'Toward a decolonial feminism', *Hypatia*, 25, 4: 742–59.

Lupton, D. (2016) *The Quantified Self*. Cambridge: Polity.

Lupton, D. (2020) 'Australian women's use of health and fitness apps and wearable devices: A feminist new materialism analysis', *Feminist Media Studies*, 20, 7: 983–98.

Maccoby, E. & Jacklin, C. (1974) *The Psychology of Sex Differences*. Stanford, CA: Stanford University Press.

MacKinnon, C. (1987) *Feminism Unmodified: Discourses on Life and Law*. Cambridge, MA: Harvard University Press.

MacKinnon, C. (1989) *Toward a Feminist Theory of the State*. Cambridge, MA: Harvard University Press.

MacKinnon, C. (1993) *Only Words*. Cambridge, MA: Harvard University Press.

MacKinnon, K.R., Ashley, F., Kia, H., Lam, J.S.H., Krakowsky, Y. & Ross, L.E. (2021) 'Preventing transition "regret": An institutional ethnography of gender-affirming medical care assessment practices in Canada', *Social Science & Medicine*, 291: 1–9.

MacSween, M. (2013 [1993]) *Anorexic Bodies: A Feminist and Sociological Perspective on Anorexia Nervosa*. London: Routledge.

Mager, J. & Helgeson, J.G. (2011) 'Fifty years of advertising images: Some changing perspectives on role portrayals along with enduring consistencies', *Sex Roles*, 64: 238–52.

Maguire, S.J. & Mansfield, L. (1998) '"No-body's perfect": Women, aerobics and the body beautiful', *Sociology of Sport Journal*, 15, 2: 109–37.

Malatino, H. (2019) 'Tough breaks: Trans rage and the cultivation of resilience', *Hypatia*, 34, 1: 121–40.

Mannheim, K. (1952 [1923]) 'The problem of generations', in: Kecskemeti, P. (ed.) *Karl Mannheim: Essays*. London: Routledge.

Markula, P. (1995) '"Firm but shapely, fit but sexy, strong but thin": The postmodern aerobicizing female bodies', *Sociology of Sport Journal*, 12, 4: 424–53.

Marques, A.C. (2019) 'Displaying gender: Transgender people's strategies in everyday life', *Symbolic Interaction*, 42, 2: 202–28.

Marshall, K., Chamberlain, K. & Hodgetts, D. (2020) 'Male bodybuilders on Instagram: Negotiating inclusive masculinities through hegemonic masculine bodies', *Journal of Gender Studies*, 29, 5: 570–89.

Martin, E. (1987) *The Woman in the Body: A Cultural Analysis of Reproduction*. Boston, MA: Beacon Press.

Martin, E. (1994) *Flexible Bodies: Tracking Immunity in American Culture from the Days of Polio to the Age of AIDS*. Boston, MA: Beacon Press.

Martin, K. (2018) *Puberty, Sexuality and the Self: Girls and Boys at Adolescence*. London: Routledge.

Martschukat, J. (2021 [2019]) *The Age of Fitness: How the Body Came to Symbolize Success and Achievement*. Cambridge: Polity.

Marx, K. (1977 [1887]) *Capital*. New York: International Publishers.

Mascia-Lees, F.E. (2011) *A Companion to the Anthropology of the Body and Embodiment*. Oxford: Blackwell.

Mathebula, M. (2022) 'Nakedness as decolonial praxis', *Body & Society*, 28, 3: 3–29.

Mauss, M. (1973 [1934]) 'Techniques of the body', *Economy & Society*, 2, 1: 70–88.

McArthur, L.Z. & Eisen, S.V. (1976) 'Television and sex-role stereotyping', *Journal of Applied Social Psychology*, 6, 4: 329–51.

McClintock, A. (1995) *Imperial Leather: Race, Gender, and Sexuality in the Colonial Contest*. London: Routledge.

McCormack, M. (2014) 'The intersection of youth masculinities, decreasing homophobia and class: An ethnography', *The British Journal of Sociology*, 65, 1: 130–49.

McKay, J., Messner, M. & Sabo, D. (eds) (2000) *Masculinities, Gender Relations, and Sport*. Thousand Oaks, CA: Sage.

McNay, L. (1992) *Foucault and Feminism: Power, Gender and the Self*. Cambridge: Polity.

McNay, L. (1999) 'Gender, habitus and the field: Pierre Bourdieu and the limits of reflexivity', *Theory, Culture & Society*, 16, 1: 95–117.

McRobbie, A. (2004) 'Post-feminism and popular culture', *Feminist Media Studies*, 4, 3: 255–64.

Mead, M. (2003 [1935]) *Sex and Temperament in Three Primitive Societies*. New York: HarperCollins.

Meadow, T. (2018) *Trans Kids: Being Gendered in the Twenty-First Century*. Berkeley, CA: University of California Press.

Mears, A. (2020) *Very Important People: Status and Beauty in the Global Party Circuit*. Princeton, NJ: Princeton University Press.

Merleau-Ponty, M. (1962 [1945]) *Phenomenology of Perception*. London: Routledge.

Messerschmidt, J.W. (2018) *Hegemonic Masculinity: Formulation, Reformulation, and Amplification*. Lanham, MD: Rowman & Littlefield.

Messner, M.A. (1988) 'Sports and male domination: The female athlete as contested ideological terrain', *Sociology of Sport Journal*, 5: 197–211.

Meyerowitz, J.J. (2002) *How Sex Changed: A History of Transsexuality in the United States*. Cambridge, MA: Harvard University Press.

Milburn, S.S., Carney, D.R. & Ramires, D.M. (2001) 'Even in modern media, the picture is still the same', *Sex Roles*, 44, 5–6: 277–94.

Mirivel, J.C. (2007) 'Managing poor surgical candidacy: Communication problems for plastic surgeons', *Discourse & Communication*, 1, 3: 309–36.

Mirzoeff, N. (2023 [1999]) *An Introduction to Visual Culture*, 3rd edn. London: Routledge.

Mitchell, J. (1971) *Women's Estate*. London: Penguin.

Möbius, P.J. (1900) *Über den physiologischen Schwachsinn des Weibes*. Halle: Verlag von Carl Marhold.

Moisio, R. & Beruchashvili, M. (2016) 'Mancaves and masculinity', *Journal of Consumer Culture*, 16, 3: 656–76.

Monaghan, L. (2008) *Men and the War on Obesity: A Sociological Study*. London: Routledge.

Moodie, T.D. (1994) *Going for Gold: Men, Mines, and Migration*. Berkeley, CA: University of California Press.

Moore, L.J. & Kosut, M. (2010) *The Body Reader: Essential Social and Cultural Readings*. New York: New York University Press.

Moore, L.J. & Lorber, J. (2011) *Gendered Bodies: Feminist Perspectives*. Los Angeles, CA: Roxbury Publishing Company.

Moore, S. (1988) 'Here's looking at you kid!', in: Gamman, L. & Marshment, M. (eds) *The Female Gaze: Women as Viewers of Popular Culture*. London: The Women's Press.

Mora, R. (2012) '"Do it for all your pubic hairs!" Latino boys, masculinity, and puberty', *Gender & Society*, 26, 3: 433–60.

Morgan, K.P. (1991) 'Women and the knife: Cosmetic surgery and the colonization of women's bodies', *Hypatia*, 6, 3: 25–53.

Moss, M. (2011) *The Media and Models of Masculinity*. Lanham, MD: Rowman and Littlefield.

Motschenbacher, H. (2009) 'Speaking the gendered body: The performative construction of commercial femininities and masculinities via body-part vocabulary', *Language in Society*, 28, 1: 1–22.

Mulvey, L. (1989 [1975]) 'Visual pleasure and narrative cinema', in: *Visual and Other Pleasures*. Basingstoke: Palgrave Macmillan.

Murray, D.P. (2013) 'Branding "real" social change in Dove's campaign for real beauty', *Feminist Media Studies*, 13, 1: 83–101.

Nagel, J. (2000) 'Ethnicity and sexuality', *Annual Review of Sociology*, 26, 1: 107–33.

Nash, M. (2015) 'Gender on the ropes: An autoethnographic account of boxing in Tasmania', *International Review for the Sociology of Sport*, 52, 6: 734–50.

Nayak, A. (1997) 'Frozen bodies: Disclosing whiteness in Häagen-Dazs advertising', *Body & Society*, 23, 3: 51–71.

Nayak, A. (2007) 'Critical whiteness studies', *Sociology Compass*, 1, 2: 737–55.

Nayak, A. & Kehily, M.J. (2013) *Gender, Youth and Culture: Young Masculinities and Femininities*. Basingstoke: Palgrave Macmillan.

Nettleton, S. (1994) 'Inventing mouths: Disciplinary power and dentistry', in: Jones, C. & Porter, R. (eds) *Reassessing Foucault: Power, Medicine and the Body*. London: Routledge, pp. 73–90.

Nilsen, A.P. (1971) 'Women in children's literature', *College English*, 32, 8: 918–26.

Nochlin, L. (1989) *The Politics of Vision: Essays on Nineteenth-century Art and Society*. London: Routledge.

Oakley, A. (2018 [1980]) *From Here to Maternity: Becoming a Mother*. Bristol: Policy Press.

O'Brien, M. (1981) *The Politics of Reproduction*. Boston, MA: Routledge & Kegan Paul.

Ochs, E. & Kremer-Sadlick, T. (eds) (2013) *Fast-forward Family: Home, Work, and Relationships in Middle-Class America*. Berkeley, CA: University of California Press.

Oliver, K. (2017) 'The male gaze is more relevant, and more dangerous, than ever', *New Review of Film and Television Studies*, 15, 4: 451–5.

Orbach, S. (1978) *Fat is a Feminist Issue*. London: Arrow Books.

Osborne, T. (1994) 'On anti-medicine and clinical reason', in: Jones, C. & Porter, R. (eds) *Reassessing Foucault*. London: Routledge.

Oudshoorn, N. (1994) *Beyond the Natural Body: An Archaeology of Sex Hormones*. New York: Routledge.

Paasonen, S. (2011) 'Online pornography: Ubiquitous and effaced', in: Consalvo, M. & Ess, C. (eds) *The Handbook of Internet Research*. Oxford: Blackwell, pp. 424–39.

Paechter, C. (2003) 'Masculinities and femininities as communities of practice', *Women's Studies International Forum*, 26, 1: 69–77.

Paoletti, J.B. (2012) *Pink and Blue: Telling the Boys from the Girls in America*. Bloomington, IN: Indiana University Press.

Pape, M. (2019) 'Expertise and non-binary bodies: Sex, gender and the case of Dutee Chand', *Body & Society*, 25, 4: 3–28.

Paradis, E. (2012) 'Boxers, briefs or bras? Bodies, gender and change in the boxing gym', *Body & Society*, 18, 2: 82–109.

Peiss, K. (1998) *Hope in a Jar: The Making of America's Beauty Culture*. New York: Metropolitan Books.

Peragine, D.E., Skorska, M.N., Maxwell, J.A., Impett, E.A. & VanderLaan, D.P. (2022) 'A learning experience? Enjoyment at sexual debut and the gender gap in sexual desire among emerging adults', *The Journal of Sex Research*, 59, 9: 1092–109.

Petersson McIntyre, M. (2018) 'Gender by design: Performativity and consumer packaging', *Design and Culture*, 10, 3: 337–58.

Pfeffer, C.A. (2014) '"I don't like passing as a straight woman": Queer negotiations of identity and social group membership', *American Journal of Sociology*, 120: 1–44.

Pink, S. (2004) *Home Truths: Gender, Domestic Objects and Everyday Life*. Oxford: Berg.

Pitts, V. (2003) *In the Flesh: The Cultural Politics of Body Modification*. New York: Palgrave Macmillan.

Plous, S. & Neptune, D. (1997) 'Racial and gender biases in magazine advertising: A content-analytic study', *Psychology of Women Quarterly*, 21, 4: 627–44.

Plummer, K. (2002) *Sexualities: Critical Concepts in Sociology*. London: Routledge.

Pollock, G. (1988) *Visions and Difference: Femininity, Feminism and the History of Art*. London: Routledge.

Preves, S.E. (2003) *Intersex and Identity: The Contested Self*. New Brunswick, NJ: Rutgers University Press.

Prosser, J. (1998) *Second Skins: The Body Narratives of Transsexuality*. New York: Columbia University Press.

Prout, A. (2000) 'Children's participation: Control and self-realisation in British late modernity', *Children & Society*, 14, 4: 304–15.

Pulerwitz, J., Amaro, H., De Jong, W., Gortmaker, S. & Rudd, R. (2002) 'Relationship, power, condom use and HIV risk among women in the USA', *AIDS Care*, 14, 6: 789–800.

Purnell, K. (2021) *Rethinking the Body in Global Politics: Bodies, Body Politics and the Body Politic in a Time of Pandemic*. London: Routledge.

Ramírez, Á. (2015) 'Control over female "Muslim" bodies: Culture, politics and dress code laws in some Muslim and non-Muslim countries', *Identities*, 22, 6: 671–86.

Ramsey, L. & Horan, A.L. (2018) 'Picture this: Women's self-sexualization in photos on social media', *Personality and Individual Differences*, 133: 85–90.

Randall, H. & Polhemus, T. (1996) *The Customized Body*. New York: Serpents Tail.

Rappaport, E. (1999) *Shopping for Pleasure: Women in the Making of London's West End*. Princeton, NJ: Princeton University Press.

Raun, T. (2016) *Out Online: Trans Self-representation and Community Building on YouTube*. London: Routledge.

Raymond, J. (1979) *The Transsexual Empire: The Making of the She-Male*. Boston, MA: Beacon Press.

Rehberg, P. (2022) *Hipster Porn: Queer Masculinities and Affective Sexualities in the Fanzine Butt*. London: Routledge.

Rémaury, B. (2000) *Le Beau Sexe Faible: Les Images du Corps Féminin entre Cosmétique et Santé*. Paris: Grasset.

Rhode, D.L. (2010) *The Beauty Bias: The Injustice of Appearance in Life and Law*. Oxford: Oxford University Press.

Rich, A. (1976) *Of Woman Born: Motherhood as Experience and Institution*. New York: Norton.

Rich, A. (1980) 'Compulsory heterosexuality and lesbian existence', *Signs*, 5, 4: 631–60.

Richardson, D. (2007) 'Patterned fluidities: (Re)imagining the relationship between gender and sexuality', *Sociology*, 41, 3: 457–74.

Riessman, C.K. (1983) 'Women and medicalization: A new perspective', *Social Policy*, 14, 1: 3–18.

Risman, B.J. (2004) 'Gender as a social structure: Theory wrestling with activism', *Gender and Society*, 18, 4: 429–50.

Rivière-Zijdel, L. (2009) 'The ignored aspects of intersectionality', in: Franken, M., Woodward, A., Cabó, A. & Bagilhole, B. (eds) *Teaching Intersectionality: Putting Gender at the Centre*. Utrecht: Athena.

Roberts, C. (2002) '"A matter of embodied fact". Sex hormones and the history of bodies', *Feminist Theory*, 3, 1: 7–26.

Rogers, M.F. (1992) 'They all were passing: Agnes, Garfinkel, and company', *Gender & Society*, 6, 2: 169–91.

Romero, M. (2018) *Introducing Intersectionality*. Cambridge: Polity.

Rose, N. (2013) 'The human sciences in a biological age', *Theory, Culture & Society*, 30, 1: 3–34.

Rottenberg, C. (2017) 'Neoliberal feminism and the future of human capital', *Signs*, 42, 2: 329–48.

Rottenberg, C. (2018) *The Rise of Neoliberal Feminism*. Oxford: Oxford University Press.

Rousseau, J.-J. (2010 [1762]) *Emile, or On Education*. Lebanon, NH: University Press of New England.

Ruberg, W. (2020) *History of the Body*. London: Red Globe Press.

Rubin, G. (1975) 'The traffic in women: Notes on the "political economy" of sex', in: Reiter, R. (ed.) *Toward an Anthropology of Women*. New York: Monthly Review Press.

Rudrappa, S. (1999) 'Normative sexuality and the production of ethnicity: Race and identity among (Asian) Indian immigrant families in the United States'. Annual Meeting of the American Sociological Association.

Sagebin Bordini, G. & Sperb, T.M. (2013) 'Sexual double standard: A review of the literature between 2001 and 2010', *Sexuality & Culture: An Interdisciplinary Quarterly*, 17, 4: 686–704.

Saguy, A. (2020) *Come Out, Come Out, Whoever You Are*. Oxford: Oxford University Press.

Said, E. (2003 [1975]) *Orientalism*. London: Penguin.

Sakaluk, J., Todd, L.M., Milhausen, R. et al. (2014) 'Dominant heterosexual sexual scripts in emerging adulthood: Conceptualization and measurement', *The Journal of Sex Research*, 51, 5: 516–31.

Salzman, M.L., Matathia, I. & O'Reilly, A. (2005) *The Future of Men*. New York: Palgrave Macmillan.

Sanders, C. (2008 [1989]) *Customizing the Body: The Art and Culture of Tattooing*. Philadelphia, PA: Temple University Press.

Sanders, R. (2017) 'Self-tracking in the digital era: Biopower, patriarchy, and the new biometric body projects', *Body & Society*, 23, 1: 36–63.

Sassatelli, R. (2007a) *Consumer Culture: History, Theory and Politics*. London: Sage.

Sassatelli, R. (2007b) 'When Coleman read Garfinkel', *SocioLogica*, 1: 1–26.

Sassatelli, R. (2010a) *Fitness Culture: Gyms and the Commercialisation of Discipline and Fun*. Basingstoke: Palgrave Macmillan.

Sassatelli, R. (2010b) 'Promotional reflexivity: Irony, de-fetishisation and moralization in The Body Shop promotional rhetoric', in: Avellini, L.,

Benvenuti, G., Michelacci, L. & Sberlati, F. (eds) *Prospettive degli Studi Culturali*. Bologna: I libri di Emil.

Sassatelli, R. (2011) 'Indigo bodies: Fashion, mirror work and sexual identity in Milan', in: Miller, D. & Woodward, S. (eds) *Global Denim*. Oxford: Berg.

Sassatelli, R. (2012) 'Self and body', in: Trentmann, F. (ed.) *Handbook of the History of Consumption*. Oxford: Oxford University Press.

Sassatelli, R. (2016) '"You can all succeed!". The reconciliatory logic of therapeutic active leisure', *European Journal for Sport and Society*, 13, 3: 230–45.

Sassatelli, R. & Mulvey, L. (2011) 'Gender, gaze and technology in film culture: An interview with Laura Mulvey', *Theory, Culture & Society*, 28, 5: 123–43.

Satrapi, M. (2003) *Persepolis*. New York: Pantheon Books.

Savigliano, M.E. (1995) *Tango and the Political Economy of Passion*. London: Routledge.

Sax, L. (2002) 'How common is intersex? A response to Anne Fausto-Sterling', *The Journal of Sex Research*, 39, 3: 174–8.

Scanlon, J.R. (2000) *The Gender and Consumer Culture Reader*. New York: New York University Press.

Schilt, K. (2016) 'The importance of being Agnes', *Symbolic Interaction*, 39, 2: 287–94.

Schilt, K. & Lagos, D. (2017) 'The development of transgender studies in sociology', *Annual Review of Sociology*, 43: 425–43.

Schneider, M. (1996) 'Sacredness, status and bodily violation', *Body & Society*, 2, 4: 75–92.

Schrock, D., Reid, L. & Boyd, E.M. (2005) 'Transsexuals' embodiment of womanhood', *Gender & Society*, 19, 3: 317–35.

Schwalbe, M.L. (2022) 'Goffman and visual studies', in: Jacobsen, M.H. & Smith, G. (eds) *The Routledge International Handbook of Goffman Studies*. London: Routledge.

Schwark, S. (2017) 'Visual representations of sexual violence in online news outlets', *Frontiers in Psychology*, 8: 774.

Scott, J.W. (1986) 'Gender: A useful category of historical analysis', *The American Historical Review*, 91, 5: 1053–75.

Scott, J.W. (1988) *Gender and the Politics of History*. New York: Columbia University Press.

Scott, S. (2010) 'How to look good (nearly) naked: The performative regulation of the swimmer's body', *Body & Society*, 16, 2: 143–68.

Scranton, P. (2001) *Beauty and Business: Commerce, Gender, and Culture in Modern America*. New York: Routledge.

Sedgwick, E.K. (2008) *Epistemology of the Closet*. Berkeley, CA: University of California Press.

Shaw, J. (2012) 'The birth of the clinic and the advent of reproduction: Pregnancy, pathology and the medical gaze in modernity', *Body & Society*, 18, 2: 110–38.

Shilling, C. (2008) *Changing Bodies: Habit, Crisis and Creativity*. London: Sage.

Shilling, C. (2012) *The Body and Social Theory*, 3rd edn. London: Sage.

Shilling, C. (2016) *The Body: A Very Short Introduction*. Oxford: Oxford University Press.

Shuttleworth, R.P. (2000) 'The search for sexual intimacy for men with cerebral palsy', *Sexuality & Disability*, 18, 4: 263–82.

Simmel, G. (1950 [1903]) 'The metropolis and mental life', in: Wolff, K. (ed.) *The Sociology of Georg Simmel*. New York: Free Press.

Simmel, G. (1957 [1904]) 'Fashion', *American Journal of Sociology*, 62, 6: 541–58.

Simmel, G. (2009 [1908]) *Sociology: Inquiries into the Construction of Social Forms*. Leiden: Brill.

Simon, R.W. (2014) 'Sociological scholarship on gender differences in emotion and emotional well-being in the United States: A snapshot of the field', *Emotion Review*, 6, 3: 196–201.

Simon, R.W. (2020) 'Gender, emotions, and mental health in the United States: Patterns, explanations, and new directions', *Society and Mental Health*, 10, 2: 97–111.

Simon, R.W. & Nath, L.E. (2004) 'Gender and emotion in the United States: Do men and women differ in self-reports of feelings and expressive behavior?', *American Journal of Sociology*, 109, 5: 1137–76.

Smith, L.J. (1994) 'A content analysis of gender differences in children's advertising', *Journal of Broadcasting & Electronic Media*, 38, 3: 323–37.

Smith, S.M. (2004) *Photography on the Color Line: W.E.B. Du Bois, Race, and Visual Culture*. Durham, NC: Duke University Press.

Sobande, F. (2019) 'Woke-washing: "Intersectional" femvertising and branding "woke" bravery', *European Journal of Marketing*, 54, 11: 2723–45.

Sombart, W. (1967 [1922]) *Luxury and Capitalism*. Ann Arbor, MI: University of Michigan Press.

Sontag, S. (1977 [1972]) 'The double standard of aging', in: Allman, L. & Jaffe, D. (eds) *Readings in Adult Psychology*. New York: Harper & Row.

Spitzack, C. (1990) *Confessing Excess: Women and the Politics of Body Reduction*. New York: SUNY Press.

Spivak, G.C. (2010 [1988]) 'Can the subaltern speak?', in: Morris, R.C. (ed.) *Can the Subaltern Speak: Reflections on the History of an Idea*. New York: Columbia University Press.

Stearns, P. (1997) *Fat History: Bodies and Beauty in the Modern West*. New York: New York University Press.

Steele, V. (2001) *The Corset: A Cultural History*. New Haven, CT: Yale University Press.

Stein, A. (1989) 'Three models of sexuality: Drives, identities and practices', *Sociological Theory*, 7, 1: 1–13.

Stoler, A.L. (1995) *Race and the Education of Desire: Foucault's History of Sexuality and the Colonial Order of Things*. Durham, NC: Duke University Press.

Stone, S. (1991) 'The empire strikes back: A post-transsexual manifesto', in: Epstein, J. & Straub, K. (eds) *Body Guards: The Cultural Politics of Gender Ambiguity*. London: Routledge.

Strathern, M. (1988) *The Gender of the Gift: Problems with Women and Problems with Society in Melanesia*. Berkeley, CA: University of California Press.

Strings, S. (2019) *Fearing the Black Body: The Racial Origins of Fat Phobia*. New York: New York University Press.

Strossen, N. (1995) *Defending Pornography: Free Speech, Sex, and the Fight for Women's Rights*. New York: Scribner.

Sullivan, D. (2001) *Cosmetic Surgery: The Cutting Edge of Commercial Medicine in America*. New Brunswick, NJ: Rutgers University Press.

Sullivan, N. (2003) *A Critical Introduction to Queer Theory*. New York: New York University Press.

Sullivan, R. & McKee, A. (2015) *Pornography: Structures, Agency and Performance*. Cambridge: Polity.

Sweetman, P. (1999) 'Anchoring the (postmodern) self? Body modification, fashion and identity', *Body & Society*, 5, 2–3: 51–76.

Swidler, A. (2001) *Talk of Love*. Chicago, IL: University of Chicago Press.

Synnott, A. (2002 [1993]) *The Body Social: Symbolism, Self and Society*. London: Routledge.

Szasz, T. (1990) *Sex by Prescription*. Syracuse, NY: Syracuse University Press.

Tabet, P. (2012) 'Through the looking-glass: Sexual-economic exchange', in: Omokaro, F. & Reysoo, F. (eds) *Chic, Chèque, Choc: Transactions Autour des Corps and Stratégies Amoureuses Contemporaines*. Geneva: Graduate Institute Publications.

Thomas, H. (2013) *The Body and Everyday Life*. London: Routledge.

Thompson, B.Y. (2015) *Covered in Ink: Tattoos, Women and the Politics of the Body*. New York: New York University Press.

Thompson, B.Y. (2019) 'Women covered in ink: Tattoo collecting as serious leisure', *International Journal of the Sociology of Leisure*, 2, 3: 285–99.

Thorne, B. (1987) 'Re-visioning women and social change: Where are the children?', *Gender and Society*, 1, 1: 85–109.

Thorne, B. (1993) *Gender Play: Girls and Boys in School*. New Brunswick, NJ: Rutgers University Press.

Thrift, N. (2000) 'Still life in present time: The object of nature', *Body & Society*, 6, 3–4: 34–57.

Titley, G. (2019) *Racism and Media*. London: Sage.

Toerien, M., Wilkinson, S. & Choi, P.Y.L. (2005) 'Body hair removal: The "mundane" production of normative femininity', *Sex Roles*, 52: 399–406.

Totman, R. (2011) *The Third Sex: Kathoey, Thailand's Ladyboys*. London: Souvenir Press.

Travis, M. (2015) 'Accommodating intersexuality in European Union anti-discrimination law', *European Law Journal*, 21, 2: 180–99.

Tseëlon, E. (1995) *The Masque of Femininity: The Presentation of Woman in Everyday Life*. London: Sage.

Tsichla, E. & Zotos, Y. (2016) 'Gender portrayals revisited: Searching for explicit and implicit stereotypes in Cypriot magazine advertisements', *International Journal of Advertising*, 35, 6: 983–1007.

Turner, B.S. (2000) 'The possibility of primitiveness: Towards a sociology of body marks in cool societies', in: Featherstone, M. (ed.) *Body Modification*. London: Sage.

Turner, B.S. (2008) *The Body & Society: Explorations in Social Theory*, 3rd edn. London: Sage.

Twigg, J. (2004) 'The body, gender, and age: Feminist insights in social gerontology', *New Directions in Feminist Gerontology*, 18, 1: 59–73.

Tyler, I. (2006) '"Welcome to Britain": The cultural politics of asylum', *European Journal of Cultural Studies*, 9, 2: 185–202.

Tyler, M. & Abbott, P. (1998) 'Chocs away: Weight watching in the contemporary airline industry', *Sociology*, 32, 3: 433–50.

Valverde, M. (1998) *Diseases of the Will: Alcohol and the Dilemmas of Freedom*. New York: Cambridge University Press.

Van Brussel, L. & Carpentier, N. (2014) *The Social Construction of Death: Interdisciplinary Perspectives*. Basingstoke: Palgrave.

Vandereycken, W. & van Deth, R. (1994) *From Fasting Saints to Anorexic Girls: The History of Self-Starvation*. New York: New York University Press.

Veblen, T. (1994 [1899]) *The Theory of the Leisure Class*. New York: Dover Publication.

Venn, S., Davidson, K. & Arber, S. (2011) 'Gender and aging', in: Settersten, R. & Ange, J. (eds) *Handbook of Sociology of Aging*. New York: Springer.

Verloo, M. (2006) 'Multiple inequalities, intersectionality and the European Union', *European Journal of Women's Studies*, 13, 3: 211–28.

Vigarello, G. (1978) *Le Corps Redressé: Histoire d'un Pouvoir Pédagogique*. Paris: J.P. Delarge.

Voas, D. & Fleischmann, F. (2012) 'Islam moves West: Religious change in the first and second generations', *Annual Review of Sociology*, 38: 525–45.

Von Scheve, C. (2012) 'Emotion regulation and emotion work: Two sides of the same coin?', *Frontiers in Psychology*, 3: 1–10.

Wacquant, L. (1995) 'Why men desire muscles', *Body & Society*, 1, 1: 163–79.

Wacquant, L. (2004) *Body & Soul: Notebooks of an Apprentice Boxer*. Oxford: Oxford University Press.

Wade, L.D. & DeLamater, J.D. (2002) 'Relationship dissolution as a life stage transition: Effects on sexual attitudes and behaviors', *Journal of Marriage and Family*, 64, 4: 898–914.

Wallis, C. (2011) 'Performing gender: A content analysis of gender display in music videos', *Sex Roles*, 64: 160–72.

Walter, T. (2020) *Death in the Modern World*. London: Sage.

Washington, M.S. & Economides, M. (2016) 'Strong is the new sexy:

Women, CrossFit, and the postfeminist ideal', *Journal of Sport & Social Issues*, 40, 2: 143–61.

Watkins-Hayes, C. (2014) 'Intersectionality and the sociology of HIV/AIDS: Past, present, and future research directions', *Annual Review of Sociology*, 40, 1: 431–57.

Weber, L. (2001) *Understanding Race, Class, Gender, and Sexuality: A Conceptual Framework*. Boston, MA: McGraw-Hill.

Weber, M. (1992 [1922]) *Economy and Society*. London: Routledge.

Weber, M. (2002 [1904]) *The Protestant Ethic and the Spirit of Capitalism*. London: Penguin.

Weitzer, R. (2009) 'Sociology of sex work', *Annual Review of Sociology*, 35: 213–34.

Wekker, G. (2006) *The Politics of Passion: Women's Sexual Culture in the Afro-Surinamese Diaspora*. New York: Columbia University Press.

West, C. (1996) 'Goffman in feminist perspective', *Sociological Perspectives*, 39, 3: 353–69.

West, C. & Ferstermaker, S. (1995) 'Doing difference', *Gender & Society*, 9: 8–37.

West, C. & Zimmerman, D. (1987) 'Doing gender', *Gender & Society*, 1: 125–51.

West, C. & Zimmerman, D. (2009) 'Accounting for doing gender', *Gender & Society*, 23, 1: 112–22.

Weston, C. (1993) 'Lesbian/gay studies in the house of anthropology', *Annual Review of Anthropology*, 22: 339–67.

Wetherell, M. (2012) *Affect and Emotions*. London: Sage.

Wheaton, B. & Tomlinson, A. (1998) 'The changing gender order in sport? The case of windsurfing sub-cultures', *Journal of Sport and Social Issues*, 22: 252–74.

Whittle, C. & Butler, C. (2018) 'Sexuality in the lives of people with intellectual disabilities: A meta-ethnographic synthesis of qualitative studies', *Research in Developmental Disabilities*, 75: 68–81.

Wiederman, M.W. (2015) 'Sexual script theory: Past, present, and future', in: DeLamater, J. & Plante, R.F. (eds) *Handbook of the Sociology of Sexualities*. Cham: Springer International.

Williams, L. (ed.) (2004) *Porn Studies*. Durham, NC: Duke University Press.

Williams, R.H. & Vashi, G. (2007) 'Hijab and American Muslim women: Creating the space for autonomous selves', *Sociology of Religion*, 68, 3: 269–87.

Williams, S.J. & Bendelow, G. (1999) *The Lived Body*. London: Routledge.

Wiseman, C.V., Gray, J.J., Mosimann, J.E. & Ahrens, A.H. (1992) 'Cultural expectations of thinness in women: An update', *International Journal of Eating Disorders*, 11, 1: 85–9.

Witt, S.D. (1997) 'Parental influence on children's socialization to gender roles', *Adolescence*, 32, 126: 253–9.

Witz, A. (2000) 'Whose body matters? Feminist sociology and the corporeal turn in sociology and feminism', *Body & Society*, 6, 2: 1–24.

Wojcik, D. (1995) *Punk and Neo-Tribal Body Art*. Jackson, MS: University Press of Mississippi.

Wolf, N. (2002 [1990]) *The Beauty Myth: How Images of Beauty are Used Against Women*. New York: Perennial.

Wollstonecraft, M. (1995 [1792]) *A Vindication of the Rights of Men; with, A Vindication of the Rights of Woman, and Hints*. New York: Cambridge University Press.

Woodman, D. & Wyn, J. (2015) 'Class, gender and generation matter: Using the concept of social generation to study inequality and social change', *Journal of Youth Studies*, 18, 10: 1402–10.

Wouters, C. (2007) *Informalization: Manners and Emotions since 1890*. London: Sage.

Wykes, M. & Gunter, B. (2005) *The Media and Body Image: If Looks Could Kill*. London: Sage.

Yancy, G. (2017) *Black Bodies, White Gazes: The Continuing Significance of Race in America*. Lanham, MD: Rowman & Littlefield.

Young, I.M. (2005 [1980]) *On Female Body Experience: 'Throwing Like a Girl' and Other Essays*. Oxford: Oxford University Press.

Young, G., Smith, M. & Batten, J. (2022) '"Social media makes it inevitable to feel bad about your body": Examining self-presentation and body image of young collegiate females', *Youth*, 2, 3: 217–35.

Zamantakis, A. (2022) 'Queering intimate emotions functioned to mitigate the effects of whiteness and cis-ness within intimate relationships', *Sexualities*, 25, 5–6: 581–97.

Zborowski, M. (1969) *People in Pain*. San Francisco, CA: Jossey-Bass.

Zimman, L., Davis, J.L. & Raclaw, J. (2014) *Queer Excursions: Retheorizing Binaries in Language, Gender and Sexuality*. Oxford: Oxford University Press.

Index